Funding a New Business

by Marc R. Butler and Eric Butow

Funding a New Business For Dummies®

Published by: **John Wiley & Sons, Inc.**, 111 River Street, Hoboken, NJ 07030-5774, www.wiley.com

Copyright © 2024 by John Wiley & Sons, Inc., Hoboken, New Jersey

Published simultaneously in Canada

For general information on our other products and services, please contact our Customer Care Department within the U.S. at 877-762-2974, outside the U.S. at 317-572-3993, or fax 317-572-4002. For technical support, please visit https://hub.wiley.com/community/support/dummies.

Wiley publishes in a variety of print and electronic formats and by print-on-demand. Some material included with standard print versions of this book may not be included in e-books or in print-on-demand. If this book refers to media such as a CD or DVD that is not included in the version you purchased, you may download this material at http://booksupport.wiley.com. For more information about Wiley products, visit www.wiley.com.

Library of Congress Control Number: 2024932427

ISBN 978-1-394-24171-2 (pbk); ISBN 978-1-394-24173-6 (ebk); ISBN 978-1-394-24172-0 (ebk)

SKY10067577_022024

Contents at a Glance

Table of Contents

Introduction

Huzzah! We're proud of you, because we know that starting a business isn't for the faint of heart, but it's one that will not only benefit you but people far and wide. As a new business, you need funding as much as your favorite vehicle needs fuel to get to each milestone on your road to the top.

This isn't just a book; it's your companion as you navigate the road and drive around any roadblocks with aplomb. So, grab your favorite beverage, sit in your comfortable chair, and we're with you for every mile of the journey. (Sunglasses are optional.)

About This Book

Funding a New Business For Dummies isn't just about understanding the nuts and bolts of startup financing. It's about transforming you into a savvy entrepreneur who not only grasps the essentials of raising capital but is also a master of the art of negotiation, strategy, and relationship building. This book will change your mindset, enrich your knowledge, and open doors to new possibilities.

Whether you're looking to connect with angel investors, thinking about venture capital, or exploring the realms of crowdfunding, we've got you covered. With each chapter, you dive deeper into the world of startup financing, becoming more informed, confident, and prepared. From refining your value proposition to navigating investment agreements and understanding the nuances of each funding avenue, this book is your comprehensive guide.

Foolish Assumptions

When writing this book, we assumed that you

>> Are curious about the world of startup financing

>> Are potentially starting a business and you desire to be a successful entrepreneur

>> Are committed to devoting time and energy to make yourself the owner of a growing, thriving business

If these assumptions are correct, this is the right book for you! We're confident that the tactics and information here will help you achieve your goals.

Icons Used in This Book

To make things easier and ensure that you don't miss important details, we have various icons throughout this book. Here's what the different icons look like and mean.

TIP

The Tip icon is a small piece of expert advice that will save you time and make funding your business easier to master.

REMEMBER

Because we cover a lot of details and information, every now and then we throw in a Remember icon to remind you of important details we've already covered. We know you're reading every juicy detail of the book; the Remember icon just helps resurface some of those tidbits.

WARNING

Yes, this book has a few warnings. When you see a Warning icon, please take a few extra moments to understand the effect of what we're saying. You're not going to sink your finances or do anything irreparable, but we want to save you from any headaches we can.

Beyond the Book

In addition to what you're reading right now, this book also comes with a free, access-anywhere Cheat Sheet that provides a handy glossary of finance lingo. To view the Cheat Sheet, simply go to www.dummies.com and type **Funding a New Business For Dummies Cheat Sheet** in the Search box.

Other extra elements mentioned in this book can be found at www.dummies.com/go/fundinganewbusinessfd.

Where to Go from Here

If you're just getting started, you may want to turn the page and start reading. If you're looking for funding sources, check out Part 2. To uncover the roles of different players in the startup ecosystem, including angel investors, venture capitalists, crowdfunding platforms, and accelerators, try Part 3. Part 4 focuses on the critical aspects of finalizing your funding, and Part 5 focuses on the post-funding phase. Regardless of what you choose, we're sure that you'll find what you're looking for!

1
Getting Started with New Business Funding

» **Moving from idea to successful execution**

» **Why do we need startup funding?**

» **How startup funding has evolved**

» **Examples of startup funding that worked**

Chapter **1**

Learning About the Funding Ecosystem

C ongratulations — you've come up with a business idea that passes the laugh test and now you may be feeling like you're taking a cross-country road trip. You're sitting in your ready-to-drive automobile, you have your phone connected to your car's computer system, and you have some notion of where you're going to go.

But when you step on the gas pedal, nothing happens. Just as a car won't go without gasoline in its fuel tank, the lack of money in your business means it won't go very far and your grand dreams will stay locked in your head.

Sadly, many fantastic concepts are never brought into the real world because the founder(s) don't have enough money to do that. When you have a new business, expansion is always the objective, which is why you're reading this book.

No matter if your objective is to broaden your customer base, expand into new geographic areas, or develop innovative new goods, you need two things to succeed: access to sufficient financial resources and financial stability so you can get around the roadblocks that you'll inevitably encounter on your trip.

As you embark on the journey toward securing funding for your startup, keep in mind that you are not on this journey alone. This book will serve as your guide and provide you with the information, strategies, and self-assurance you need to acquire the capital you require and accomplish the objectives you have set for your company.

So, fasten your seat belts, put your favorite beverage in your cup holder, and get ready to enter the exciting world of startup financing. There's excitement up ahead.

Understanding Funding Terms and Definitions

Before we start your trip into the intricate world of startup financing, we need to stop for a moment to acquire a solid understanding of the 30 fundamental funding terms and definitions. After all, you need to know what the signs and road markings mean on your journey before you go.

Whether you are an experienced businessperson or just getting your feet wet in the world of entrepreneurship, these definitions will also serve as your compass.

Accelerator: An organization or a program that offers early-stage entrepreneurs' resources, funding, and coaching in exchange for a share of the company's ownership. A *demo day* is typically the finale of an event, and it is during this time that startups give presentations to potential investors.

Angel investor: A generous individual who possesses additional financial means and recognizes the potential in a newly established business. They offer monetary assistance to a company throughout its formative years to aid in its growth and development. Angel investors typically offer not just financial support but also useful connections and direction for the entrepreneur.

Bootstrappers: People who finance the expansion of the business primarily through their own personal resources and the revenue generated by the company itself, typically avoiding the need for outside financing.

Bootstrapping: Refers to a method of beginning a business that makes use of the founder's resources or the revenue generated by the business itself. It is like having resourcefulness and independence, as well as beginning your business from scratch without receiving capital from outside sources. The practice of bootstrapping typically involves adhering to a stringent budget and making effective use of the resources that are already available.

Burn rate: The amount of money that a business spends in order to meet its operating expenditures before it starts to experience positive cash flow.

Business plan: A comprehensive document that describes every aspect of a business. This document provides an overview of the company's goals, strategies, day-to-day operations, financial projections, and marketing initiatives. It's your company's road map that not only helps founders and investors grasp the potential of the business but also tells you, your team, and the plan's readers the path that it will take to achieve success.

CAC (client acquisition cost): The cost of acquiring a new client is referred to as CAC. It compensates for expenses incurred in connection with operations including marketing, advertising, and sales.

Convertible note: A convertible note is a type of financial instrument that is used to finance businesses. It is a loan that is provided to a company by an investor with the option of being converted into ownership equity (shares) later, typically when the startup receives more significant funding. Convertible notes are a form of early-stage financing that enables startups to access capital without committing to a specific ownership interest right away.

Crowdsourcing: The practice of soliciting monetary contributions from a large number of individuals (referred to collectively as the *crowd*) to finance the development of a product or the operation of a business. It happens rather regularly on several websites.

Due diligence: This term refers to the process of investigating and assessing a business in great detail. It is analogous to performing a comprehensive check of everything to ensure that everything is in order before making a significant financial investment. With the use of due diligence, investors can discover the risks and opportunities associated with a business.

Equity: Another name for an ownership stake in a business. When you have equity in a company, it indicates that you are the owner of a certain number of the company's shares. Think of it as having your own slice of the pie, or your proportionate share of the overall value of the company.

Equity financing: Entails selling ownership shares, often referred to as equity, to investors. In exchange for a share of the company, these investors provide financial backing to the business to facilitate its growth and daily operations.

Exit: In the context of new businesses, an exit refers to a favorable event in which the company's founders and investors receive a return on the money they invested. Common exit strategies include selling the company, going public through an initial public offering (IPO), or merging with another business.

Exit strategy: A well-thought-out plan that outlines how founders and investors anticipate departing from or profiting from their engagement in a corporation. It encompasses possibilities such as selling the company, going public via an IPO, or fusing with another business.

LTV: This is an acronym for *customer lifetime value*, which is a metric that estimates how much money a company can anticipate receiving in total from a single customer over the period of that buyer's relationship with the company. LTV can be used by both new businesses and established companies.

MVP: This is not an acronym for *most valuable player* — in business, it means *minimum viable product*. This term refers to the most basic model of a new good or service that a newly established business can create and introduce to the market-place. A test version was created to gather feedback and determine whether there is interest in the product before investing a significant amount of money in its development.

Monetization: The process of generating cash or profit from a product or service offered by a startup company. It requires determining how the organization will earn revenue, which could be accomplished by subscriptions, advertising, sales, or some other approach.

Pitch: A brief and persuasive explanation of a company concept given by an entrepreneur to prospective customers, partners, or investors to gain their business's support. It is analogous to putting up a compelling argument as to why individuals ought to back or invest in the company.

Private equity: Investing in or purchasing ownership stakes in privately-held companies. It is typically not traded on public stock exchanges and typically involves higher investments in established companies with the purpose of either promoting expansion or boosting the operational efficiency of the business. Private equity investors could improve their earnings by purchasing, reorganizing, or selling enterprises in the market.

Product-market fit: When the product or service offered perfectly satisfies the requirements and expectations of the market it intends to serve. This ultimately results in a huge uptick in customer satisfaction and adoption rates.

ROI: This is an acronym for *return on investment*, which is a method for determining the profitability of an investment by making a comparison between the gains or profits gained from the investment and the capital invested. It makes it easier for investors to assess the performance of their investments and determine whether they made a sound financial choice.

Runway: This term defines how much longer a business can continue operations before it runs out of money. It considers a variety of factors, such as the cash reserves that are accessible, routine spending, and projected earnings.

SaaS: This is an acronym for *software as a service*, which refers to a type of business model in which customers obtain software programs via the cloud on a subscription basis rather than in the traditional manner of installing software on their own computers.

Scaling: The process of expanding the customer base and operations while maintaining or increasing profitability. Scaling can be accomplished in multiple stages. It often involves increasing production capacity or penetrating new markets.

Seed investment: The initial infusion of funds that a company receives to commence its operations, and it is also known as seed funding. This early-stage finance helps ideas become achievable items or services, funds preliminary research, and lays the framework for expansion of the business.

Series A, B, C: Following the initial seed money, the first major fundraising round is often the Series A funding, which is then followed by the Series B funding, the Series C funding, and so on. Each round represents a new degree of development and often comprises increasingly substantial contributions.

Term sheet: An early agreement between an investor and a startup company that states the primary terms and conditions of the funding deal.

User acquisition: The process of gaining new customers or users for a product or service offered by a startup company. It comprises making use of marketing strategies in order to both bring in and retain customers.

Valuation: The process of estimating the amount of money that a company or startup is worth. It is critical for investors to have an accurate understanding of the value of their ownership stake, as this factor plays a role in the terms and conditions of equity financing arrangements.

Venture capital: Refers to the funding that is provided by accredited investors or venture capital firms to newly established businesses, both large and small, that have a strong potential for future growth. Venture capitalists typically demand ownership percentages for their investments and actively support the expansion and development of the businesses they back.

TIP

If you want to read an in-depth glossary that's updated often, visit the article *The Definitive Startup Glossary: 210 Words Every Founder Should Know* on the OpenVC website at https://openvc.app/blog/startup-glossary.

Moving from Idea to Successful Execution

You're here reading this book and ready to start this journey because you believe that your brilliant idea has the potential to make a huge impact on the entire world, or at the very least a sizable chunk of it. After that, what? What steps would need to be taken to turn that idea into a legitimate and lucrative business?

The power of ideas to influence

A fantastic idea is the foundation upon which every prosperous business is built. The journey from having an idea to carrying it out is a matter of research, planning, and an adaptable mindset. Don't forget the intangibles, either — your dogged determination, unwavering commitment, and eagerness to absorb new information will set you apart from the competition.

That said, the first step is to act by driving to your first destination: your research and its results.

Pay attention to the research

It is imperative that you research your journey first as you would with any long road trip. Through conducting market research, you may better understand your company's operating environment and plan for the trip ahead.

When you're starting a new business, market research is analogous to getting a map that you can use. You need to become familiar with the surrounding area before you put your foot on the gas in your fancy vehicle. There are three primary aspects of market research.

Determine who your ideal customer is

When you throw a party for your friends, you want it to be amazing, don't you? Certainly, you do. As a result, you think about the people you want to invite by identifying your target demographic or market. Which segments of the population are most likely to be interested in the products and services that your organization provides? To find out the answer to this question, ask yourself these questions:

>> What piques their interest?

>> Where do they typically go to pass the time?

>> Which of your ideal customer's needs remains unfulfilled?

>> Which of those needs can only be satisfied by your idea?

REMEMBER

Be as specific as possible with your answers to these questions, because specificity will help you craft not only better products and services, but also a better message to reach your target audience.

Analyze industry trends

It's vital to pay attention to your industry. What exactly is going on just this minute? Are there any major shifts that are going to take place soon? Are people's preferences evolving throughout time? By being aware of these things, you can better prepare yourself for new opportunities — and roadblocks.

It's just as important to keep a watchful eye out for trends that are just beginning to take shape. Being an early user of a technology or a service might help you better understand in which direction the market is going.

Research your competition

Think of your competitors as other explorers who are involved in the same trip as you are — it's a cross-country race! (We leave you to think of your favorite movie about road trips and racing before we continue.)

Pay close attention to other businesses in the industry that are analogous to your own. Where do they particularly shine? Which aspects of them do their customers find particularly appealing? In what instances do they fall short of expectations? Is there any way you can make it better?

You need to identify potential gaps that your business can fill. Are there any services that customers want but that your competitors do not provide?

Analyze your customers

Your customers are your traveling companions. If you want to be sure that you are heading in the right direction, you need to be sure that you completely understand what they are saying.

Get in touch with individuals who could be interested in the product or service you are offering. Inquire about their needs, problems, and personal preferences.

Your customers are the ones watching your compass and telling you what direction to go to make the trip enjoyable for you and for them.

Analyze your finances

Your company's finances are the fuel that makes it go, and you can't do anything at all without keeping that gas tank full enough to keep everything moving.

Give a lot of thought to how you'll bring in money and keep it coming in. Will you get income through purchases or subscriptions? When do you think you'll first see a profit from your investment in your product or service?

REMEMBER

You also need to figure out how much money you need to offset your expenses, because your company is always burning fuel, and also set aside a reserve for unforeseen expenses such as inflationary costs making product production more expensive than you expected.

Prepare a business plan

When you have all your research notes together, it's time to put together a business plan, which acts as your itinerary for your trip. A plan not only solidifies your idea in your mind, it's also a crucial tool when you're looking for funding or partnering partnerships. Here's an outline you should use in your business plan:

>> **Your business concept:** Describes the objectives of your organization as well as the qualities that set it apart from others.

>> **Market analysis:** Here you discuss the findings of your research into your business sector, your competitors, and your ideal customers.

>> **Marketing strategy:** Describes your plan for attracting new clients and keeping the ones you now have. That is, how do you plan to communicate with the people who make up your target audience?

>> **Financial projections:** A description of your startup expenses, anticipated revenue, and anticipated earnings. When you create your estimates, be conservative and practical.

>> **Operational plan:** Describes the day-to-day business activities of your company including the policies, processes, and controls you're planning to put into effect.

>> **Your team:** Make a list of the roles that will need to be filled, the abilities that each member of those roles will need to have, and at what points you'll hire them, such as when you reach a financial milestone.

Take baby steps

After you have your business plan, you need to test your product or service in the real world. Though it's tempting to just start looking for funding immediately, potential funders will want to see your idea in action.

To do that, you need to launch a prototype or a minimal viable product (MVP). It's like a customer test drive for the car that you're driving on your road trip. This simplified version of your product or service will give you the feedback you need from genuine customers so you can make improvements, which is like tuning up your car for the best performance.

WARNING

Don't be caught in feature creep as you develop your product or service. You can easily fall into the trap of not producing your product or service until it's just right, so before you start MVP development, be sure to clearly define what it will take for your product or service to be released to the masses.

Why Do We Need Startup Funding?

Now you're ready for your road race in the competitive world of business, and you've come to an essential question that you need to answer: Why do you seek capital for a startup? In this section, we discuss the convincing arguments that demonstrate why collecting financing is frequently a vital stage in the process of turning your company's dreams into a reality.

Fostering creative activity and economic development

Putting money into research and development is essential to produce brand-new products or improve upon those that already exist. With the support of finance, you can experiment, discover fresh solutions, and go through iterations.

As your business grows, you'll need resources so that you may extend your operations, acquire additional personnel, and serve an expanding consumer base. You'll also need resources to fulfill that expanding consumer base.

Don't forget costs associated with marketing. An efficient marketing strategy is essential to bringing in new customers. With the assistance of startup financing, you will have the ability to carry out marketing initiatives in more channels (like paid social media), attract a broader audience, and increase brand awareness.

Getting past the startup stage

When you start a new business, there's a good chance that you're not making much money yet. When you approach financers, you need to spell out where you need financing now and where you need it down the road. There are six important areas your potential investors will want to know about.

Covering operational costs and expenses

Rent, energy, payroll, and other operational costs can be paid by startup financing, which acts as a bridge and ensures you can keep running your day-to-day business as you work toward being profitable.

Bringing in the best possible talent

To launch a successful company, you need more than just a fantastic idea. You also need the ideal people to carry it out and make it a reality. When you have access to your financial fuel, you will have the ability to employ qualified individuals who can contribute to the success of your company by offering them competitive pay and other incentives.

Adjusting to variations in the market

The nature of business is inherently dynamic, and the conditions of the market are subject to rapid change. You need to ensure that you have the right level of funding so your business can adjust to unforeseen curves in the road.

Making course corrections when necessary

It's not always the case that one must wait for the opportune moment before seizing opportunities. The availability of funding helps you capitalize on advantageous opportunities, such as the acquisition of a competitor or the entry into a new market.

Creating a reputation of credibility

In the eyes of potential investors, business partners, and customers, having money to start can significantly boost your reputation. The financial investment from investors demonstrates that other individuals have faith in your idea. And this could result in more investors and customers because financial support implies stability and a dedication to growing your business.

Reducing the danger

You know that running your own business and driving on your journey isn't easy. You'll have to weather bad economic downturns and obstacles in the road, and there is no guarantee of future financial gain. The provision of financing, in the form of a financial safety net, is an important aspect of risk management.

How Startup Funding Has Evolved

In the realm of startup finance, a landscape that was formerly dominated by traditional methods has given way to a landscape that features a diverse ecosystem of funding possibilities. Before we talk about the current state of startup funding, let's take a quick tour of the history of startup finance and how it has evolved over the years.

In the early stages of the business startup industry, it was common for business owners to invest their own money and resources in their ventures, which is better known as bootstrapping. It was an age that was distinguished by innovation, which emerged as a result of a combination of unyielding drive and limited resources.

As their businesses grew, the proprietors of those businesses approached the banks in their communities in search of loans. They also sought the support of family and friends who believed in the cause that they were fighting for. These loans were often secured with the personal assets and relationships of the borrower.

Venture capital

The 1960s and 1970s were pivotal years in the development of the venture capital industry, and the use of venture capital proved to be a big improvement over previous financing methods. Wealthier individuals and institutional investors began providing substantial amounts of capital to newly established enterprises in exchange for ownership holdings in those businesses.

Silicon Valley developed and became a hub for venture capital activity, which fueled the expansion of major technology companies such as Apple, Intel, and Microsoft. This was made possible by the region's evolution. The atmosphere in this region is one that is favorable to innovation, which has resulted in the attraction of investors who are prepared to back ventures that are breaking new ground.

The use of venture capital was linked to higher levels of risk, but it also offered the opportunity to generate significant returns on investment. Investors were aware that not all new enterprises would be successful, but that investors might potentially make great gains from those businesses that did succeed.

Crowdfunding

In the 2000s, online crowdfunding platforms became a popular form of funding new businesses, Creators can present their projects on crowdfunding platforms such as Kickstarter and Indiegogo and collect monetary contributions from supporters in exchange for gifts or early access to the products that they make.

The practice of equity crowdfunding, which enables investors to purchase shares in new enterprises, has begun to be implemented in a growing number of countries. The ability to invest is available to smaller investors, who were subsequently able to take part in early-stage businesses as a result.

Angel investors

Angel investors are people who have significant money and a strong motivation to support entrepreneurial endeavors. These investors have come together to form networks in order to facilitate the sharing of information and resources among themselves. These networks offered new enterprises a technique of collecting finance that was more structured and organized.

Incubators and accelerators

Startups might potentially receive funding, coaching, and access to resources from groups such as Y Combinator and Techstars in exchange for a stake of ownership in the company. These programs act as both incubators and accelerators, and we talk about how they've worked for businesses in the next section.

Examples of Startup Funding that Worked

There is a plethora of examples of entrepreneurs whose businesses have become big success stories as a result of receiving startup capital, and here are three examples from different industries that may inspire you.

Airbnb

In 2007, Joe Gebbia and Brian Chesky rented out air mattresses from their apartment in San Francisco in order to bring in some extra money and cover their living expenses.

Airbnb began with a seed investment of around $20,000, and that money helped Gebbia and Chesky grow their business into one that's known around the world as a service that connects travelers with unique places to stay, for better and for worse.

Today, Airbnb has raised over $7 billion in total investments and has over 4 million hosts in over 100,000 places around the world.

Stripe

In 2010, brothers Patrick and John Collison established Stripe with the intention of simplifying the process of accepting payments online. Because their technology was so user-friendly, businesses had an easier time tracking transactions and accepting payments with it.

The Collison brothers received $20 million in seed funding in 2011, and they focused primarily on the software developer market, and that was the key to their company's success.

Today, Stripe has received over $2 billion in cumulative funding, and they're a leading payment processing platform with a valuation of $50 billion as of 2023.

Beyond Meat

Ethan Brown founded Beyond Meat in 2009, and you may know them from their signature product Beyond Burger. Beyond Meat is known for developing plant-based meat alternatives that mimic the taste and feel of traditional meat products.

Beyond Meat was bootstrapped at the beginning, but venture capital firm Kleiner Perkins was the first to invest in the company in 2011. As more consumers who were looking for veggie meat that tasted more like meat bought Beyond Meat products, more investors flocked to the company.

Today, Beyond Meat has raised about $1 billion from 28 investors, and you can buy not only burgers but also veggie chicken, sausage, and jerky.

Chapter 2

Finding the Funds You Need

Now that you're on the road with your business, it's time for your first stop: finding the funds you need that will turn your dreams into reality and ensure you can reach your final destination (and beyond).

In this chapter, we give you the grand tour of the environment of startup finance and make the complex concepts simple. We start by discussing the different sources of startup financing and move on to the art of matching your financial demands with your business goals.

After you know those demands, you'll learn how to assess the capital needs of each business function to strike a balance between necessary and nice-to-have investments.

Different Business Stages Have Different Funding Needs

It's trite because it's true: There is no one-size-fits-all approach to startup finance. Depending on the stage of development, a business's finance needs can change dramatically.

Any entrepreneur hoping to obtain the appropriate financial support at the appropriate moment must know about these various stages and their accompanying funding requirements. We're here to provide that road map for you, and here are the five stages you need to know about.

The concept stage

Your business concept is still in its infancy at the concept stage. You have a vision that consumes your soul, but your product or service may not be fully formed, and you're probably not making any money.

So, you have two funding options:

» Investments from friends and family or angel investors who support your business plan.

» Bootstrapping, where your personal funds or savings are used to meet startup expenditures. We talk more about bootstrapping in Chapter 4.

But you just don't show up with excitement and an idea if you want people to give you their money. You need to provide the following three things:

» A proof of concept that shows investors that your idea has the potential to succeed (and at least pay the investors back).

» A concise business plan that outlines your concept, market research, and long-term goals.

» An MVP (minimum viable product) or prototype that proves the viability of your product or service.

TIP

To draw in early-stage investors, concentrate on validating your idea and creating a prototype or MVP.

The initial stage

When you get past the idea stage, you're officially in the startup stage. That is, you have an MVP or prototype of your product or service and you're ready to test it in the market.

Funding sources

You probably aren't raking in the dough, either, and so these three funding sources will give you the highest chance of success:

>> **Seed funding:** Continue looking for venture capitalists and angel investors to invest in your business.

>> **Angel investors:** These people invest money in new businesses in exchange for equity.

>> **Crowdfunding:** To raise money from a large audience, use websites like Kickstarter or Indiegogo.

What investors are looking for

Before you start going after money, here are the four things investors want you to show them:

>> **Market validation:** Investors want to know if the market needs your product or service.

>> **Scalability:** Emphasize how your company can expand quickly with the appropriate resources.

>> **Pitch presentation:** Create an engaging pitch that highlights the potential and distinctive value of your company and its capacity to earn profit.

>> **Profit potential:** Your startup idea and pitch needs to demonstrate the ability to drive revenue and become profitable.

TIP

Use networking opportunities to meet possible angel investors or think about using crowdfunding to get started quickly.

The growth stage

Congratulations! Your startup is now in the growth stage and the company is gaining momentum. Your revenue is rising and you have a customer base. To scale quickly, you need to make more investments, though.

Now you can look for venture capital companies that have a focus on your sector or industry and seek Series A funding, which is the initial, significant round of venture capital funding.

What's going to get these potential investors to pay attention to you?

>> **Proof of traction:** Investors want to see sustained growth and a route to profitability.

>> **Company model:** Clearly state your intended market penetration strategy and your company model, which is your core strategy for doing business profitably.

>> **Team strength:** Highlight your team's skills and how you'll retain your team over the long term because investors frequently stake their money on the company's employees.

REMEMBER

Be ready for due diligence from potential investors, because investors in venture capital will examine your company carefully before they make an investment.

The expansion stage

You have funding from the startup stage and now your company is growing quickly. You're probably close to profitability or you've already reached it. After you've taken a little time to celebrate and breathe, it's time to think about increasing growth, penetrating new markets, or buying rival businesses.

If you want to keep growing, you need money, and now you're able to explore Series B, C, and D funding. These rounds include more equity capital to support growth and market dominance.

Potential investors are looking for businesses that are positioned to dominate their respective industries. What's more, if you intend to buy other businesses, be ready to defend your plan and the advantages it offers.

REMEMBER

To draw later-stage investors, make sure your company has a clear path to profitability and sustained growth.

The exit stage

If your company is prepared for a significant liquidity event, such as an IPO or being purchased by a bigger business, you're looking for an exit strategy.

In an initial public offering (IPO), you're getting ready to sell shares to the general public on a stock market. If you want someone to buy your company, you're looking for potential suitors yourself.

As with many things in life, timing is everything when you're planning your company exit. You need to start by ensuring that your finances are in tip-top form. If they're not, potential buyers will find where you've come up short and sound the alarm so other potential buyers will know about it.

That means you'll have to fix your problems and then be transparent about what happened the last time you presented your business for an IPO or put it up for sale.

TIP

To overcome the difficulties of going public or negotiating an acquisition, seek the advice of financial consultants and legal professionals.

Aligning Your Financial Needs with Your Business Objectives

We talked about timing earlier, and if you don't secure the right funds at the right moment and for the right reasons (not just dollars), your business could find itself wasting money on initiatives that don't improve the value of your business.

Now that you know about the different types of funding at different stages, you need to align those needs with your business goals so you can get the most bang from your (and investors') buck.

Establish your business goals

Take a step back and carefully describe your business goals before you're too far into your business road trip. What do you hope to accomplish with your startup, both now and in the future? Your goals ought to be SMART, which is an acronym for *specific, measurable, achievable, relevant, and time-limited*.

Think about some of these typical corporate goals and how many of them apply to your business:

>> **Growth:** Increasing your clientele, breaking into new markets, or growing your business.

>> **Profitability:** Achieving a level of revenue that is greater than expenses and is sustained.

> » **Innovation:** The process of creating and introducing new goods or services.
>
> » **Market dominance:** Becoming the undisputed leader in your specialized field or sector.
>
> » **Exit strategy:** Your strategy that gets your company ready for an acquisition or IPO (initial public offering).

Make a financial needs analysis

After you know what your company's goals are, it's time to evaluate your financial demands. This entails carefully examining the financial needs of your startup at every step of development.

Startup costs

Determine the amount of money needed to start your business. This covers costs for things like marketing, product development, legal fees, and office space.

Operational costs

Calculate continuing costs for things like rent, utilities, employees, and advertising campaigns. Think about how these expenses will change as your business expands.

Working capital

Calculate the amount of capital required to pay for ongoing costs and preserve liquidity.

Growth capital

Determine the amount of money needed to support expansion, whether it is expanding into new markets, hiring more employees, or increasing output.

Contingency funds

Create a contingency fund to prepare for unforeseen costs or economic downturns.

Match funding sources with goals

Now you have your funding sources and the goals that money needs to fuel to keep your ride going, you need to connect those sources to your business goals. It's like the line from the fuel tank to your engine.

Each funding source has a unique role to play in the development of your firm, and not all are created equal. Following are some popular funding options and how they correspond with business goals:

>> **Angel and seed investors:** These investors are great for early-stage entrepreneurs looking to develop their product or validate their idea.

>> **Venture capital:** Suitable for startups looking to grow quickly and take the lead in their industry.

>> **Bootstrapping:** A choice for entrepreneurs who wish to keep total control while gradually expanding their company without outside funding.

>> **Debt financing:** This option is helpful for financing working capital and operational needs, but it may also require interest payments.

>> **Crowdfunding:** A practical choice for early adopters and product-based firms looking for investment.

>> **Initial public offering (IPO):** This is the route you should pursue if you want to become a publicly traded company and raise a sizable amount of money from the public market.

A financial road map

You can't drive to your desired destination without a road map, and your financial road map for your business needs to have four parts that you and your executive team need to understand the old proverbial backwards and forwards:

Milestones

Identify significant milestones that your firm hopes to reach, such as product releases, financial goals, or market expansion.

Funding rounds

Indicate the dates by which you intend to raise money through different rounds, such as seed funding, Series A, B, and so forth.

Budgets

Create thorough budgets for each stage that specify how money will be distributed.

Contingency plans

Foresee foreseeable problems and describe your financial response. Financial requirements and corporate objectives can change over time.

REMEMBER

Regularly review and adjust your financial road map as your startup grows to make sure it stays in line with your goals. Be ready to modify your finance plan in response to shifting market conditions, client feedback, and expansion prospects.

Evaluating the Capital Needed for Each Business Function

To operate your company efficiently, each component of your firm needs a certain amount of capital. Understanding and analyzing the capital required for each business activity, whether it be product development, marketing, operations, or talent acquisition, is essential for effective resource allocation.

Product development

A key task for many businesses is product development. It entails developing and perfecting the core offering that will satisfy the needs of your clients and generate income. These products can be hard products such as earplugs or services such as product delivery.

REMEMBER

If your business only provides services, you know that your service is your product. So, take note that you have to go through the same development process described in this section with a service.

When you start developing your product that will change the world, the obvious area is research and development, better known by the acronym R&D. Of course, this means you have to set aside money for planning, prototyping, and research.

But don't forget that you have to make resources available for testing, quality assurance, and issue remedies. When you send your prototype out for testing by a small number of trusted followers, you need to have enough money invested so you can make timely changes to customer feedback.

REMEMBER

Product development can be expensive, especially for startups in the technology sector. To prevent overinvesting too soon, carefully evaluate your minimum viable product (MVP) needs.

Advertising and client acquisition

No matter how fantastic your product is, you still need strong marketing to reach your target market and persuade them to become paying customers. So, here are the three marketing areas to research and allocate money to:

>> **Digital marketing:** Set aside money for social media marketing, search engine optimization, and online advertising.

>> **Content creation:** Set aside money to create blogs, videos, and other resources that will interest and inform your audience.

>> **Customer acquisition:** Include costs associated with business development, inclusive of partnerships, promotions, and user acquisition efforts.

WARNING

Marketing can be expensive, and results aren't always apparent right away. Keep an eye on the results of your marketing activities and make any necessary adjustments.

Facilities and business operations

If you're going to have a brick-and-mortar business, you need to understand everything about your daily business operations, from inventory management to logistics. So, here are the areas that you need to look at:

>> **Office space:** Set aside money for rent, utilities, and office equipment.

>> **Technology and tools:** To make processes run more smoothly, spend money on necessary software, hardware, and tools.

>> **Inventory or supplies:** If necessary, provide funds for the first purchase of inventory and/or office supplies like staplers and compressed air canisters.

WARNING

Overhead expenses might pile up very rapidly. Take into account cost-cutting strategies like working remotely or using shared offices. This is especially true if your company provides services online, though in those cases you may still need to provide technology to your team such as software and cloud storage accounts.

Talent identification and workplace culture

Finding and keeping the appropriate talent is essential to the success of your startup, because you can't run the business by yourself as you grow no matter how hard you try. (Unless you like ending up in the hospital.) You need to delegate product development, marketing, and overall operations to your team so you can focus on growing the business.

With that said, there are three people areas that require capital:

» **Salaries and perks:** Budget money for attractive salaries and perks to draw in top talent.

» **Recruitment costs:** Include charges for hiring firms, job ads, and onboarding.

» **Training and development:** Make an ongoing training investment to develop the skills of your team and yourself. Becoming a leader and a people manager for the first time is not easy and is often ignored as a critical skill for success.

Turnover is inevitable, and you'll need to factor that into your calculations. High turnover can be expensive to the point of threatening. To keep talent, concentrate on designing a favorable workplace culture as part of your initial business planning.

Your company culture is like the hub in a wheel. Without a strong hub, the wheel can't function very long, and in no time you'll have a confused look on your face as you wonder why you're in a ditch.

Companies that have standout cultures treat other employees and customers with fairness and respect, and as a result, they get all the good stuff:

» They attract the best talent.

» They have high employee engagement scores.

» They have happier customers.

» They generally perform better than companies that don't.

Humans aren't perfect, so no workplace is perfect. However, it's essential to think about what kind of culture you want and emulate the success of company cultures you admire. What's more, if you remember companies with negative cultures from your own experience, draw from that as examples of what not to do.

TIP

If you're still skeptical, don't forget the famous phrase by legendary management consultant Peter Drucker: "Culture eats strategy for breakfast."

Regulatory and legal compliance

Business requires regulations so that everyone has the same type of road to travel. The road conditions may change from time to time, but you want to be sure you avoid bad weather by adhering to federal, state, and local regulations that could impede or even stop the development of your business as it grows.

If you don't know where to start, here are the three areas you need to allocate your money to stay compliant:

>> Legal advice and counsel, possibly on a retainer basis.

>> Expenses related to insurance, licenses, permits, and compliance fees.

>> Data security initiatives to protect yourself and your employees, and this is even more necessary if you deal with consumer data.

REMEMBER

We live in a litigious society, and if you don't set compliance standards as a top priority in the early days of business development, you'll soon be cursing yourself for not doing so as you spend much of your time and money battling lawsuits and government investigations.

Have an emergency fund

When you have a business, life doesn't happen to you any differently. You'll have emergencies and unforeseen potholes in the road that require you to pull over and make any repairs, and so you need to be ready by having a contingency reserve. Without one, you may have to live in your parents' basement instead of the mansion with the heated pool and home theater you've been dreaming of.

Start by setting aside a portion of your company income at least once a month to your emergency fund so you have it stored in the metaphorical company car trunk ready to use.

You may have already figured out that you need to purchase insurance plans, such as professional liability insurance, to protect yourself when lawsuits arise. Research insurance companies carefully to find out what they offer so they can not only serve your business well now but also as you grow.

TIP

Don't forget to keep in contact with your insurance agency regularly to ensure that you'll be able to pay for increases in insurance premiums that come with growth. Otherwise, you'll have to dip into that emergency fund unexpectedly.

Scaling and expansion

After your firm starts to speed up on the road, you'll need money to scale and diversify into new products or market segments so you can keep rolling. So, you need to set aside money in three areas:

>> Market analysis, market expansion, and growth plans.

>> Plan for scaling your operations by adding more production, personnel, and infrastructure.

>> If they are a part of your growth strategy, budget money for possible mergers or acquisitions of competitors and complementary businesses.

WARNING

Like our metaphorical car, scaling too quickly can put a burden on resources and cause your growth plans to stall. Make sure your growth strategies are long term.

Analytics and reporting

It may seem obvious, but decision-making based on data is crucial for your company's long-term success. If you're not sure if spending to analyze data is important, keep in mind that if you don't analyze data, you'll miss opportunities, make decisions that cost money, and put your business at risk.

Here's where you'll need to allocate money so you can analyze data properly:

>> **Analytics tools:** Spend money on systems and software for analytics.

>> **Data management:** Set aside money for tools for managing and storing data.

>> **Skills:** Employ or train personnel with knowledge in data analysis.

Balance-Required Funding versus Nice-to-Have Funding

In our personal lives, we all know about the essential need for money that will pay for things like food and shelter and the "nice to have" money that's set aside for things like enjoying your favorite drink at Starbucks. In your business, understanding the difference between essential capital and the nice-to-have money can decide if the car that represents your business keeps going or runs off the road into a ditch.

We talked about the essential funding that's critical earlier in this chapter. That includes product development, operational costs, working capital for ongoing costs, marketing, and customer acquisition.

Nice-to-have funding: The road to innovation and growth

Nice-to-have money isn't needed for your company's ongoing survival, but that money enables your firm to pursue growth prospects, innovation, and competitive advantages over the long term. For example:

>> **Scaling initiatives:** Funds to expand into new markets or regions.

>> **Research and development:** Spending on new product features and innovation.

>> **Talent acquisition:** Finding top talent to support development and growth.

>> **Marketing expansion:** Stepping up marketing initiatives to reach a wider audience.

Getting the balance right

Finding the ideal balance between essential money and nice-to-have money is always a challenge in our personal lives and in business. A focus on one over the other can result in financial instability or missed possibilities for growth.

How do you strike that balance? Here are three general rules to abide by:

>> **Set priorities:** To ensure the longevity of your firm, make sure the most important money is obtained first.

>> **Calculate ROI:** Assess the possible return on investment for nice-to-have funding.

>> **Determine the growth potential:** Will it considerably improve your chances of development or competitive advantage?

Timing is important

Here's another trite saying for you: Timing is everything. Not only does the amount of capital you secure matter when it comes to balancing essential funding and nice-to-have funding but also when you secure it.

Easier said than done, you say, but we're here for you with three tenets to follow:

» **Secure needed funding first:** Before dedicating resources to nice-to-have initiatives, prioritize getting needed funding.

» **Set growth milestones:** Match funding for nice-to-have projects with certain growth targets. For instance, when your firm hits certain revenue goals, secure expansion finance.

» **Sustainability:** Before undertaking aggressive expansion plans, be sure your firm has a strong financial base.

As you put your financial plan together, another life lesson applies: Be adaptable. Your startup's funding mix of necessary and nice-to-have investment may change as it develops and the market environment changes.

and pitch deck

» **Building detailed P&L(s) scenarios**

» **Sample P&L Excel templates just for you**

Chapter **3**

Getting Your Finances in Good Order

Now you've arrived at your next destination, and it's one that everyone has to stop at if you want to keep going. Before you can turn your idea into reality, you need to create a strong business case and a convincing pitch deck if you want to get the cash you need to fuel your ambitions.

These crucial resources act as your startup's business card, attracting the interest and backing of potential investors, lenders, and collaborators. In this chapter, we give you the manual for perfecting the skill of making a persuasive business case and pitch deck for your target audience.

In this chapter, we go into the nuances of turning your novel idea into a compelling story packed with data-driven insights that show the viability of your firm. This chapter gives you the information and abilities to present your startup in the best possible light, whether you're looking for funding from venture capitalists, angel investors, or crowdfunding sites.

Creating a Compelling Business Case and Pitch Deck

It may be tempting to create your pitch deck before your business case because it's exciting to create a presentation where you tell everyone about the wonderfulness of your business. But you need to know what you're going to talk about first, so let's start with the business case.

The business case

The business case is the narrative of your startup. It's a thorough document that tells the tale of your company from its genesis to its objectives for the future. You have the chance to give investors a comprehensive picture of your company.

But where do you start? Let us show you the sections of the business case that you need to write about.

A succinct summary

Start with an executive summary that effectively conveys the essence of your startup and grabs the reader's attention. Emphasize the most important components, such as your client value proposition, market opportunity, and financial predictions.

Issue and resolution

Clearly express the need that your product or service fills. Look closely at the problems that your target audience has. Then demonstrate how your product successfully addresses this issue and improves your client's quality of life.

Market research

Provide a thorough study of the market, including:

>> Information on its size, which is often referred to as the TAM (total addressable market)

>> The growth rate

>> Trends

>> Competitive environment

Be sure to highlight the potential and market gaps your firm plans to exploit.

Your sales and marketing plan

Describe how you will find and convert clients. Which sales and marketing techniques will you use? Next, describe your distribution plan and sales outlets. Finally, identify the different customer personas that you will be focused on.

Offering value to the client

Describe the competitive advantage of your startup. What distinguishes your product in either an untapped market or a crowded market? How large is the potential of the market you are going after? After you answer that question, describe how your unique approach, talented team of people, and innovation will lead to success.

Your business strategy

Explain how your startup intends to make money. Is it done through the sale of products, membership fees, advertising, or some other form of monetization? After you explain that, share details about your pricing strategy, revenue forecasts, and your path to becoming profitable.

Talk about your team

Describe your team members' roles and responsibilities, accomplishments, and how they will contribute to the success of your startup.

What's more, emphasize any accomplishments and industry domain knowledge amongst your team that is relevant to further establish your credibility and likelihood to succeed.

Financial projections

Provide financial projections, such as income statements, balance sheets, and cash flow forecasts, that are reasonable and whose assumptions can be backed up.

Be open and honest about the assumptions guiding your financial projections and the reasoning behind your figures. You will be asked how you'll handle situations when, not if, everything doesn't go according to plan. It's important to think through worst-case scenarios and how you will respond to them, such as:

>> What if you don't get X number of customers or Y revenue by Z date?

>> What if your key person gets into a car accident and is in a body cast for weeks?

>> What if your strongest customer suddenly becomes your weakest?

TIP

Provide different financial scenarios and categorize them. For example, you can use Conservative, Moderate, and Aggressive. Be sure you define what your categories mean because investors may ask.

Funding demand

Clearly outline the amount of financing you need and exactly how you plan to spend it among the various aspects of your company and over what time frame.

Then offer a convincing justification for why this money is essential for the expansion and success of your firm. To the greatest extent possible, tie the need for funding back to revenue targets in your financial projections.

REMEMBER

Investors aren't putting money into your business only out of the goodness of their hearts — they're investing so they can make money. So, don't forget to tell investors how they'll get their money and when. If you don't, they'll ask you with pointed stares.

Timeline and milestones

Describe the important milestones your startup has reached or aspires to reach. This offers information about your track record to date and your vision for the future,

Next, create a timeline that depicts your path, from the founding of the firm to its upcoming milestones.

The pitch deck

Now that you have a clear idea of what you're going to present to investors, you need to create an engaging presentation to convince them that your business case is worth their time and money.

Your chance to deliver an engaging presentation that simply captures the core of your startup is with the pitch deck. It's about leaving a lasting impression and arousing interest quickly.

In many cases, it makes sense to hire a professional to help you with the creation of your pitch deck and help you with delivering it. Before you hire a pro, familiarize yourself with what your pitch deck requires with these handy-dandy guidelines.

Cover slide

Start with a visually stunning cover slide that features the name, logo, and a catchy tagline or core message for your firm. This slide needs to establish the atmosphere for an engaging presentation.

Problem proposition

Explain the unmet need your product or service solves in the first sentence of your pitch. Stress the importance and relevance of the issue.

Next, explain why it is important to solve this issue and the outcome of solving for this issue, which should at least in part be lots of money.

The solution you provide

Clearly explain your solution and how it successfully solves the problem you've identified. Use visuals to clarify complex ideas and improve understanding, such as diagrams and/or product photos.

The market potential

Give a quick overview of the market opportunity, emphasizing its size, growth potential, and allure. Then describe how your startup is positioned to take advantage of this opportunity.

Milestones and progress

Highlight any significant achievements that your startup has had so far. This could include statistics on users, earnings, collaborations, honors, or noteworthy accomplishments.

Then talk about the progress you're making in other areas that will lead to more wins — and when you think those wins will come.

Your revenue strategy

Provide a succinct description of your revenue strategy and the way you intend to make money from your product or service.

Though the text can be in one or more slides, be sure that the text is relatively brief but hangs together. You don't want to get the dreaded "PowerPoint poisoning" where people are forced to read a long paragraph in one slide.

Your unique value proposition

Describe how your startup has a competitive advantage. What distinguishes you from already-available options or rival companies?

Your team

Introduce the members of your core team, highlighting their responsibilities, areas of expertise, and contributions. What's more, have the team members express why they're dedicated to the success of your startup.

TIP

If a team member can't be present for your presentation, record a quick and professionally edited video so you can play it at the appropriate time.

Financial projections

Provide high-level financial predictions with an emphasis on profitability and growth possibilities. The goal is to emphasize your startup's financial appeal as an investment opportunity.

Request and financial use

Clearly outline the amount of funds you are requesting as well as how you plan to use them to advance your company. You also need to describe how the funding will be distributed among your company's many divisions.

Final thoughts and a call to action

Conclude your pitch with a strong statement that highlights the potential of your startup. Then give your audience a strong call to action, such as asking for a meeting, an investment, or a collaboration.

The five guides to success

Now that you have a script, here are five presentation guidelines to follow when you create your pitch deck for potential investors:

>> **Simplicity and clarity:** Keep your pitch deck and business case simple and straightforward. Steer clear of technical jargon and superfluous details.

>> **Visual appeal:** To increase understanding and engagement, include visuals like graphs, pictures, and infographics.

>> **Practice makes perfect:** Practice delivering your pitch several times to ensure a polished and assured performance. Anticipate questions the people you are presenting to will have and be prepared to answer them.

- **» Tailor to the audience:** Whether you are pitching to partners, consumers, or investors, make sure your pitch is tailored to the audience you are speaking to.

- **» Ask for input:** To improve both your business case and pitch, show your draft to mentors, advisors, and peers so you can get their input and polish your presentation to a glowing shine. What's more, accelerators and groups of investors can give you great feedback.

Building Detailed P&L Scenarios

Understanding and accurately predicting your profit and loss (P&L) is more than simply a financial exercise in the world of startup finance; it's a strategic requirement.

Your startup will be guided by your P&L statement as it navigates the complex landscape of revenues, costs, and expenses. It gives you a complete picture of your financial performance, assisting you in evaluating the strength and potential of your company for investors, lenders, and internal team members.

One of the critical hires for your team is someone who understands finance and can help build and explain your financial model. Remember, most of your investors are going to be finance people, and having someone who can speak their language is essential.

You need to understand the basic structure of a profit and loss statement before starting to develop complex P&L scenarios, because if you don't have a firm grasp of what's happening with your books, you won't be able to hold conversations with potential investors. As the owner or CEO of the company, why should an investor give their money to someone who doesn't appear to understand their own financials?

The elements of a P&L

As always, we're here to get you up to speed. A typical P&L includes the following essential elements:

- **» Revenue:** Your startup's revenue, which represents the inflow of funds produced by primary operations, is at the center of your P&L. This includes earnings from the selling of goods, the provision of services, or any other sources of income.

>> **Cost of goods sold (COGS):** COGS examines the direct expenses related to manufacturing the products or services you provide. It includes costs for things like labor, materials, and other direct manufacturing costs.

>> **Gross profit:** The difference between your revenue and COGS is your gross profit. This indicator shows how much money your firm makes before deducting additional operating costs.

>> **Operating expenses:** Operating expenses cover a wide range of charges, including rent, staff wages, marketing costs, and utility prices. Although they are not directly related to production, these are necessary for running your firm.

>> **Operating income:** Operating income, also known as operating profit, is the amount left over after operating costs are deducted from gross profit. It displays the operating income produced by your primary business operations.

>> **Interest and taxes:** The financial commitments listed in your P&L statement include loan interest costs, as well as income taxes owing to the government.

>> **Net income:** The final number on your P&L is your net income, which is calculated by subtracting interest, taxes, and any other non-operating costs from your operational income.

Developing complete P&L scenarios

Now that you have a grasp of the P&L basics, it's time to create intricate P&L scenarios, which involves creating a mosaic of potential outcomes. Each outcome explores different revenue, cost, and expense trajectories. This may seem daunting, but we have the detailed eight-part instruction manual for building these outcomes here in your hands.

Sales forecasts

Start by estimating the revenue from sales. Create a variety of sales scenarios based on industry trends and the potential of your product, ranging from cautious growth to aggressive expansion. These scenarios should reflect assumptions about how much of your product can be produced within a given time, how long your sales cycles might be, and when customers actually pay you.

Your projections of costs and expenses

Create thorough predictions for your costs and spending, taking into account both fixed and variable components. Include contingency funds to prepare for the problems and events you can't see, as well as increases in costs on at least an annual basis. A great example of this are people on your team, who will expect raises annually to at least cover the cost of inflation.

Sensitization evaluation

Run sensitivity analyses by adjusting important parameters like pricing, sales volume, or production costs. Determine the effects these variances have on your P&L and overall financial health. It shouldn't surprise you that you need to know if your projections result in a surplus or deficit and how you plan to deal with each scenario.

Flow of cash projections

Create cash flow estimates while paying close attention to when cash comes in and goes out. These estimates will tell you if your startup will have enough capital on hand for tough times, and if it doesn't, that will probably lead to discussions with your team about how to shore up your cash flow. Here's something else that shouldn't surprise you: Mismanagement of cash flow is one of the key mistakes made by startup business owners.

Worst-case suppositions

Speaking of worst-case scenarios, you need to take into account any considerable obstacles or unforeseen setbacks. You may think of hypothetical situations that may be stuff only Hollywood scriptwriters would think of, but a lot of businesses didn't have a global pandemic shutting down operations on their bingo cards in 2020.

So, go through a bunch of hypothetical scenarios from a possibility, such as an economic recession, to the unthinkable, such as the loss of one or more key employees. These situations will help you check your business model's ability to withstand financial shocks and show investors that you are ready.

How you'll spend the money you receive

Clearly describe your intended use of the requested funding and show how it is consistent with your P&L projections. Investors want confidence that their money will support the expansion of your firm and their personal profit.

A financial model's function

Fortunately, you don't have to do this from scratch. There are financial modeling software apps available that can substantially simplify the process of creating intricate P&L scenarios. By financial modeling, we mean that you're building mathematical representations of your startup's financial performance under various circumstances.

But why should you consider investing in this software? Besides making your life easier, let us count the (three) ways:

» **Accuracy:** Financial models carry out intricate calculations with accuracy, lowering the possibility of mistakes in your P&L projections.

» **Scenario testing:** Models let you test multiple situations in a methodical manner to gain insights into possible outcomes.

» **Investor confidence:** Strong financial models inspire investor trust by demonstrating your dedication to meticulous financial planning.

Accepting realism

Entrepreneurship is fueled by hope, whereas startups are grounded by realities. Avoid the temptation to make too optimistic estimates because they could cause investors to become skeptical.

You should always be realistic before you present your proposal, because it'll be a lot harder to convince an investor to overcome the objection you gave them with your numbers.

It should be obvious that you need to base your expectations on data-driven estimates. Transparency counts for a lot too, so be open and honest about your underlying assumptions by outlining them explicitly in your financial predictions.

Investors respond favorably to thoroughness and honesty, which promotes trust. Investors are your passengers on your journey, so they want to trust that you're not going to drive off and crash into a cow pasture.

Always evaluate and update as needed

Creating P&L scenarios is a continuous process that you need to leave in the trusted hands of your CFO (Chief Financial Officer) or Controller. That person's job is to constantly review your financial model and talk with you and other team members (as needed) about updating your P&L forecasts.

As your startup matures, market dynamics change, fresh information appears, and your estimates must also mature. That not only lets you make wise financial decisions but also keeps your investors happy.

Your financial statements tell a story. They tell you what happened in the past and predict on some level what is going to happen in the future.

Sample P&L Excel Templates Just for You

Microsoft Excel is a popular spreadsheet tool in business, and you can use it to create P&L statements. If you want to see what sample P&L templates look like, we've put some together in Excel that you can download from this book's page on the Dummies.com website.

Each of the three templates covers a core component of your financial model: the balance sheet, a cash flow forecast, and a profit and loss statement. Those three templates appear below (as Figures 3-1, 3-2, and 3-3, respectively) so you can see what they look like before you download them.

After you download them, you can change the numbers for your business. At the least, you'll be able to get a rough idea of the numbers you need so you can build out your model.

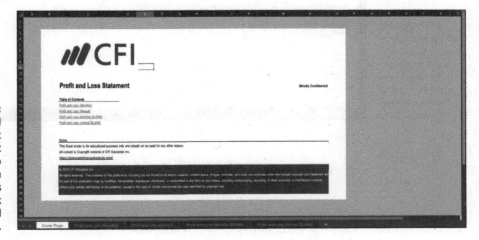

FIGURE 3-1: The profit and loss statement spreadsheet has links to worksheets with sample data as well as blank monthly and annual sheets.

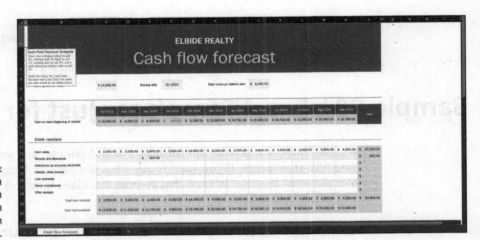

FIGURE 3-2:
A sample cash flow forecast with sections for cash on hand and cash flow receipts.

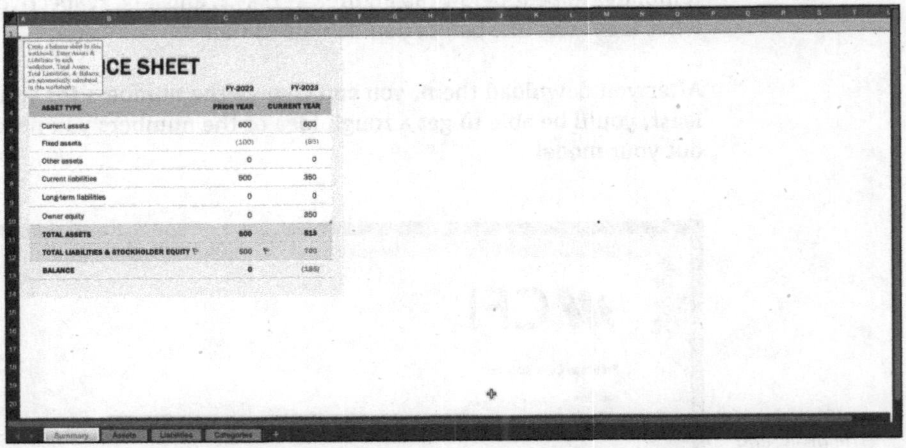

FIGURE 3-3:
The balance sheet template with a summary, assets, liabilities, and categories in separate worksheet tabs shown in the bottom-left.

2
Exploring Funding Options

Chapter **4**

Bootstrapping: Starting with What You Have

Bootstrapping is one of those words associated with startups because the term evokes romanticism about the intrepid entrepreneur scraping and clawing to become successful.

This chapter offers a deep dive into the skill of developing a business not by external financial help but rather by pure persistence, resourcefulness, and a willingness to start with what you already have.

As we proceed through this chapter, you'll learn the fundamentals, methods, and success stories that illustrate the path of entrepreneurs who have begun their ventures on a modest scale but have aspirations on a much larger scale.

What Is Bootstrapping?

The term bootstrapping is a phrase taken from the concept of "pulling oneself up by one's bootstraps," which refers to the determination and self-sufficiency that are required to do something meaningful.

In terms of startups, bootstrapping refers to the practice of developing and expanding a company with little to no money from outside sources, typically beginning with the proprietor's own resources and ingenuity.

As your guides, we're here with some guiding ideas that define bootstrapping that will help you better understand what's involved if you go down this route.

Responsible growth

Bootstrapped firms place a higher priority on achieving sustainable growth than they do on rapidly increasing their operations. They are not interested in chasing inflated valuations or success in the short run. Instead, they put their attention toward laying a solid foundation and making certain that each phase of growth can support itself financially on its own.

Streamlined and efficient operations

Bootstrapping a business means cutting costs wherever possible, including administrative ones. They steer clear of superfluous bureaucracy and hierarchical structures, which enables them to make decisions more quickly and adapt more readily to shifting market conditions.

Lower risk profile

Although bootstrapping does involve risk, it encourages risk-taking that is calculated and in moderation rather than recklessly taking chances. The company's founders weigh the possibility of gain against the dangers of the venture and then make decisions based on that analysis.

Going beyond personal resources

In addition to using personal resources, bootstrapped businesses typically investigate alternative financing sources such as crowdfunding, microloans, and grants at some point in the company's lifecycle. Without having to give up equity, these sources can provide your business with a much-needed financial boost.

In pursuit of profitability

This is typically one of the first goals of bootstrappers from the very beginning. They plan to start bringing in money early on in the company's lifetime in order to reduce their need for outside financing.

Staying adaptable

Founders who have grown their businesses through bootstrapping channel their inner Darwin by understanding adaptability is essential. They're open to adjusting their business models or strategies in response to feedback from the market that indicates they need to change direction.

Advantages and Disadvantages of Bootstrapping

Okay, now that you know what's involved in bootstrapping, you're undoubtedly wondering what the benefits and drawbacks are before you put your own money into your business car's fuel tank. We've told you that every business is different one or ten times before in this book, so read this section carefully to see if bootstrapping matches what you're trying to do with your startup.

Advantages

We start with the good news first: There are four benefits that come with bootstrapping your new venture.

Independence and control

When you rely on your own resources and labor, you keep complete control over the decisions, methods, and directions that your company takes. What's more, there is no requirement for you to water down your business idea in order to win over outside investors and launch your startup.

Learning opportunities

Because bootstrapping is an approach that emphasizes hands-on work, it offers a well-rounded education in entrepreneurship. As a founder who is funding their company from their own resources, you'll have to wear multiple hats and you'll get invaluable expertise in many areas of your company. Because of your extensive knowledge, you have the abilities necessary to effectively confront obstacles.

Lower (but not zero) risk

In general, the financial risk that is associated with companies that are self-funded is far lower than that which is associated with firms that receive funding from outside sources. You are free to concentrate on creating a viable business at your own speed now that you are not under the burden of having to repay significant loans or satisfy the expectations of investors. The alleviation of some of the strain placed on your finances can be beneficial to the long-term success of your endeavor.

Encourages long-term thinking

Bootstrapped startups always work toward the goal of being profitable as quickly as feasible. Not only does this self-sufficiency give financial security, but it also minimizes the need for outside financing sources. You're also free to reinvest money in the expansion and improvement of your company.

The inevitable disadvantages

Yes, there's bad news that you have to be aware of, too. The drawbacks come in six different areas and will test your patience. As you read through this section, ask yourself if you can avoid being the back-seat kid asking, "Are we there yet?"

Limited financial resources

Bootstrapped businesses typically have limited access to financial and other resources, which can make it difficult for them to achieve their full growth potential. Your capacity to scale operations to meet growing demand may be hindered if you do not have sufficient funds to spend on marketing, employ critical talent, or scale operations.

Growth that's not as fast as you want

Organizations that are self-funded through internal resources typically see growth that is less rapid as compared to organizations that receive significant finance from outside sources. Without sufficient resources, it might be difficult to grow your consumer base, access new markets, or rapidly innovate new products or services.

Wearing lots of hats

Entrepreneurs wear a lot of hats, and though this gives them a lot of experience, they may also experience burnout at some point. Maintaining a healthy equilibrium between one's professional and personal life is essential for long-term success, so you need to plan ahead to handle this stress in your life.

Competitors may be better funded

A disadvantage in the marketplace is that your bootstrapped startup may find it hard to keep up in the race with rivals that are supported by considerable capital. Competitors who have access to significantly more resources may be able to conduct extensive marketing efforts, make investments in innovative technology, or grow at a faster rate than your company can.

Financial shortfalls

Your bootstrapped business may run into financial shortages at various stages of your growth. These voids can make it difficult to carry out expansion plans or restrict your ability to capture opportunities that are time-sensitive. You need to plan carefully and have a lot of flexibility if you're going to navigate these winding, curvy stretches in the road.

Limited expertise

Because bootstrapping typically involves working with a small team, there is a possibility that the team will lack expertise in certain key areas. It can be difficult to find highly skilled workers who are also affordable, which can have a negative impact on a company's capacity to compete effectively.

Creating Strategies for Minimizing Expenses

To be successful as a bootstrapper, you need a strong knack for managing resources effectively. Every dollar that is put aside in the form of savings is a dollar that may be put toward the expansion of your company. We see you nodding your head with a confused look on your face because you're not sure how to do that. We have the strategies to do just that for you in this section.

Adopt a lean way of operating

Utilizing a lean strategy to run business operations is essential to the success of a business that is self-funded. This necessitates carefully analyzing each step of the process, as well as every expense, to pinpoint the areas in which you can get the most bang for your buck. Here are the four steps to become a lean, mean operating machine:

1. **Get rid of waste:** Identify and get rid of any activities or resources that aren't directly contributing to the value proposition of your company. This may involve paying for software subscriptions that you don't need, having meetings that could be emails, or going through superfluous processes.

2. **Outsource wisely:** Give some thought to outsourcing projects that are not directly related to your company's key skills. This enables you to take advantage of particular skills without incurring the costs associated with employing someone full-time. The provision of any and all services, from customer assistance to graphic design, can be outsourced.

3. **Work remotely:** Take advantage of working from home whenever the opportunity presents itself. This not only eliminates the requirement for actual office space, but it also enables you to access a larger talent pool without being limited by geographic location.

4. **Trade and barter:** Investigate the possibility of doing business the old-fashioned way by trading or bartering your services or products with other companies. If you are able to contribute something of value to another organization, then it is possible that they will provide you with the goods or services that you require in return.

Minimize fixed costs

The burden of fixed costs such as rent and electricity can be particularly difficult for firms that are self-funded. Keeping your financial options open requires that you reduce these expenses as much as possible, so here are three ways to make sure every penny counts.

Working from home

If you decide to run your business out of your home, be sure that your working space is clean, well-organized, and a place that encourages productivity. Also be sure to minimize your distractions, because YouTube videos are not your friend.

Coworking spaces

If you find that you need a dedicated workspace, you should investigate coworking spaces. These shared work settings typically provide more adaptable lease terms in addition to a wider variety of amenities at a cost that is far lower than that of standard office rents.

Be energy efficient

To lower your monthly utility bills, consider switching to LED lighting, improving heating and cooling systems, and turning off equipment when it is not in use.

Technology that is compatible with bootstrapping

Cheap and easy access to technology has made bootstrapping easier than ever before, and before you get your startup out on the road, stop to shop for software in three areas.

Open-source software

If you have the option, you should look into employing open-source software alternatives. The use of these applications is typically free of charge, despite the fact that they could be just as capable as their paid equivalents.

One popular tool is the Google Docs Editors suite that includes Google Docs for word processing and the Google Sheets spreadsheet.

Cloud computing

Use cloud computing and platforms that provide software on a subscription basis, also known as software as a service (SaaS). These solutions frequently offer price models that are scalable, which means that you may pay just for what you require, which lowers the initial investment. Office 365 and Adobe Creative Cloud are two examples.

Automation

If you have a lot of repetitive work, you should invest in automation tools. This not only helps save time, but also reduces the number of additional staff that is required. Marketing automation is one such example, with popular tools like Mailchimp and HubSpot for Startups used for email marketing and customer relationship management.

Engage in discussions and look for discounts

Never underestimate the power of bargaining with service providers, merchants, and suppliers. Many businesses are eager to provide discounts, particularly to repeat consumers who have been loyal to them. Here are three things to do before and during negotiations to make them successful for your business:

>> **Do your research:** Investigate several different vendors to have a better understanding of the pricing variances. Make use of this information as a bargaining chip during the negotiation process.

>> **Discounts for loyalty:** If you have been a consistent client, you may be eligible for discounts or rewards programs if you inquire about them.

>> **Get payment terms:** If you want to increase your cash flow, you should negotiate favorable payment terms with your vendors, such as extended payment windows.

Manage your cash flow well

It's easy enough to say keep close watch over your company's expenditures and conduct regular audits to see where your money is going. That's true if you're bootstrapping your company or not. How to do that is the catch, but there are easy ways to do that nowadays.

Use accounting software

On a daily basis, use accounting software designed to manage expenses and break spending down into different categories. Popular software includes QuickBooks, FreshBooks, and Xero.

Also set up frequent financial audits to evaluate the value and necessity of each expenditure. You can review your previous month's finances at the beginning of every month and see what expenses are slowing you down.

TIP

You may also want to hire a CPA or a bookkeeper to audit your books on a regular schedule to catch anything that you missed, as well as get pointers from the CPA about any financial issues coming that will affect your finances for good or ill.

Make investing in your business your top priority

Although it is important to keep costs as low as possible, your company still needs to make some investments to grow. Use discretion while deciding how to distribute your financial resources. Investing in ways that will immediately affect revenue generation or long-term sustainability should be your priority.

Keep cash on hand

The ability to effectively manage one's company's cash flow is absolutely necessary for bootstrapped startups. Always make sure you have enough cash on hand to cover emergency costs as well as any other costs that may arise. By carefully controlling both your receivables and payables, you can prevent overextending your resources.

Good Examples of Successful Bootstrapped Startups

A running theme of this chapter is that you're talking to real people, and so a core tenet of online etiquette is to treat others respectfully. That's especially true when they make mistakes and violate the rules of your meeting or your classroom, or when they flout online etiquette in the wild.

Basecamp

Basecamp is a popular project management and online collaboration software app that is a renowned example of a business that was successfully bootstrapped. Initially established in 1999 under the name 37signals, the company started off providing web design services before shifting its focus to software solutions. The success of their main product, Basecamp, may be attributed to the ease of use and impressive results it delivers in the field of project management.

Founders Jason Fried, Carlos Segura, and Ernest Kim implemented their bootstrapping strategy by concentrating on developing a solution that catered to their personal requirements and difficulties. They resisted the impulse to chase venture financing, which allowed them to keep their staff small, embrace remote work, and maintain flexibility. They instead relied on the income made from their products to drive their expansion.

The most important thing to remember is that the success of Basecamp demonstrates the potential of developing a product that addresses actual issues and places an emphasis on profitability from the very beginning. They were able to maintain control over the direction their company was headed in while also becoming evangelists for the bootstrapping method.

Dell

Michael Dell, who was still a college student at the time, laid the groundwork for what would become the successful computer technology business Dell in 1984.

Michael had the ambitious goal of circumventing the established approach of computer retail by selling fully customized PCs to end users directly. Dell saw phenomenal growth and emerged as a dominant force in the competitive computer business.

Based on his personal resources, Dell's early success was predicated on a direct-to-consumer model that allowed for cost reductions and personalization.

This strategy is known as a *bootstrapping strategy*. The corporation placed a strong emphasis on effective operations and preserved tight control over its distribution network. It went public while maintaining a substantial degree of control over its operations.

The most important thing to take away from Dell's path is that it demonstrates how success can be achieved even in highly competitive industries by having a clear vision, effective processes, and a direct connection with customers.

GoPro

Nick Woodman established the firm that would become known as GoPro in 2002. The company is famous for its action cameras and the accessories that go along with it.

Nick wanted to take high-quality action shots when he was on a surfing trip, which is when he came up with the idea for GoPro. It was using a 35-millimeter film that he created the first GoPro camera, and from there the company expanded.

GoPro's early success was motivated by the company's focus on providing a unique product that catered to action sports enthusiasts. The profits were plowed back into the corporation for further research and development of products, as well as marketing.

The most important takeaway from GoPro's history is that amazing success can be achieved by the combination of a passionate entrepreneur and a focus on meeting the specific requirements of individual customers.

Meta

Mark Zuckerberg established the platform, which was initially established as "The Facebook," in 2004 while Zuckerberg was enrolled as a student at Harvard University.

Facebook eventually morphed into the social media behemoth that is now known as Meta. With platforms such as Facebook, Instagram, WhatsApp, and Oculus VR, the firm revolutionized how people connect with one another and exchange information online.

In the early days of Facebook, founder Mark Zuckerberg and his team concentrated their attention on developing a platform that was popular among college students. Although they were successful in attracting early funding, the company put an emphasis on achieving rapid development and expanding their user base.

The most important thing to take away from this story is that it demonstrates the potential of a game-changing vision and relentless execution, even if it requires initial investment. The transformation of the corporation into a global technology powerhouse exemplifies the significance of innovative thinking in the early years of the social media era.

Chapter **5**

Tapping into Personal Funding Options

After the euphoria of your business idea wears off, the next question you're probably asking is more sobering: "Where can I find the money to make it happen?"

Although the road ahead provides a plethora of opportunities for obtaining financing for your startup, one source of capital that is frequently ignored is one's own pockets. In this chapter, we will discuss the power of personal finance choices and how you may make the most of your own financial resources to transform your vision of entrepreneurship into a reality.

Using Personal Savings, Credit, and Assets as Funding Sources

Starting a business requires a leap of faith, and for many would-be business owners, that leap of faith begins with their own personal wealth.

There is a common misconception among entrepreneurs regarding the significance of personal funding. After all, your funds, investments, and assets can serve as a solid foundation for your new venture. What's more, your own assets, credit lines, and savings can be extremely useful tools that can help you fuel your startup as it cruises down the road.

Using your own reserves and savings

Your own personal funds are the most easily available and straight forward source of finance for your startup business. This is the starting point. It refers to the money that you have set aside for a certain purpose, whether in the form of a savings account, investments, or some mix of the two.

Using this money gives you a number of benefits, including independence. You're not dependent on investors and so you have complete control over the path that your organization takes.

However, reliance on one's personal money does not come without its share of potential pitfalls. You're putting your money where your mouth is, and the road ahead is filled with risk and uncertainty.

TIP

Consider beginning with a strategy that is friendly to your finances in order to reduce your risk. Before you scale up, you should first develop a more streamlined version of your product or service, try it out in the market, and verify your overall concept. This is a win-win: You not only lower your risk, you get valuable feedback and hone your product or service.

Taking advantage of your own credit

Credit can be a literal lifeline for entrepreneurs who don't have considerable personal savings and don't have access to credit lines or credit cards. But (and it's a big but) because these choices come with high-interest rates, it's essential to make responsible use of them and make prompt payments toward balances in order to avoid accruing even more debt.

If you own a home, you could choose to access your home's equity by taking out a home equity loan or a home equity line of credit (HELOC). In comparison to interest rates offered by credit cards, loans, and unsecured credit lines, the rates offered by these alternatives are frequently cheaper.

WARNING

Keep in mind that your home will act as collateral for the loan, placing your property at risk in the event that your company runs into financial trouble. That could lead you to become penniless — and possibly divorced.

Using your own resources

There are a number of assets you own that you can use as fuel to not only get you on the road but keep you going to the next milestone.

The sale of personal assets

By personal assets, we mean stocks, bonds, or precious goods, is another way to get fuel for your business. Although this can give an initial infusion of cash, take care to evaluate the long-term consequences of parting with these assets. These implications include the possibility of incurring capital gains taxes as well as the opportunity cost of missing out on future earnings.

TIP

At the risk of sounding like Gollum from *Lord of the Rings*, precious things are anything with a resale value such as jewelry, vehicles, and equipment. (You probably read this in Gollum's voice, didn't you?)

Retirement accounts

401(k) rollover for business startups (ROBS) and *self-directed individual retirement accounts (IRAs)* are two examples of the types of retirement accounts that some business owners look into using in order to access their retirement funds in order to finance their businesses.

These accounts may be able to generate large amounts of money, but they come with a host of complications and hazards, including the possibility of incurring tax penalties and putting your retirement savings in jeopardy.

TIP

Rollovers for business startups (ROBS) are discussed in greater depth on the following page of the IRS website: `https://www.irs.gov/retirement-plans/rollovers-as-business-start-ups-compliance-project`.

Consider this

Now that you know the options that are available to you, you need to get your favorite beverage, sit in a comfortable chair, and absorb your reality to find out if your business engine will rev up when you step on the gas.

Consider your current financial situation

Before you spend any of your own money, analyze your current financial condition carefully. Determine the overall amount of money you have saved, take a close look at your regular costs, and research your legal and ethical responsibilities regarding spending money in and for your business.

On this book's webpage on www.dummies.com, we've given you a downloadable personal monthly budget sheet that you can update for your needs and use as a guide for managing your personal finances. Figure 5-1 shows you what it looks like.

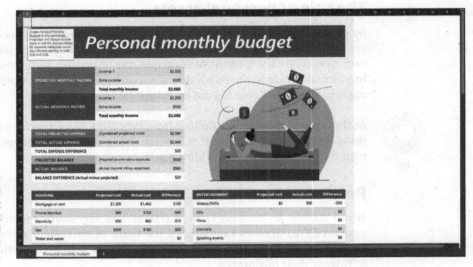

Personal monthly budget

PROJECTED MONTHLY INCOME	Income 1	$2,500
	Extra income	$500
	Total monthly income	$3,000
ACTUAL MONTHLY INCOME	Income 1	$2,500
	Extra income	$500
	Total monthly income	$3,000

TOTAL PROJECTED EXPENSE	(Combined projected cost)	$2,060
TOTAL ACTUAL EXPENSE	(Combined actual cost)	$2,040
TOTAL EXPENSE DIFFERENCE		$20
PROJECTED BALANCE	(Projected income minus expenses)	$940
ACTUAL BALANCE	(Actual income minus expenses)	$960
BALANCE DIFFERENCE (Actual minus projected)		$20

HOUSING	Projected cost	Actual cost	Difference		ENTERTAINMENT	Projected cost	Actual cost	Difference
Mortgage or rent	$1,500	$1,400	$100		Videos/DVDs	$0	$50	-$50
Phone Number	$60	$100	-$40		CDs			$0
Electricity	$50	$60	-$10		Films			$0
Gas	$200	$180	$20		Concerts			$0
Water and sewer			$0		Sporting events			$0

Personal monthly budget

FIGURE 5-1:
The personal monthly budget lets you track projected and actual income and expenses.

Make a budget for your startup

Take the time to create a detailed budget for your new business. Provide an accounting of your starting costs, ongoing business expenses, and anticipated levels of revenue. You will gain a better understanding of how much cash you require and how your own personal finances will be spent as a result of reading this.

Consult with a qualified expert

Consult with professionals in the fields of finance, accounting, and the law who are familiar with the repercussions of using one's own personal assets as a source of funding for a new venture. They can offer insightful advice, assist you in navigating difficult financial decisions, and ensure that you are in conformity with any legislation.

TIP

If you don't know of good financial and legal experts, consult your local chamber of commerce. They'll be happy to give you contact information of business pros who want to help business owners in your community.

Increase the variety of funding sources

It can be perilous to rely only on your own resources for financial support. Investigate many different avenues of funding, such as grants, loans, or crowdsourcing, in order to diversify the sources of your money and minimize the risk to your personal finances.

Preserve money set aside for emergencies

Be sure to keep your startup cash and an emergency reserve in different accounts. This reserve should cover personal emergencies and other unforeseen expenses so you can ensure that your personal financial stability is not compromised.

Be a wise manager of your debt

If you use credit cards or take out loans, be sure you do it responsibly. Quickly paying off debts with high-interest rates is the best way to prevent accruing further interest charges. We're also putting on our Captain Obvious hat here to remind you not to make late payments and avoid going beyond the limits of your available credit.

A lot of great business owners aren't good stewards of their debt, and if you think you can't manage it, enlist a trusted team member or an external financial expert to do that work for you.

Think carefully about your equity in your home

Carefully consider the repercussions of leveraging the equity in your house if you're thinking about using a home loan or line of credit as business fuel. Be aware of the potential negative effects on the financial stability of your home as well as the hazards involved in placing your property at risk.

Be very careful with your retirement accounts

If you even have an inkling that you want to draw from your retirement account(s) to fund your startup, consult with a financial advisor before you start. Your advisor will review potential financial repercussions, including taxes and fines, as well as the long-term effect on your ability to retire comfortably.

Keep accurate records

It's time to put on our full Captain Obvious uniforms to note that you need to meticulously record every single financial transaction related with your company. Maintaining accurate financial records is critical for monitoring the performance of your company and complying with tax obligations. Battling with the IRS and your state tax agency are no one's idea of a good time.

Observe and make changes

Maintain a close eye on your own personal financial status and the overall financial health of your new business at the same time. Always make adjustments to your business funding strategy in the event that the conditions change or if your company faces obstacles that you and your team never thought of before they happened.

TIP

Schedule a "money day" once a month where you and your financial team review your actual income against your projected income as well as what's coming in the next 30 to 90 days. That review will tell you if you're in good shape to keep going down the road or pull over to effect repairs.

Ensure that your expectations are realistic

One hard lesson we all learn is that life never happens quite the way we want or plan, so always keep in mind that developing a successful startup takes some time. You need to ensure that your expectations about the time when your company begins to generate a profit and when you can anticipate a return on your investment are both grounded and reasonable.

Ensure the safety of your private credit

Take precautions to protect your own credit score, such as monitoring your score regularly through the three credit agency bureaus here in the United States or an outside credit monitoring service. If you ever find yourself in need of a loan or credit line, having a solid credit history can be extremely beneficial.

Strike a balance between risk and reward

Just like a car needs to have a balanced water temperature in its tank to make sure that the engine will run smoothly, you need to ensure that your personal financial goals and your overall business objectives are balanced. If they're not, you'll see the dreaded check engine light flash before your eyes.

Look for help and guidance from others

Make connections with other business owners who have launched successful companies with only their own money. They are able to offer advice, share their experiences, and provide insights that can be used to navigate the problems.

REMEMBER

Professional organizations like chambers of commerce and industry events are two ways to connect with people both online and in person to get the support you need to keep you focused on the road ahead.

Knowing the Risks and Benefits of Using Personal Finances for Your Startup

Some of the information in this section may seem repetitive if you've read everything up to this point, but we're listing the risks and benefits for those in the back who decided to skip to this section (though you're allowed to go back and read this chapter from the beginning).

The bad

We start off with the risks first so you have those fresh in your mind as we follow up with the benefits.

Exposure to financial risk

In the event that your company experiences challenges or is unsuccessful, the state of your personal finances could be jeopardized. It's a high-stakes risk that could have an effect on how well off you are financially.

A reduction in financial safety

If you allocate personal cash to your startup, you will have less of a financial buffer to fall back on in the event of personal emergencies or unexpected needs. Due to the limited scope of this financial safety net, if that net disappears then you may be left to depend on the support of friends, family, and maybe the community.

Debt with a high-interest rate

A dependency on personal credit, such as that provided by credit cards, loans, and credit lines (secured and unsecured), can lead to the accumulation of debt with an unmanageable rate of interest. If you can't manage this debt, it can lead to a snowball effect of increased interest costs and more money going to credit card payments than to developing your business.

A threat to your assets

When you use assets like home equity or funds for retirement as a source of finance, and you don't pay back the debts that are secured by these assets, you could end up losing the property or putting your retirement savings at risk.

More stress and pressure

When you use your own money to launch a business, you take on the burden of handling a tremendous amount of stress on top of the daily stress of running the business. Your mental health and ability to make sound choices can suffer when you are worried about losing money.

Stressed personal relationships

The stress of managing your startup's finances can put a strain on your personal connections, particularly if members of your family or your partner's relationship are financially dependent on you for stability. Startup owners often ignore their family and friends, sometimes for years. What's more, if you have to go to family and friends for help when you're in dire straits, prepare to be berated on more than one occasion.

The good

Okay, we're done with all the scary stuff, and you can lift your hands off your face. If you've caught your breath, we're ready to talk about the good stuff that comes with using your own money to fuel your business.

Autonomy while maintaining control

You have unrestricted authority over every facet of your enterprise. You are not required to answer to any outside investors or give up any ownership part in the company. Because of this liberty, you are able to mold your firm in your vision.

Direct obtainability of financial resources

You can access your personal finances at any time. The procedure is quick and uncomplicated regardless of whether you are withdrawing money from savings or investments or making use of credit. Having instant access to finance can be a game-changer in the frenetic world of startup companies.

There is no dilution of equity

Personal finance, as opposed to soliciting outside investments, does not necessitate selling out a portion of your company's ownership stake (also known as *equity*), so you can keep more of the profits for yourself. Because you won't have to divide the profits with investors, the entire sum will be yours to keep regardless of how well your company does.

A more adaptable allocation system

If you finance your company using personal assets, you have the flexibility to distribute resources in a manner that best meets the specific requirements of your company. You have the option to prioritize spending based on the priorities and growth plan of your firm, regardless of whether it's product development, marketing, or operating expenses.

Keeping Your Personal Finances and Credit in Order

Now that you know about all your options to personally finance your business, as well as all the bad and the good things that come with the territory, it's time to build your "go bag" that tells you how to keep your focus on the road ahead. (Yes, you can do this.)

Here's your road map

When you drive into areas that you're not familiar with, you need a road map so you don't end up in the middle of a field somewhere with no cell service — or, worse, end up in a snowed-in area where you can't drive out and can't get help. (There have been plenty of news stories about GPS mishaps.)

The same is true when you plan to finance your business, and you need to have that map in place. It won't give you the answer to all your funding problems, and it won't keep bad weather away, but a map gives you more control so you can better adapt to changing conditions.

Risk mitigation techniques

Put risk mitigation techniques into action to lessen the possibility that your financial exposure will have a negative impact. Keeping an emergency fund, being responsible with debt, and obtaining funding from a variety of sources are all examples of this.

Thorough financial planning

Work with financial pros to create a complete financial plan that describes how personal assets will be spent, the projected return on investment, as well as a contingency plan for when unexpected obstacles arise.

Emotional and financial readiness

Get yourself ready mentally for the potential emotional and financial strains that may come your way. For assistance in coping with the pressures, you should look for support from mentors, advisors, coaches, and/or mental health professionals in your community and your industry.

TIP

Online business networks such as LinkedIn (https://linkedin.com) and Alignable (https://alignable.com) are good places to find other businesspeople and ask questions about how to run your business. Don't forget your local chamber of commerce networking events, too.

Framework makes the finances work

Just like the different parts of a car are built on a framework to ensure that everything works together, you need a framework for managing your personal finances while safeguarding your personal financial stability and creditworthiness.

Maintain a separate financial entity

Keep your personal and professional finances completely separate from one another. In order to keep your personal funds separate from those of your company, it's a really good idea to open one or multiple bank accounts as well as a credit card that are solely for the use of your company.

Grow and replenish your financial resources

As your company begins to generate a profit, you should establish a detailed financial strategy that details how you will add to your personal savings and any monies set aside for unforeseen circumstances. It is essential to replenish any personal financial resources you may have depleted in order to support the operation of the firm.

Regularly monitor credit reports

Keep a close eye on your personal credit reports at all times. Take immediate action to fix any inconsistencies or errors that have been found. Consider subscribing to a credit monitoring service so that you can be apprised of any shifts that may occur in your credit profile.

Administer debt effectively

If you have used personal credit to fund your business venture, making payments on that debt should be your top priority. So, set aside a payment each month that's larger than your minimum payment. You'll save money on interest payments, improve your credit rating, and best of all, you'll get that payment off the books faster.

REMEMBER

Ideally, your monthly payment should be as high above the minimum as possible.

Diversify your sources

Explore other avenues of funding for your company in order to reduce the risk that your personal finances are exposed to. This could involve looking for investors from the outside, applying for loans for the firm, or investigating the possibilities of crowdsourcing.

Consult with experts in the financial industry

When it comes to financing your business and paying taxes on the money you receive, don't rely on the advice from your relative or what you see on the Internet. Instead, seek the advice of seasoned accountants and financial consultants who are real life people.

These professionals focus their practices on assisting business owners. Their thoughts and methods can assist you in navigating the complex interplay of personal and business finances, as well as tax laws.

Chapter **6**

Borrowing Money: Debt Funding Basics

A t first, you may think that borrowing money is a bad idea. After all, you say, that's contrary to the all-American bootstrapping system that makes small business great!

But hold up there, champ. Debt funding is a common way for business owners to fuel their cars to get to their dream destinations much as debt financing helps people buy cars in the real world. There are several compelling reasons to consider borrowing money:

>> Debt funding gets you access to capital without requiring you to sell ownership interests in the company to one or more people.

>> You have full control over your business while still getting the money you need. (That's a good definition of win-win.)

>> There are plenty of different options for financing your business that you can fit to your needs.

Sounds exciting, but as Master Yoda said, excitement is not something one craves if you want to approach your craft seriously. So, this chapter starts by telling you what debt funding is and what it isn't so you know what fuel your shiny business car needs to go, as well as the advantages and disadvantages of getting that fuel.

Like different types of gas and electric charging, you have options that you need to be aware of. Then we talk about interest rates and payment terms so you can find out how to manage that debt you take on responsibly. We don't want to run out of fuel in the middle of the desert.

Understanding What Debt Funding Is . . . and Isn't

You probably guessed what debt funding is because it's a staple of modern life: One entity, like a business, borrows from another entity with money such as a bank. The entity giving the money has the certainty that the money will be repaid.

Debt Funding 101

But what's a debt, specifically? Put simply, it's money that's been borrowed and needs to be paid back over a predetermined amount of time, typically with interest. So, let's put on our thinking caps and review all the terms you need to know. (Feel free to quiz yourself afterward.)

borrower: The party that is asking for financing is referred to as the borrower, regardless of whether that entity is an individual or a business.

collateral: Certain types of loans, such as secured loans, require the borrower to provide collateral, which is an asset that acts as security for the loan. If the borrower does not make their payments on time, the lender has the right to exercise their security interest in the collateral and take it.

creditworthiness: Lenders look at a borrower's creditworthiness to figure out whether or not they can trust them to repay the money they borrow. Their decision depends on factors such as income level, credit history, and current amount of outstanding debt.

debt instruments: Loans, bonds, promissory notes, and lines of credit are all examples of debt instruments that can be used as debt funding. Each of these instruments comes with its own set of terms and conditions.

interest: The cost of borrowing money is the interest that accrues on the loan. It refers to the additional money you pay on top of the principal, expressed as a percentage of the total principal amount. The interest rate that you are charged on a loan can vary depending on the type of debt funding you leverage and how creditworthy you are.

lender: The organization or person that provides the money is known as the lender. Lenders are most commonly financial institutions like banks, credit unions, and private investors.

principal: The initial amount of money that was borrowed and is expected to be repaid in full. This is the amount that has been provided to you as a financial advance for business reasons.

repayment terms: The length of time that the borrower has committed to paying back the loan. There is a range of possibilities for the terms of the payback from several months to several years.

Different forms of debt funding

In the past, banks were the only source of funding available to businesses. One of the perks of living in the 21st century is that we have many different kinds of debt funding available, and here's a list that you should become familiar with. Yes, you guessed it, you'll become more familiar with these forms later in this chapter.

Traditional bank loans

We start with the tried-and-traditional bank loan, which is still the form of debt funding that people use most often. These loans can be secured (backed by collateral) or unsecured (based on creditworthiness), depending on the circumstances.

Credit lines

A credit line gives a company the ability to borrow up to a certain limit, which is predetermined. Only the funds that have been borrowed will have interest collected on them.

Bonds

Organizations can provide investors with the opportunity to purchase bonds, which are just another name for promissory notes. Investors purchase bonds, and after doing so, they are entitled to interest payments from the issuer until the bond matures and the principal is repaid.

Promissory notes

A written promise to pay back a given sum of money by a specified date is referred to as a promissory note, and it is written in the form of a note. Figure 6-1 shows you the first page of a standard promissory note.

STANDARD PROMISSORY NOTE

1. **THE PARTIES.** This Standard Promissory Note ("Note") made on _____, 20____ is by and between:

    Borrower: _____, with a mailing address of _____ ("Borrower"), and

    Lender: _____, with a mailing address of _____ ("Lender").

2. **LOAN TERMS.** The Lender agrees to lend the Borrower under the following terms:

    a. **Principal Amount:** $_____
    b. **Interest Rate:** ____% compounded per: (check one)
        ☐ - Month
        ☐ - Annum
        ☐ - Other: _____
    c. **Borrower to Receive the Borrowed Money on:** _____, 20____

    Hereinafter known as the "Borrowed Money."

3. **PAYMENTS.** The full balance of the Borrowed Money, including all accrued interest and any other fees or penalties, is due and payable in: (check one)

    ☐ - **A LUMP SUM.** The Borrower shall repay the Borrowed Money as a lump sum, in full, in the amount of $_____ (principal and interest) by _____, 20____ ("Due Date").

    ☐ - **INSTALLMENTS.** Borrower shall pay principal and interest installment amounts equal to $_____ with the first (1ˢᵗ) payment due on _____, 20____ and the remaining payments to be paid: (check one)
        ☐ - **Weekly** with any remaining balance payable on _____, 20____ ("Due Date").
        ☐ - **Monthly** with any remaining balance payable on _____, 20____ ("Due Date").
        ☐ - **Quarterly** with any remaining balance payable on _____, 20____ ("Due Date").

    Hereinafter known as the "Repayment Period."

4. **PAYMENT IS DUE.** Any payment made by the Borrower is considered late if made more than ____ day(s) after any payment due date ("Payment Due Date"). This shall include, but not be limited to, any payment made related to the Repayment Period, the Due Date, or any other payment mentioned in this Note.

Page 1 of 4

FIGURE 6-1:
The first page of a four-page promissory note template.

Peer-to-peer lending

A modern day form of financing debt in which private individuals, as opposed to banks, provide money to businesses through the use of Internet-based platforms.

Getting the Lay of the Land

Okay, now that you know the terms you need to navigate the road, you need to know what debt funding roads are available for you to choose from.

Some of those roads have different features, such as straight shots on desert highways and winding roads with inclines and declines. After you know the advantages and disadvantages of each route, you'll know the best one to take.

The good news

We like to look on the bright side, so we start by reviewing the advantages of financing your business with debt.

You maintain your ownership

One of the most significant advantages of using debt funding is that it enables you to keep full ownership and management control of your business.

In contrast to equity financing, which entails the sale of ownership shares in your company, debt funding is essentially an arrangement in which money is borrowed from a third party. You are still in complete control of your company even though you are obligated to pay back the principal amount of the loan along with the accrued interest.

Tax deductions

Here's a fact that will excite you: The interest paid on a loan is typically an expense that you can deduct from your taxes. Because of this, it is possible that your taxable income will drop by a significant amount, which will result in a lower total tax liability for your business. Tax deductions are only exciting when you can deduct expenses after you've made enough money to pay taxes.

Predictable repayment terms

The terms of payback are more foreseeable when using debt funding. In most cases, the terms and circumstances of the loan, including the interest rates and the repayment schedule, are discussed and agreed upon at the beginning of the process.

No dilution of equity

When you use debt funding, neither your ownership of the company nor your interest in it are affected in any way. As your business grows, you won't have to give investors a cut of the profits or cede decision-making authority to anybody else.

Creates a record of credit history

Your company's ability to establish and maintain positive credit can benefit from effective management of its existing debt. It's possible that this will come in handy when searching for more loans or negotiating better terms with creditors.

The bad news

Yes, you knew it was coming, but being the intrepid business owner you are, we know you're undaunted by learning about the disadvantages of debt funding so you can plan ahead and manage them.

The responsibility to make repayments

The necessity to repay the money borrowed, in addition to interest, is the primary drawback associated with debt funding. If your company is experiencing financial difficulties or other unplanned setbacks, it may become more difficult to fulfill your responsibilities.

The costs of interest

The total cost of borrowing is increased by the interest expenses that relate to debt funding. Although interest payments may be deducted from taxable income, this does not change the fact that they are an additional expense that cuts into a company's profit.

Conditions of collateralization

When applying for some loans, particularly secured loans, you could be required to provide collateral in the form of a piece of personal or business property. If you're unable to repay the loan, the lender may confiscate the collateral that you provided as security for the debt.

The risk of mediocre credit

When it comes to debt funding, the trustworthiness of your firm is essential. If you have a credit history that is less than perfect, you may find it difficult to obtain loans, be subject to higher interest rates, and be required to comply with more stringent requirements.

The consistent timetable

When taking on debt, one implicitly agrees to a certain schedule for making payments. This predictability may be good, but it can also work against you if your company has a variable income or you deal with changing market conditions. When the weather gets bad on the road, your fuel tank may not have enough to keep making your fixed payments.

Knowing the Types of Debt Funding Options

It's great to know about the different types of financing just like it's good to know about the types of fuel available to get your car moving. But just as you decide whether to use conventional gasoline, a hybrid gas-electric system, diesel (people still buy those cars), or all-electric for your next car, you need to think just as carefully about the debt funding that will fit your business.

REMEMBER

Even if you use one type of debt funding now, you may want to use a different type in the future when your business is bigger and thriving, so put a flag on this page so you can refer to it when you're ready for the next leg of your business journey.

This is the section where you can get the good and not-so-good in every type of debt financing there is (at least as of this writing).

Traditional bank financing

Loans are typically offered by financial institutions like banks and credit unions. There are many different loans available, some of which include equipment financing, term loans, as well as revolving credit lines.

The good:

>> Competitive interest rates.

>> Reliability and security are provided by well-established firms.

>> Repayment schedules are organized in a manner that is conducive to budgeting.

The not-so-good:

>> There are strict restrictions for approval, which may include requiring collateral and conducting credit checks.

>> It's possible that the application and approval processes will take a long time.

Loans from the U.S. Small Business Administration

The U.S. Small Business Administration (SBA) issues loans, commonly called SBA loans, to aid small businesses. They can be obtained through a variety of schemes, including microloans, CDC/504 loans, and 7(a) loans, among others.

The good:

>> There are favorable terms such as shorter terms and lower initial payments.

>> The guarantees provided by the SBA make the approval process for startup firms much more straightforward.

The not-so-good:

>> It's possible that the application procedure might require additional work that you may not be prepared to make time (and maybe spend money) to complete.

>> Restrictions and prerequisites imposed by the terms of the SBA loan program may be a factor.

Alternative lending options

In the 21st century, the proliferation of peer-to-peer (P2P) lending and online lending platforms has grown the amount of capital that is readily available to startup companies. Borrowers can connect with individual investors as well as huge financial organizations through these online marketplaces. Figure 6-2 illustrates how the system works.

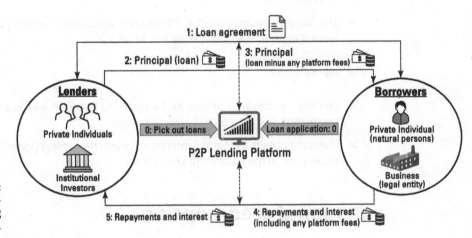

FIGURE 6-2: How a peer-to-peer lending system works.

The good:

>> The application and approval processes can be completed more quickly.

>> Accessibility has been increased in recent years, and so loans are available to borrowers with a wider range of credit profiles.

>> There are plenty of options as you'll see when you put **p2p lending platforms** into your favorite search engine.

The not-so-good:

>> There is a possibility that the interest rates will be higher than those associated with traditional bank loans.

>> A lack of regulatory supervision may lead to a variety of loan conditions as well as additional fees that you have to pay.

Financing for machines and equipment

Equipment financing is available to companies who want to buy or lease vehicles, machines, or other types of equipment. Most of the time, the sponsored item also serves as the loan's collateral.

The good:

>> The company can save its working capital to use in paying for other business expenses.

>> The fact that the equipment itself can serve as collateral removes the requirement that other assets be put up for security.

The not-so-good:

>> The only permissible purpose for the loan is to finance the acquisition of new machinery.

>> There is a possibility that the interest rates and repayment periods will vary depending on the equipment you finance.

Personal credit options

Entrepreneurs may choose to employ personal loans or personal lines of credit to finance their businesses. These loans are considered secured because they are guaranteed by the creditworthiness of the individual borrower.

The good:

>> The application process isn't as complex.

>> In most cases, losing one's personal possessions is not a consideration.

The not-so-good:

>> There is a possibility that the interest rates will be greater than those applicable to company loans.

>> Should the company run into financial difficulties, it is possible that this will impact the individual's credit.

If you want to learn more about using your own personal credit or loans, bookmark this page and go back to Chapter 5.

Understanding Interest Rates and Repayment Terms

When it comes to debt funding, having a firm grasp on interest rates and payback terms is analogous to knowing what all the measurement indicators on your car dashboard mean. When you borrow money, you need to understand how much you have to pay back, because you don't want the dreaded fuel light to come on because your shiny business car unexpectedly ran out of gas.

What are interest rates, anyway?

Interest rates are the cost for using the money that belongs to someone else. The additional fees you must pay when you borrow money are called *interest rates*. There are many variations of interest rates, and it is essential to have a solid understanding of each one:

Interest rates that never change

Imagine you're driving along on a straight, flat road when you think about a rate of interest that is fixed. It won't change at any point during the duration of your loan. Because of this, you know that both your total interest costs and your monthly payments will continue to be predictable.

Variable interest rates

On the other hand, having variable interest rates is like riding in the mountains. These rates are subject to change and could go up or down depending on a variety of circumstances, such as the current state of the market or the terms and conditions of your loan agreement. These rates may start out lower than fixed rates, which might be exciting at first, but they have the potential to increase over time. Just like your car, moving up a mountain expends more fuel, and you have to make higher monthly payments.

The annual percentage rate

The *annual percentage rate*, commonly known by its acronym APR, is analogous to the full formula for the loan. It includes the interest rate on your loan in addition to any other fees that may apply. Therefore, when comparing different loan options, it is important to take into consideration both the interest rate and the APR. It gives you an accurate depiction of the situation and assists you in understanding the total cost of the loan.

The prime rate

As the name implies, prime rate refers to the annual percentage rate (APR) of interest that commercial banks offer to their best customers. The prime rate serves as a connecting point for loans with variable interest rates. This suggests that your interest rate might change in tandem with the prime rate as it moves up and down. It feels as though your financial situation is precariously balanced on a seesaw. An increase in the prime rate will result in an increase in both your interest rate and your monthly payments.

Repayment terms

The *repayment terms*, also known as the instructions for repaying your loan, have two parts: the duration of the loan and how much you need to pay every month.

The duration, better known as the term

The length of time you must repay the loan is indicated by the loan term, which is also sometimes referred to as the loan length. It could be anything from a few months to several years, depending on the kind of loan that was taken out.

When you have a loan with a shorter term, your regular payments will typically be higher; however, the total amount of interest you will pay will be lower. The result of a loan with a longer duration is lower interest rates and monthly payments, but the overall interest rate is greater.

The amount that must be paid

One portion of your payment goes toward the principal (the overall amount of the loan), and the other goes toward the interest on the loan. These two parts make up your monthly payment. As payments are made, the principal portion of the loan increases, the interest portion decreases, and your debt gradually is paid off. (And your lender is happy, too.)

Plan for amortization of debt

Amortization is the process of paying off debt over time in regular installments of principal plus interest so you can repay the loan in full by the due date.

When you get a loan, you get an amortization schedule so you can keep track of the payment amount that's applied to the reduction of your debt as well as the amount that is applied to the interest on your debt. Because a bigger amount of your payments will be applied toward the reduction of your debt as time passes, you will be able to pay off the loan more quickly.

You may be able to make additional payments or pay off the balance of some loans ahead of schedule. You can cut costs and save money by choosing a prepayment option, which has lower interest rates, so don't forget to ask your lender about your options!

TIP

Managing Debt Responsibly

If you have used personal credit to fund your business venture, making payments on that debt should be your top priority. So, set aside a payment each month that's larger than your minimum payment. You'll save money on interest payments, improve your credit rating, and best of all, you'll get that payment off the books faster.

Personal guarantees: No good, very bad

Personal guarantees should be avoided at all costs whenever it is practicable to do so, even though they may be required for some types of loans. If a loan for your company is not returned, a personal guarantee will hold your own assets, such as your home or savings, responsible for the debt. The moral of this story is to protect your own finances by reducing the number of personal pledges you make.

Keep your financial condition in good shape

Lenders will usually examine the financial health of your firm before deciding whether to provide credit just as they would look under the hood of your car to make sure it looks good before they ride with you.

Make sure that your financial reports are correct and up to date, and that they exhibit your company's capabilities regarding profitability, cash flow, and debt management in a clear and concise manner. Being in a healthy financial position can increase the chances for a loan with terms more to your liking.

Establish a liquidity buffer

Having some money in the bank always acts as a kind of financial safety net for you. During difficult circumstances, it might be helpful in meeting unexpected costs, such as loan obligations, which may arise. Establish a "rainy day fund" that your company can rely on in times of difficulty so that it can continue operating normally.

Establish precise objectives

Make sure that your organization has well-defined, measurable goals under consideration before taking on further debt. Your goals, whether they are to expand into new markets, launch a new product, or simplify existing procedures, will determine the kind of borrowing options available to you.

Create a payment strategy

Responsible management of debt means you need to prepare thoroughly to settle your loans before you ask for one. Develop a repayment strategy for your company that is compatible with its existing cash flow.

If you want to avoid incurring late fees or penalties, you should make sure that you have the necessary funds on hand when the return dates get near. Your company's creditworthiness will increase if payments are paid in a consistent manner and on time.

Increase the variety of your funding sources

You've heard of the axiom that your parents may have told you a dozen times before: "Don't put all of your eggs in one basket." In business, it's especially important to diversify your funding sources so that you can reduce your exposure to risk. Investigate the various options that are available to you, such as loans from banks, credit lines, financing from peers, and business credit cards.

Make investments in order to decrease your debt

Put some of the profits your firm brings in aside for the repayment of your company's debt. It's possible to reduce the overall amount of interest paid on a debt by making consistent additional payments, regardless of how small these payments may be.

Conduct frequent audits of your debt portfolio

As your company expands, you should make it a habit to conduct regular audits of your debt portfolio. Review the terms of your existing debts, and if it's at all possible, investigate the possibility of refinancing your debt in order to secure more favorable terms. For example, refinancing your mortgage in your brick-and-mortar space could result in cheaper interest rates or longer loan terms, both of which would lighten your overall financial load.

Create an effective business strategy

A well-written business plan should be the foundation of any successful business strategy. It explains the company's goals, as well as its strategies, finances, and overall vision.

A comprehensive business plan not only demonstrates to potential investors that you are committed to responsible management but also helps them understand the potential and risk associated with your company. When asking for money, having a detailed plan can help you increase your credibility with potential funders.

Make a deal that is favorable to you

When it comes to getting debt, negotiation is frequently an available choice. Get advice from others who have been through these types of negotiations so you can negotiate favorable terms with the lenders, such as reduced interest rates, prolonged payback schedules, or the elimination of fees. Financing arrangements may turn out to be more attractive because of successful negotiation.

Be vigilant about the debt-to-equity ratio

Your company's total debt, as well as its total equity, are both factors that are considered when calculating the debt-to-equity ratio. This ratio compares a company's total liabilities with its shareholder equity, and you can use this to assess the extent of your company's reliance on debt.

The degree to which you can maintain control over this proportion may indicate how stable your company's finances are. If there is a large amount of debt in comparison to the amount of equity, lenders and investors may back away. So, always be sure to keep a healthy ratio that is in line with the criteria set for your business.

Mitigate the risk

It's always good to pack an emergency bag before a long trip in case you get stuck, and in business you need to prepare in advance and plan for challenges that cannot be anticipated.

Think about creating that rainy day fund so that you can repay loans if you experience temporary financial difficulties. In addition, there are many insurance options available, such as business interruption coverage and disability insurance, which can provide protection against unanticipated disruptions.

Change up your financing

If your organization has multiple debts that remain outstanding, you may want to investigate consolidation or refinancing possibilities.

Consolidating multiple obligations into a single obligation under the terms of a loan makes payments simpler. Refinancing a loan can enhance the terms of the loan and lower interest rates, both of which will make it easier to make payments.

What's more, consider establishing a debt management plan even if you are dealing with challenging circumstances. You can negotiate with your creditors for lower interest rates and debt consolidation if you use a debt management program, which will make your obligations to make repayments simpler.

Examining your loan agreements often

Make it a habit to regularly go over the terms and conditions of any loan agreements you have. Be sure that you continue to abide by the conditions that were set, and that you have a full understanding of any covenants or restrictions that may apply. If you find something that's a problem, contact your lender to ask questions and get advice.

Seek professional advice

Speaking of advice, if you're having trouble managing your debt or feel overwhelmed by it, don't be hesitant to seek the counsel of a financial specialist. Professionals in the fields of accounting, financial planning, and business consulting can offer you information and guidance on how to handle your debt in a responsible manner.

TIP

A great place to look for financial professionals is your local chamber of commerce. You may also find pros on social media sites that focus on business such as LinkedIn and Alignable.

Stay up to date on regulations

Just as the rules of the road can be different in specific states as you travel on the road, laws and regulations pertaining to debt funding can change over time. So, as part of your financial auditing processes, stay up to speed because if you don't, you'll get pulled over and face fines or other legal headaches.

REMEMBER

This is another good reason to find and work with financial professionals, because it's their job to know what the regulations are and keep you from being pulled over.

Chapter **7**

Sharing the Pie: Equity Funding Explained

W hen you're on a road trip and you have people riding with you, you may want to have them chip in to help with expenses like fuel for the car. In your business, the idea of equity is simple: In return for the money your company requires, you give investors a piece of the ownership pie.

There are plenty of benefits to this arrangement:

>> Money, which we think we can agree is good.

>> Priceless knowledge from your equity partners, which is also good.

>> The contacts your equity partners have that can help your business.

>> The possibility of mentorship from your equity partners as you grow your business.

But if you've read any other chapter in this book, you know that it's not all roads with smooth asphalt and clear weather. So, this chapter takes you on the full tour of equity funding including what it is, what it means for your ownership, and examines the various sources of equity investment.

We take a magnifying glass to two of those main sources: angel investors and venture capitalists. Then we explore the area of crowdfunding, a newer but rapidly gaining method of raising equity capital. As we proceed through these parts, we arm you with the information and understanding you need to successfully negotiate the world of equity finance.

What's Equity Funding, Anyway?

Equity funding, which is also known as *equity investment*, is at its core the exchange of financial resources for ownership in a company. It is a potent substitute for conventional debt financing, in which a company borrows money that must be repaid with interest.

Equity funding involves selling shares or ownership holdings in your company to outside investors as an alternative to taking on debt. These financiers, also known as equity financiers or shareholders, offer crucial funding for the success of your company.

This is like dividing a pie, which is a common (some might say trite) metaphor in finance. In your business, an ownership stake is represented by one piece of the pie. By choosing equity funding, you are essentially cutting your pie in a slice of a certain size and giving these pieces to investors. These investors give your company the capital it needs for growth and development in exchange.

Before we continue exploring, we need to pull over and check to make sure that we're all on the same wavelength when it comes to equity funding.

Ownership share

At the center of equity funding is the ownership share. You are giving investors a stake in your company when you distribute equity to them. They are entitled to a portion of the company's revenues as well as a voice in decision-making thanks to this ownership stake.

Equity investors

Equity investors come in a variety of shapes and sizes, from individual angels and venture capitalists to supporters of crowdfunding initiatives. They include anyone willing to buy ownership shares in your company and invest in it.

Exit strategy

Equity funding is not an open-ended arrangement; hence it has an exit strategy. Investors typically plan on making an exit at some point so they may get a return on their investment. This departure could take the form of your company going public through an initial public offering (IPO) or your company being bought by a bigger organization.

Valuation

A crucial component of equity investment is figuring out the worth of your company. It has a big impact on the ownership stake you give investors. A higher valuation usually entails giving away a lesser portion of your ownership.

What Equity Funding Means for You

Equity investment adds one more managerial bag (or three) to the trunk of your fancy business car on your road to glory.

On the one hand, equity investment offers access to significant money infusions, which are frequently necessary for quick growth and market penetration.

On the other hand, it requires giving up some control and sharing future benefits with investors.

At the heart of the equity funding process is the skill of striking the ideal balance between maintaining your vision and allowing outside ideas. To illustrate this, we give you four scenarios based on the state of a company's growth and how equity funding can affect its development.

The founders' share

A startup's founders own 100 percent of their company upon launch. Due to their full ownership, they are able to make decisions, determine the company's course, and reap the rewards of their labors. However, the startup is likely to need money to expand. So, the founders turn to equity investors for this cash, whether they are angel investors, venture capitalists, or backers of crowdfunding campaigns.

The founders gradually give up bits of ownership as equity investors join the picture. The amount of capital transferred and the agreed-upon terms determine how much ownership is being purchased. For example, if the value of your company is

$500,000 and angel investors contribute $100,000 for a 20 percent equity invest-ment, your ownership stake drops to 80 percent, or $400,000. Ownership of the company by the founders may decrease further as it develops and receives more rounds of funding.

Getting on the fast track

A new tech company has an original and creative idea, and the founders currently own all of the company when they approach equity investors to raise the signifi-cant funds necessary for rapid growth.

These investors bring important knowledge and contacts to the table, but in exchange they demand a sizable ownership stake. Consequently, founder owner-ship may decrease to a minority interest when the business secures numerous rounds of venture money. As a founder, it's also likely you'll give investors a seat or two on your board.

A long-standing business wants to grow

Equity funding is frequently used by well-established organizations to support growth, introduce new products, or enter new markets. The ownership structure is already in place in this case, with stockholders that might include the compa-ny's founders, early investors, and employees who were granted stock options.

Established businesses can issue more shares or sell their current shares to out-side investors in order to receive equity finance. In exchange for ownership hold-ings, these investors provide financial support to the company. The ownership structure of the business changes as a result. The amount of equity issued and the investment's terms will determine how much of a shift occurs.

The IPO

A company's equity capital may reach its apex with an initial public offering (IPO) for some businesses. The first time a firm distributes shares of stock to the gen-eral public is known as an initial public offering, or IPO. This change in status from private to public has broad ramifications for ownership.

The ownership structure before the IPO may include the founders, early inves-tors, and possibly venture capitalists. After the initial public offering (IPO), shares are freely traded on the stock market, and a wider range of shareholders, including institutional investors and regular people who buy shares on the stock exchange, come into ownership.

Although a larger range of shareholders must partake in the decision-making process, founders and early investors sometimes retain a sizable amount of ownership if they're savvy negotiators.

The moral of our story

Each of these situations involves a redistribution of ownership along with growth potential brought on by equity finance. Entrepreneurs must carefully strike this balance, maintaining their vision while acknowledging the advantages equity investors offer.

Making decisions about the future of your company should start with an understanding of how equity investment affects ownership. So let's continue our exploration of the complex world of equity investment to learn more about how it affects the ownership and course of your company.

Prospecting for Equity Funding Sources

There are three popular equity funding sources, and you can probably guess them all: angel investors, venture capital, and crowdfunding.

These funding sources act as three separate paths that all lead to the same place — a well-funded, successful firm. However, each path has its own distinct qualities, possibilities, and considerations.

Guardian angels

Angel investors, who are frequently seasoned businesspeople or wealthy individuals, bring more than simply money to the table. They provide support, direction, and a wide range of relationships.

Angel investors are renowned for their readiness to invest their own money and take on early-stage risks. In return, they receive stock in your business. In addition to financial assistance, they may also offer priceless advice and direction. Is taking flight with an angel investor right for your business?

The advantages

Let's start with the good stuff: the four advantages of working with angel investors.

>> **Capital injection:** Angel investors might provide the crucial financial help to launch or advance your firm. They can offer the startup money needed for your business's expansion, marketing, or product development.

>> **Mentorship and knowledge:** Angel investors offer more than simply money; they also bring significant knowledge to the table. Many of them have business expertise and market knowledge that can help you make business decisions.

>> **Opportunities for networking:** Angel investors frequently have wide networks in the business environment. Their relationships may provide access to new clients, partners, and investors.

>> **Fast cash:** Angel investors can make funding decisions more quickly than other institutional investors, on average. When you need to seize a developing opportunity, this quickness can be quite important.

The disadvantages

Don't get too excited about angel investors, because their wings can be a bit too heavy for your business — or be unable to flap them to make your business go faster.

>> **Equity sharing:** In exchange for their investment, angel investors receive equity in your business. Because you'll be splitting ownership and possible income with them, your ability to make independent decisions may be impacted.

>> **High expectations:** Angel investors frequently look for a big return on their capital. You can be under a lot of pressure to accomplish ambitious growth goals in addition to the need to generate results.

>> **Limited resources:** Because angel investors often contribute their own money, their ability to make large investments may be constrained. If your company needs a lot of money, you might need to find several angel investors or explore for other funding options.

>> **Personality:** Your relationship with your angel investor may be good, bad, or downright ugly. What many founders learn is that people with money are often, shall we say, eccentric. Pick your partners wisely!

Where to find angel investors

Angel investors aren't hard to find, and there are three places to search both in person and online.

>> **Angel investing networks:** Joining neighborhood or regional angel investing networks is a great method to meet possible backers. These networks frequently offer pitch events where business owners can pitch their concepts to a panel of angel investors.

>> **Online platforms:** A number of online resources, like AngelList and Gust, facilitate connections between entrepreneurs and angel investors. These platforms make it simpler to connect with a larger community of angels.

>> **Face-to-face:** Attend networking events, startup meetups, and conferences in your sector. The best approach to discover angel investors is frequently through personal ties.

Approaching angel investors

So now that you know where to find angel investors, how do you talk to them about your business and why they should invest in your business? As always, we're here for you with three helpful tips:

>> Craft a persuasive and succinct proposal that highlights the value proposition of your company, the market opportunity, and your qualifications to manage this endeavor.

>> Angels want to see evidence that your project has promise, so show that it has traction. Showing traction, whether it be through a functional prototype, early sales, or a strong customer base, might improve your prospects.

>> Establish genuine relationships. They are investing in you and your goals, not just giving you money. A solid, trustworthy friendship may make all the difference.

Matchmaking tips

Making contact with potential angel investors and giving them information about your company is important in establishing a relationship. They're going to research you, so you need to research them by doing four things.

>> **Do your homework:** Research the investor's interests, investing history, and preferences. If they don't match with your outlook and where you want to take your company, don't go forward.

- >> **Be transparent:** Be open and truthful about the risks and difficulties facing your company. Potential investors can develop trust by being transparent.

- >> **Negotiate wisely:** If necessary, obtain competent legal counsel when considering equity and terms. Make a contract that supports your long-term objectives.

- >> **Use their knowledge:** If an angel investor has experience in your sector, use their advice and insights to figure out if this investor would be valuable for your company.

Venture higher

When your company's goals soar to new heights, venture capital (VC) can be your ideal ally. Institutional investors who manage diverse sources of funding are known as venture capitalists. They are quite picky, looking for firms with tremendous growth potential.

VC businesses contribute not only substantial sums of money but also a plethora of connections and information about the sector. Venture capitalists get shares in your company in return for their investments. This investment can help your business grow and attain its full potential by enabling it to reach a larger audience and enter new markets.

What are the advantages?

Venture capital is popular because it provides a big upgrade for your business just like putting a bigger engine in your car.

- >> **Significant capital injection:** Venture capitalists (VCs) frequently spend bigger quantities of money than angel investors, making them a good fit for firms with strong growth potential. Significant efforts in development, marketing, and scaling can be supported by this money.

- >> **Expert advice:** Venture capitalists contribute more than just money; they also have a wealth of strategic knowledge. They frequently have in-depth knowledge of market trends, business scalability, and operational effectiveness, which can be extremely helpful.

- >> **Networking possibilities:** Venture capitalists have wide networks in the business community. Their networks may be able to connect you with possible clients, investors, and business partners.

- >> **Street cred:** Having a respected venture capital firm to support your startup might give you more credibility in the eyes of clients, partners, and other investors.

Disadvantages of venture capitalists

You have to tread carefully when you deal with venture capital because there are significant challenges that you have to plan for before you sign on that dotted line.

>> **A rigorous review:** Due diligence is rigorously performed by VCs, who examine every facet of your company. So, make sure your business operations, legal documentation, and financial records are in order. This process could take a while and be a distraction to the regular operations of your company.

>> **Stock dilution:** In exchange for their investment, venture capitalists demand a sizable stock stake in your business. You could have to give up a considerable amount of ownership and decision-making authority.

>> **High growth expectations:** Venture capitalists (VCs) anticipate high growth and significant returns on their investments. This can put a lot of pressure on you to meet ambitious goals.

REMEMBER

Because of the loss of stock and potential decision-making authority, not to mention the constant drive to hit growth targets, relying only on venture capital investment can be dangerous. To lessen the dependency only on venture capitalists and to give you a better chance of keeping organizational control, think about varying your funding sources.

How to find venture capitalists

Like angel investors, it's pretty easy to find venture capitalists in their native habitats.

>> **Venture capital companies:** Conduct online research to find VC companies with expertise in your sector or stage of development. Many of these companies have websites with details about their investment emphasis and standards.

>> **Online platforms:** Resources like Crunchbase and Pitch Book offer thorough databases of venture capital companies and their history of investments.

>> **Events:** Your online research will help you understand where VCs attend industry-specific conferences and events so you can connect with them. Face-to-face introductions and personal relationships can make a bigger impression than a cold email message.

Connection advice

Speaking of connections, you need to come prepared to meet with VCs because they're going to be just as picky as you are, if not more so, about who they work with. So, come prepared.

>> **It's destiny:** When you research VCs, you need to ensure that your vision and the venture capital firms' expectations for your company are in sync. Then you can talk with your VCs about your vision and how you and the VC fit together like the proverbial hand in glove.

>> **Create a powerful pitch deck:** Put together a thorough and persuasive pitch deck that emphasizes the team, market opportunity, and special value proposition of your company.

>> **Get traction:** You need traction to get up hills, and you need to show VCs that your business also has traction in the market. That is, customers need to be using your product and/or service and bringing in enough money that shows there's potential for strong growth.

>> **Get an attorney:** The terms and conditions of venture capital agreements might be complicated. To navigate and negotiate these agreements, seek legal guidance.

Work the crowd

Visualize a sizable group of people who agree with your proposal and are willing to put skin in the game with a financial contribution, with people putting in a small sum that adds up to big results.

Entrepreneurs can pitch their ideas to the public on websites like Kickstarter and Indiegogo and invite people to contribute in exchange for stock. By democratizing the investment process, crowdfunding gives regular people the option to invest in firms they support. It's a route that not only guarantees funding but also nurtures a committed group of backers.

The good things

There are a lot of good things about crowdfunding that attract business owners to use it to jump-start their business.

>> **A diverse funding pool:** Through crowdfunding, your project can attract a large number of potential backers that share your enthusiasm for the project.

>> **Validation and market testing:** A prosperous crowdsourcing effort can demonstrate the viability of your idea and confirm that there is a market for your good or service.

>> **Early brand engagement:** This gives you the opportunity to interact with early adopters and create a brand community before your product even hits the market.

>> **Full control:** Contrary to venture capital or angel investing, crowdsourcing often doesn't involve giving up equity in your business. Instead, backers frequently get gifts or swag.

The not-so-good

Crowdfunding sounds exciting, but it also comes with its own set of challenges you need to prepare for before you start.

>> **Dedication required:** It takes a lot of work to run a successful crowdfunding campaign, because you need to:

- Develop an effective proposal
- Have a rock-solid delivery model
- Promote your cause with a great marketing team
- Have a productive sales team
- Interact with potential backers

>> **Maybe an all-or-nothing approach:** Some crowdfunding platforms work on an all-or-nothing approach, in which case you only get money if you raise enough money to cover your objective. If you fall short, you may have to start over.

>> **Costs and fees:** Fundraising websites often charge a fee for their services. You might also need to pay for the fulfillment of gifts or benefits for backers, which can add to your expenses.

Effective platforms for crowdfunding

There are plenty of popular online platforms to choose from for crowdfunding your new product or service.

>> **Kickstarter:** An all-or-nothing crowdsourcing platform that has launched numerous successful companies, Kickstarter at https://www.kickstarter.com (see Figure 7-1) is renowned for its inventive and creative initiatives, such as the Grandiloquent Word of the Day calendar (with bonus bookmarks) that Eric contributes to every year.

FIGURE 7-1:
The Kickstarter
website home
page tells you
how many
projects they've
funded.

>> **Indiegogo:** The Indiegogo crowdfunding website at https://www.indiegogo.com/, which is shown in Figure 7-2, provides both all-or-nothing and flexible fundraising choices. It's popular for a variety of ventures including movies and technological devices.

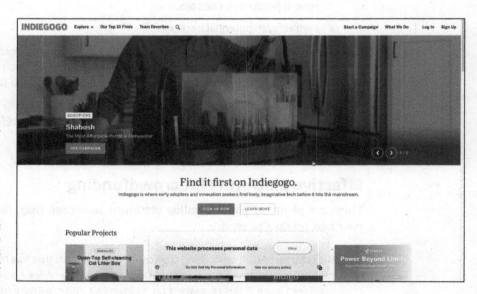

FIGURE 7-2:
The Indiegogo
website spotlights
their latest
campaigns.

>> **GoFundMe:** Although frequently connected with individual causes, GoFundMe at `https://www.gofundme.com` (see Figure 7-3) is also used often for commercial endeavors as well as charity endeavors.

FIGURE 7-3:
Click the Start a GoFundMe button on the home page to get started.

>> **StartEngine:** Startups can raise money by selling investors shares on the StartEngine equity crowdfunding platform (`https://www.startengine.com`) shown in Figure 7-4. If you're willing to give up a stake in your business, StartEngine is a platform to consider.

How to crowdfund successfully

Crowdfunding has the potential to be an effective method for raising money and creating a passionate following for your project. Thoughtful preparation, a captivating pitch, and proactive communication with backers are all necessary for crowdfunding success.

All good, you say, but wait: We have a five-step plan to entice the crowd to say, "Shut up and take my money!" (Bonus points if you know what TV show that's from.)

1. **Pitch:** Create a pitch that clearly communicates the value and possible effect of your initiative.

FIGURE 7-4:
The StartEngine website shows startups that have raised the most money in the past few days.

2. **Engage your community:** Get your network and community established as soon as possible. Use events, email newsletters, and social media to interact with possible backers.

3. **Create practical goals:** Your financial objective ought to be appropriate for the size of your project and practical. Overly lofty objectives may turn away supporters.

4. **Transparency:** Be open and honest about the status, dangers, and difficulties of your project. Customers value honesty just as you do.

5. **Reward your funders:** Plan ahead for efficient reward or perk fulfillment to your backers so you can fulfill your commitments to them. If you tell your funders you're going to give them a backpack, make sure you have enough to give every backer one in a timely manner.

Understanding Startup Valuation and Dilution

A key idea in startup financing is valuation, which involves figuring out how much money your startup is worth. Because that value directly affects how much equity you offer to investors in exchange for their money, accurate valuation is essential. We're here for you with a list of typical techniques you can use to value your startup.

Market valuation

This method considers recent market transactions for businesses that are similar. Your startup might be valued similarly, for instance, if a business of a similar nature just obtained investment at a certain valuation. This approach bases its evaluation of your value on actual data.

Investors frequently use a multiple to the revenue or profitability of your startup in order to determine its value. For instance, if comparable businesses have been valued at five times earnings and your startup earns $500,000 in yearly revenue, your valuation may be $2.5 million. This approach links your financial success and worth directly and better yet, it's simple.

Discounted cash flow (DCF) analysis

This method is more intricate but quite thorough. It makes an estimate of the future cash flows of your startup. In essence, it takes into account how much your potential earnings are currently worth. You arrive at a valuation that takes into account the time value of money by estimating your cash flows and using a discount rate.

The idea of dilution is one that you need to consider as your business expands and draws more investors. When a startup issues more equity, the ownership percentage of current shareholders — including the founders — effectively decreases.

This is how it usually goes: Imagine that you and a co-founder create a business and that you both initially hold 100 percent of the company's shares. You make the decision to sell an investor 20 percent of the business in order to raise capital. Currently, the investor owns 20 percent of the business, and you and your co-founder each control 40 percent.

In subsequent rounds, your ownership percentage will further decline if you ask for more money in the following round and issue more shares. For instance, if you sell an additional 20 percent of the business, you and your co-founder could wind up with 32 percent of the company, whereas the investor would still hold 20 percent.

So how do you and other members of your founder team protect yourselves?

Retain control

It's necessary to set up the governance of your startup in a way that guarantees you retain control over important choices. Even as your ownership proportion declines, this includes choosing important executives and board members.

REMEMBER

Anti-dilution rules should be taken into consideration when establishing contracts with investors. In the event of further investment rounds with reduced valuations, these restrictions may preserve your ownership stake. The two types that they generally take are full ratchet and weighted average. Full ratchet offers more security but may not be as appealing to investors.

Go preferred

Investigate the idea of issuing preferred shares with particular preferences and privileges. These shares may include anti-dilution protection, for instance. Share structure should reflect both your long-term business and ownership strategies.

WARNING

This strategy may provide safety, but it may also make the equity structure of your firm more complicated.

Seek experienced advisors

Don't negotiate funding rounds and agreements yourself. Speak with knowledgeable specialists including attorneys, mentors, and advisors every step of the way. You'll have a far better chance of safeguarding your ownership and making wise selections with their help.

3

Navigating the Funding Landscape

Chapter 8

Finding Free Money: Grants and Subsidies

You have all these great ideas to get your business on the road to glory and the life you want for yourself, but if you've read any of the chapters before this one, you know that getting the money can be daunting and may require you to sacrifice too much.

Do you have to win the lottery? What if we told you there were plenty of free ways to get money that aren't scams but instead supported by the U.S. government and reputable institutions?

We figure that's why you're here, and this is a chapter that you may want to read with Post-It flags at the ready to bookmark the pages you need when you need more fuel for the road. We cover grants, subsidies, and government programs that you can take advantage of right now. We also have examples of grants for specific industries and regions that can unleash your bloodhounds.

All About Grants, Subsidies, and Government Programs

The number of grants, subsidies, and government programs can seem like the menu at The Cheesecake Factory, and we can't avoid the feeling of overwhelm in this chapter. However, we broke down the information into easily digestible chunks for you, and we provide the good and not-so-good things about each of these three sources.

Grants

Grants are non-repayable cash prizes provided by a variety of entities, including corporations, government agencies, foundations, and nonprofits. They are made to aid particular initiatives, fields of study, or companies. Grants can be given in a variety of ways, such as research grants, project awards, or grants for business development.

The good stuff

There are three good things about getting a grant:

>> **No reimbursement:** Maybe the most important thing is that grants do not have to be paid back, which lessens the risk and financial load for your business.

>> **Support for innovation:** Grants frequently focus on projects that are creative, stimulating creativity and pushing the limits of industry and technology.

>> **Credibility:** Getting a grant can improve your company's reputation and increase its investment appeal.

The challenges to overcome

Sounds great, right? Take your rose-colored glasses off for a second, because there are also three challenges that you need to be prepared for before you submit your first application:

>> **Potential competition:** Grants can be fiercely competitive, with numerous applications fighting for a small pool of funding.

>> **A high bar:** Grant applications frequently have stringent qualifying requirements, reporting requirements, and compliance standards.

>> **A potentially long process:** Securing a grant could take some time, which could put your project or business ambitions on hold.

Where do you start?

If you're in the United States, the federal government offers the Grants.gov website at (you guessed it) https://www.grants.gov/ as you can see in Figure 8-1. It's a great place to learn about grants, search for grants, and apply for a grant.

FIGURE 8-1: Apply for a grant by clicking the Apply for a Grant Using Workspace button.

TIP

If you're outside the United States, contact your local government representative or government agency that supports small businesses to get connections with funding in your country.

The U.S. government's Small Business Innovation Research (SBIR) program at https://www.sbir.gov (see Figure 8-2) offers grants and partnership possibilities to small firms for innovative research and development for startups focusing on technology solutions or innovation.

Grantify (https://grantify.io/us/) shown in Figure 8-3 is another fantastic resource for startups to learn more about the grants that are available and work with specialists to assist you during the application process. They can also give you free use of a range of software programs that will help your new business.

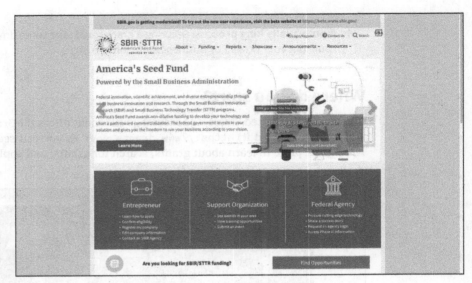

FIGURE 8-2:
The SBIR website touts itself as America's Seed Fund.

FIGURE 8-3:
The Grantify website makes it easy for you to check your eligibility.

Subsidies

Governments use subsidies as financial inducements to lower the costs of particular products, services, or endeavors in specific industries or geographic areas. Subsidies can promote corporate expansion, encourage investment, and generate employment by reducing certain costs.

What will excite you

There are a lot of good things about subsidies, with the most obvious being lower costs. By considerably reducing operational expenses, subsidies might bring starting and maintaining your company from pipe dream to reality.

What will test you

Subsidies may not be easy to get. Navigating complicated application procedures and compliance requirements may be necessary to access subsidies.

Though subsidies can be offered at different levels of government including local, state, and federal, the availability of subsidies could be here one year and gone the next thanks to budget constraints.

Be sure to contact various government agencies about subsidies that may be available to you. For example, Eric lives in California and a quick online search for California business subsidies brought up the California GO-Biz website shown in Figure 8-4.

FIGURE 8-4: The California GO-Biz Incentives, Grants, & Financing webpage.

Your government is here to help (really)

So, what kind of programs do governments support for ambitious new companies and company owners like you? Here are some programs you should research thoroughly.

TAX CREDITS

Businesses that take part in certain activities are given tax credits by the government. For instance, companies performing research and development can take advantage of tax incentives through the Research and Development (R&D) Tax Credit.

OPPORTUNITY ZONES

Opportunity zones are areas with a fragile economy where new businesses may qualify for preferential tax treatment. If an entrepreneur is beginning a business in an Opportunity Zone, they have access to a wide range of services from the U.S. Department of Housing and Urban Development. Visit https://opportunityzones.hud.gov/entrepreneurs/smallbusiness for more information (see Figure 8-5).

FIGURE 8-5:
The Opportunity Now webpage has plenty of links to useful funding resources.

STATE AND LOCAL GOVERNMENT SUBSIDIES

Many states and local governments offer financial aid to companies, particularly those operating in specific sectors or geographic areas. These awards may be used to fund initiatives like innovation and workforce development.

FEDERAL INCENTIVES

Federal incentives like the Investment Tax Credit (ITC) and the Production Tax Credit (PTC), which offer financial benefits for renewable energy projects, are available to enterprises in the renewable energy sector. Visit https://www.eia.gov/energyexplained/renewable-sources/incentives.php (see Figure 8-6) for more details on federal and local incentives.

EXPORT SUPPORT

The U.S. Commercial Service, a division of the Department of Commerce, provides services and initiatives to aid companies in expanding into foreign markets, such as support with export financing.

SUBSIDIES FOR AGRICULTURAL AND RURAL DEVELOPMENT

To encourage rural development and agriculture-related projects, there exist programs that offer financial assistance, grants, and subsidies to firms in the agricultural and rural sectors. You may see a list of the U.S. Department of Agriculture's programs at https://www.rd.usda.gov/programs-services/business-programs (see Figure 8-7).

GRANTS AND LOANS

State and municipal governments may provide grants or low-interest loans to businesses for things like expansion, capital investment, workforce development, and infrastructure development.

FIGURE 8-7:
The USDA Rural Development website offers plenty of programs for your agricultural and/or rural business.

ENTERPRISE ZONES

Some governments have designated some locations as enterprise zones where enterprises can take advantage of a number of tax breaks, laxer regulations, and financial aid.

PROPERTY TAX EXEMPTIONS

To help bring down the cost of real estate, local governments may provide property tax exemptions to companies who make significant investments in their areas.

SALES TAX EXEMPTIONS

For some goods or services, such as manufacturing equipment or data center equipment, certain states exempt firms from paying sales tax.

CREDITS FOR RESEARCH AND DEVELOPMENT

States encourage companies to invest in research and development, better known as R&D, by providing tax credits or deductions for related costs.

CREDITS FOR THE FILM AND ENTERTAINMENT INDUSTRY

Quite a few states, like Pennsylvania (where Marc lives), offer credits to entice enterprises that produce movies and television shows, thereby boosting the regional economy.

HISTORIC PRESERVATION

Businesses active in the preservation and restoration of historic structures may qualify for tax credits to help fund these initiatives.

NEW MARKET TAX CREDITS

By offering tax incentives for eligible equity investments, these credits seek to promote investments in low-income neighborhoods.

Startup incubators and accelerators

Local governments may provide funding for or support for startup incubators and accelerators that give early-stage entrepreneurs access to resources, mentoring, and workspaces.

Business incubators and accelerators offer education, workspaces, and mentorship to businesses in various stages of the startup stage. Additionally, some offer funds in the form of grants, contests where monetary awards are awarded, or connections to investors when their program is complete.

These initiatives frequently target underrepresented demographics. For instance, the Seattle-based organization Head Boss in Charge Headquarters (HBIC HQ) at `https://hbichq.com` supports minority- and women-owned startup companies (see Figure 8-8). For graduates of numerous of its educational programs, it provides merit-based awards.

FIGURE 8-8:
The HBIC HQ
website.

TIP

Even if you are searching for a grant program in your area, try to find one by searching Google for **[Your City] business incubator** with [Your City] replaced by your city or region. Local business incubators frequently offer consulting, training, and lectures that can aid in the development of your business idea.

Private Sector Support Aplenty

There is no shortage of support in the business community to help your business succeed if you decide to take advantage of it.

For example, if you're in the rapidly expanding biotech and health technology industries in the state of New York, the nonprofit organization Accelerate Long Island at https://accelerateli.org (see Figure 8-9) offers grants in collaboration with financial partners, helps entrepreneurs with state tax benefits, and locates workspaces.

FIGURE 8-9:
The Accelerate
Long Island
website.

Here are more examples of more specialized initiatives that various organizations frequently offer to aid startups and entrepreneurs in various industries to jump-start your search for help:

>> **Business networking events:** To connect local firms and entrepreneurs, chambers of commerce routinely conduct networking events.

- » **Business support seminars:** You may see seminars from private organizations and chambers of commerce on a range of business-related subjects, from marketing to legal concerns.

- » **Business counseling:** These groups may offer one-on-one advice and guidance to business owners.

- » **Training and workshops:** Organizations such as chambers of commerce frequently host workshops and training sessions on vital business skills.

- » **Physical space:** Coworking spaces are popular and they might provide your business with inexpensive office space when you want to have a private space and/or meet with clients and other team members in a professional setting.

- » **Community revitalization grants:** These grants promote the growth of the local economy by aiding small companies in specific communities

- » **Workforce training:** Assist with the professional development of manufacturing workers.

- » **Marketing assistance:** Private business associations, especially those in a specific community, can help market your business within their wider promotion of the community. The same is true of chambers of commerce.

- » **Infrastructure support:** Organizations can help develop your infrastructure such as information technology services, disaster recovery, and facilities.

Examples of Grants for Specific Industries and Regions

If you're looking for grants and other support in a specific industry and region that's more specific than the broad support we discussed in the previous section, you can research grants, subsidies, and other incentives offered by industry associations, trade organizations, and locally based organizations.

Businesses normally need to be members of relevant industry associations or business group in order to get these incentives. The requirements for eligibility and the accessibility of particular subsidies will differ from organization to organization.

REMEMBER

The accessibility of these programs may differ by region, sector, and size of the company. In order to efficiently obtain these subsidies, entrepreneurs must also be ready to fulfill specified qualifying conditions and adhere to the program's rules.

We're your compass, so let us point you in some directions that could match your true north.

Agricultural support

There are grants for sustainable farming, agricultural ventures, or research; instructions on sustainable farming methods; and events promoting agriculture that include shows, markets, and fairs.

Grants for research and development (R&D)

To promote research, product development, and innovation within their industry, business organizations in the technology and innovation sectors may offer R&D grants.

Training and workforce development

Some business organizations provide financial aid to members so they can train their staff members and improve workforce capabilities. Grants for specialist training courses or certifications fall under this category.

Grants for market expansion

Business groups may offer grants to help members broaden their customer bases locally and abroad. Costs associated with marketing, advertising, and market research may be covered by these funds.

Sustainability initiatives

Business organizations that are committed to the environment and sustainability may provide members with grants or subsidies to help them implement environmentally friendly procedures or technologies.

Assistance with trade shows and exhibits

To make exhibiting at trade shows, exhibits, and conferences more reasonable for their members, many industry groups offer financial assistance.

Research cooperation

Business organizations frequently promote collaborative research endeavors among their members by contributing funds to cooperative research projects, technology development, or market research.

Access to capital

Some business groups run financial initiatives that put their members in touch with financiers, venture capital firms, or investors, making it possible to get funding more quickly.

Export and trade promotion

By granting financial aid for market research, trade missions, and export strategies, associations involved in international commerce can assist members who are trying to break into new markets.

Innovation and startup incubation

Some business associations provide financial assistance, mentoring, or access to shared resources and incubator facilities to startups and innovative enterprises.

Technology adoption grants

Organizations in technology-focused industries may offer financial assistance to businesses interested in using cutting-edge systems or technologies to boost productivity and competitiveness.

Chapter **9**

Demystifying Angel Investors

Do you know the name Mike Markkula? If it wasn't for him, we wouldn't have Apple — no Mac computers, no iPod, no iPhone, none of that. Markkula was the original angel investor at Apple Computer, Inc., in 1977.

Not only did Markkula provide critical early funding to launch the Apple II computer, he provided managerial support for founders Steve Jobs and Steve Wozniak. Jobs even convinced Markkula to join Apple as its first chairman and second CEO.

In popular culture, angels are bright, luminescent winged creatures. Though angel investors don't have wings, they are guiding lights of the startup world because they help startup companies and founders. (Hey, that's you!) Angel investors support firms financially in exchange for ownership stock or convertible debt.

How Angels Help You Fly

Angel investors play a far bigger role than just supplying capital. They are growth catalysts, risk-takers, mentors, and connections to the proverbial movers and shakers in your industry. If you find a particularly valuable investor as Steve Jobs did, you may want to have the angel investor come.

For entrepreneurs seeking their support as well as for anybody interested in the mechanics of startup finance, we're here to unpack the suitcase that angels bring with them on your road trip to help turn your business into a flying ride.

Providing money for young ventures

As a new business, sources of finance like banks or venture capital firms, are typically not available because the business is too new or risky.

Angel investors are a lifeline for entrepreneurs (hey, that's you!) hoping to get their initial round of investment, frequently called seed funding. Angel investors often bridge this gap by providing your business with the critical funding it needs to get from concept to execution.

What's more, you can use the investor's money to improve your products, enter the market, and reach the next leg in your journey.

Providing knowledge and guidance

Angel investors are not just passive financiers; they frequently have extensive business or professional experience that's just as helpful as the cash infusion.

For example, Mike Markkula was able to establish Apple as a corporation in early 1977 and bring on his pal Michael Scott from their days at Fairchild Semiconductor to be Apple's first CEO.

This move from a partnership with Jobs and Wozniak working out of a garage into an actual brick-and-mortar business with a real corporate structure helped the founders navigate Apple's growth stage. What's more, having people working on corporate stuff freed up Jobs and Wozniak to bring the Apple II to market.

Resources and networking

Angel investors are good at introducing new business founders to their network of contacts. Their network may include other investors, potential clients, strategic allies, and/or consultants.

Even if a potential angel investor isn't interested in an investment at that time, they may know other angel investors who are a fit. With Apple, Jobs and Wozniak approached marketer Regis McKenna and Don Valentine, and Valentine introduced Jobs to Markkula.

Promoting future growth

Your new adventure may require more money than the initial seed round as you grow your business. For example, there was a UPS commercial from the 1990s where all the employees were gathered around a computer screen as they watched orders coming in for the holiday season.

As the number of orders grew exponentially, the employees' initial excitement at getting orders turned to shocked silence as they realized they didn't have the infrastructure to serve all those customers.

The commercial said that UPS could help that fictional company, but it was also very clear they'd need a lot more. Angel investors could be on option to meet the immediate needs of fulfilling orders as well as company expansion based on the demonstrated interest in its products.

Finding the exit ramp

Angel investors will eventually want to get off your ride at a stop along the road, and they'll expect significant returns on their investment when they disembark.

We can hear you scratching your head already about what an exit strategy is. Your angel has a clear idea: They want to sell their ownership at a profit, which can come from an acquisition by another company or an initial public offering, better known by the acronym IPO, in the stock market.

That exit strategy will not only help you understand what you want from your company, it will also entice angel investors. Yes, you guessed it, we go into more detail later in this chapter.

Present a Compelling Attraction

Angel investors are picky about where they spend their money because they want to profit from their investments just as you would. When you've decided to pursue angels, you don't look for them first. You need to be able to show that your company just isn't a shiny toy but something that is actually useful and can serve your target market(s).

A reliable, devoted team

You need to show that there are people who are devoted to your business as much as you are, even if it's just one partner like Wozniak was to Jobs. Here are the three things you need to show angels.

Highlight your team's relevant experience

Highlight how team members' talents match those of the startup by sharing their major accomplishments in prior positions. For instance, emphasize the experience your lead developer has with similar projects or the success your sales manager has in establishing important alliances.

Diverse skill sets

Describe the team's various skill sets and give instances of how those skill sets have already helped the startup grow. Talk about how your marketing director's inventiveness and your technical co-founder's coding expertise combine to produce cutting-edge products and/or services.

Passion and commitment

Provide examples of the team's steadfast commitment, such as staying up late to fulfill deadlines or making personal investments in the project. Describe how your team's passion has helped them overcome obstacles and change course when necessary.

Strong customer value proposition

You need to show that you have a product and/or service that not only sells but that people are using. There are three areas you need to call out.

Show them your customers

Provide thorough customer reviews and case studies that show how your product or service can alleviate particular consumer problems. Video interviews with potential clients who can describe their unmet needs and how your solution meets it should be included.

Show what makes you different

Compare yourself thoroughly to rivals, highlighting not only what makes you special but also how this distinction gives you an edge over the competition. Customer preference surveys and in-depth feature-by-feature analysis should be provided.

Show them numbers

Support the distinctiveness of your product using a range of market research information, consumer polls, and test findings. A/B testing results and user comments should be shared to demonstrate why your product is superior.

Market potential and future growth

If you don't research your market and know that information cold, angel investors will not only shun you like an introvert shuns parties, they'll tell their friends that you're a waste of time. So, know the following three things that clearly demonstrate your potential in the market.

Total addressable market (TAM)

Segment your TAM to give a clear picture of the market's dimensions, features, and potential for growth. Independent and credible market-sizing research reports for your industry will get you bonus stars.

Market trends

Describe market trends and support your analysis of where the industry is headed by providing figures, studies, and professional opinions. Share your own in-depth trend assessments and emphasize how your company fits in with them.

Client segmentation

Showcase how you have effectively reached and engaged with various client segments in addition to defining your ideal customer. To demonstrate the success of targeted marketing efforts and customer acquisition tactics, use precise data. Vague data gets pointed and maybe uncomfortable questions.

Validation and progress

By the time you look for an angel investor, it's likely that you already have customers that are buying. After all, Apple sold several Apple I computers to show their computers were viable before they approached angel investors.

In keeping with our theme of threes, here are three things you need to show that your business is moving down the road in the right direction.

Customer testimonials

Include in-depth comments from pleased customers (or pilot customers), detailing the particular difficulties they had and how your product resolved them. Include case study documentation and video testimonials.

Revenue growth

Provide a well-organized graph or table outlining historical revenue or sales growth, along with an explanation of any peaks or valleys. Share quarterly and yearly financial reports and emphasize the sources of revenue.

Alliances and partnerships

Provide examples of strategic alliances that have improved brand recognition, boosted sales, or generated cost-saving synergies. Include results such as increased sales or collaborative initiatives, as well as signed collaboration agreements.

Scalability

Draw a diagram of your business plan to show how it scales well. Discuss how your model would cope with an increase in the number of users or clients. Provide flowcharts that show your business processes can scale as the company grows.

Next, illustrate how your business model can effectively scale, including particulars on cost reductions and revenue increases if applicable. To demonstrate your scalability, highlight key performance indicators (KPIs) like user base growth and cost per acquisition.

A clear exit plan

And here we are with more for you about putting together an exit strategy. When you talk with an angel investor, talk about various exit options, such as possible acquisitions or an initial public offering (IPO). Give each option's benefits and drawbacks, supported by past instances of businesses that employed comparable tactics.

Describe the timeline for the prospective exits and the milestones or circumstances that may cause them. Point out businesses in your sector that have used comparable exit strategies and their results.

Your competitive advantage

Emphasize the competitive advantage that your intellectual property (IP) or proprietary technology offers. Include any patent information or technological advancements that distinguish you.

Next, describe how your company has erected substantial entrance barriers that make it difficult for rivals to duplicate your success. Wrap up by giving examples of successful businesses in your field and describe the challenges they tried to overcome.

Making Your Pitch

Now that you have all that information ready, it's time to find investors, put together your pitch, and actually meet with these people who could move your business along the road faster than you ever thought possible.

REMEMBER

Be ready for numerous encounters with prospective investors. It takes time to develop relationships but maintaining them can result in money in the future if not right now.

Searching for angel investors

Angel investors aren't mythical like angels in popular culture with the halos, shiny human bodies, and big white wings. You can find angel investors in your communities so you can meet them in person as well as online. There are also angel investor communities you can find in directories to match your location and/or industry. As Calvin said in the last line of the *Calvin and Hobbes* comic strip, let's go exploring.

Boost your network

Don't merely request recommendations. Inquire about warm introductions from shared acquaintances. Your chances of having a meeting considerably increase with a personal introduction from someone the investor knows and trusts.

If you're not attending industry-specific events and conferences already, set up your calendar to go to some and foster strategic networking. It is more likely that you will discover investors who have a real interest in your market if you attend events that are related to the niche in which your firm operates.

Platforms for angel investors

There are websites where angels congregate, and a popular one is AngelList at `https://www.angellist.com`, and their home page is shown in Figure 9-1.

FIGURE 9-1:
The AngelList
website.

When you develop a profile on AngelList or a similar site, make sure to highlight your startup's market potential and traction in a straightforward and compelling manner.

Make use of these sites not merely for visibility but also for thorough investor research. Recognize their investment history, preferred industries, and any particular investment philosophies they have.

TIP

If you want to expand your search, you can type **angel investor platforms** in your search engine of choice.

Groups of angel investors

You can sign up with groups of angel investors, and one place to start is the Meetup website at `https://www.meetup.com/topics/angel-investors/` (see Figure 9-2). These are great places to connect with angel investors in person that are (hopefully) reasonably close to you.

TIP

You can also find groups of angel investors closer to your area, such as in the state where you live, by typing **angel investor groups near me** in your favorite search engine.

FIGURE 9-2:
The Angel
Investing page on
the Meetup
website will help
you find groups
in your area.

Directories of angel investors

It's easy to find angel investor directories through a search engine, and a great place to start is with the Angel Capital Association website at `https://www.angelcapitalassociation.org/directory/` as shown in Figure 9-3.

FIGURE 9-3:
The Angel Capital
Association
Member
Directory has a
list of groups
from around
the world.

Laws of attraction

Whenever you apply for funding, you need to create as strong of a presentation as possible to get your angel investors to pay attention and make them realize that you're a good match for them and their cash. And we're happy to share our match-maker's playbook to help you get the angel investor you deserve.

Be clear and compelling

Make sure the content of your pitch deck is both clear and succinct. Include slides outlining the issue your startup addresses, the size of the market, your solution, your revenue model, your financial predictions, your team, and the reasons why your startup is a special investment opportunity.

Your pitch deck also needs to be compelling. You can do that when it has relevant images and infographics that support what you're saying without a lot of text or unnecessary jargon.

Understand your market

Address the specific interests and areas of expertise of the angel investor in your proposal. Show how your firm fits within their portfolio by citing their prior investments. And if you and an investor share a personal connection or a common interest, mention it in your pitch.

What's more, show how thorough market research has shaped your company's strategy and helped to reduce any potential market hazards down the road.

Beginning with a powerful elevator pitch

Start your presentation with a compelling, one-sentence elevator pitch that sum-marizes the key value proposition of your startup. This is the hook that will get the investor's attention.

What's your why?

Create a captivating narrative that highlights your entrepreneurial path, the fac-tors that motivated you to launch the company, and the background of your prod-uct or service.

Humans are storytellers, so make your elevator pitch memorable and relatable with stories that connect to your investor. For example, you can talk about what excites you about your industry, the problems you found in your experience, and how those problems motivated you to launch your company and fix them.

The investor's values and interests should be reflected in your story, because a connection with your angel investor during your presentation can mean a stronger connection when your investor joins you for the ride.

Display progress and achievements

Include pertinent metrics like user acquisition, revenue, client testimonials, partnerships, and other noteworthy accomplishments in your metrics and data. Specify how your milestones confirm that there is a market for your product and/or service.

Show your finances

Offer thorough financial forecasts that cover income sources, costs, profit margins, and significant financial milestones. Clearly describe how the invested money will be used to scale up and grow your company.

If you don't do this, your angel investor will ask you some very pointed questions including why you didn't have this financial information in your pitch deck.

Your plan for the opportunity

Focus on your market opportunity's finer points, such as target market demographics, industry trends, and possible growth areas. Then describe your tactical plan for breaking into the market while highlighting your competitive advantages.

IP management

Intellectual property, or IP, is the lifeblood of your business because it gives you an advantage over your competition and gives your new venture a better chance of getting where you want to go. So, your pitch deck must describe your IP strategy and how it safeguards your company.

The ask

Be transparent, because this is a relationship for keeps. Clearly outline your equity offering and finance needs, which will be the starting point for negotiations.

Be flexible in negotiations while maintaining a clear ask. Investors might recommend changing the terms, so talk about it with them.

Practice, practice, practice (and practice some more)

Before you approach your angel investor, repeatedly work on your pitch. Make sure you are fully familiar with your pitch deck and practice until you feel comfortable.

Practice answering tough questions by holding practice Q&A sessions with your company team, mentors, and/or advisors. Encourage them to comment on and provide suggestions for changes to your presentation.

Follow Up

This pitch is just like a sales pitch to a customer you want to buy your product or service in that you should answer questions or requests for information as soon as possible. If you don't at least tell the investor that you'll get back to them as soon as possible because other things are stopping you, your angel may fly away.

Chapter **10**

Venturing into Venture Capital

enture capital, better known by its acronym *VC*, is probably the most popular form of raising capital because it's fueled the growth of many of tech companies like Apple, Amazon, and Google. But venture capital likes non-tech companies, too — SpaceX, DoorDash, and Airbnb have plenty of venture capital backing them up.

If you're thinking of using venture capital as another fuel source for your business, you've come to the right place. Within this chapter, we take a tour of the VC ecosystem and its denizens. VC funding comes in stages, so we spend some time with each one.

When you're ready to (*ahem*) venture forth, we tell you the secrets of what attracts VC investors so you can show them that investing in your business is a no-brainer.

What's Venture Capital All About, Charlie Brown?

Welcome to the VC ecosystem, which is well defined with four participants in this game:

>> **Entrepreneurs:** Yes, you! Entrepreneurs are the starting point and the inspiration for new concepts. In order to make their concepts a reality, entrepreneurs look for venture funding.

>> **Venture capitalists:** These investors, known by the acronym VCs, exist in a variety of shapes and sizes, including private individuals, institutional investors like pension funds, venture capital companies, and corporate venturing arms.

>> **Private investors:** These investors work together with VCs and want high returns for their investments.

>> **Investment bankers:** These investment bankers need companies for selling stock.

If you want to see how these four players work together along with corporations and government as well as with public markets and operations, Figure 10-1 below shows the relationships between all the players.

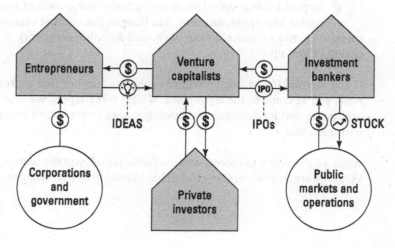

FIGURE 10-1: How the venture capital ecosystem works.

The inner workings of venture capital

Venture capital functions according to a common model, though it can be tweaked depending on the deal. For the purposes of our exploration, we cover all of the parts of the venture capital machine here for you, and then we go into what VCs actually do.

Although it can be tailored to certain deals, venture capital functions according to a common model. Here's a detailed explanation of how it operates:

Funding rounds

Venture capital funding typically comes in several stages, such as Series A, Series B, and Series C, each of which reflects a different stage in the growth and development of the company.

Pitch and due diligence

A pitch is the beginning of the journey for entrepreneurs, followed by due diligence. They have to persuade venture funders of the transformative potential of their company during this presentation. The VC performs due diligence, a detailed analysis of the startup's state, including its business model, staff, intellectual property, and financials, if interest is aroused.

Term sheet

Following the completion of the due diligence, a term sheet is discussed and negotiated between the parties. The investment terms are described in this document, including the amount of money invested, the equity stake the VC receives, and any safeguards that protect the investor's interests.

Exit strategy

Venture capital investments are focused on an exit strategy that generates significant profits. This might happen either by the startup going public in an initial public offering (IPO) or being acquired by a bigger company. At this point, both the founders and the venture capitalist are aware of the benefits of their investment.

Risk vs. reward

Venture capital investments are by their very nature hazardous to their bottom lines. Although not every company succeeds, venture capitalists frequently invest in a portfolio of businesses in the hopes that a few notable successes will more than offset the losses in other ventures.

What do VCs actually do?

Venture capitalists just give out money, right? After all, capital is in their name. But VCs do a lot more and expect a lot more from their investments in four areas.

Mentor and advisor

Venture capitalists usually have extensive knowledge of entrepreneurship and particular industries. They increase the likelihood that the startup will succeed by providing founders with mentoring, strategic advice, and coaching.

Network facilitator

Venture capitalists connect entrepreneurs with prospective partners, clients, and other investors through their extensive networks, promoting the growth of their companies.

Governance

As equity owners, VCs frequently have a voice in the management of the company. They might serve on the board of directors and actively participate in making strategic choices. It's critical to put care and attention into how your board is structured and how you manage the board members. If you aren't attentive, you could suddenly find yourself ousted from the company you founded.

Exit strategist

To ensure that both the startup and investors successfully exit the venture, VCs collaborate closely with founders to develop and implement exit plans.

Platform Stages

The VC ecosystem also includes various stages of funding depending on where your startup is on your road to glory. As you get farther down the road, you'll find fuel stations with more money to get you to the next milestone.

Pre-seed stage

At the pre-seed stage, business owners depend on their own funds or gifts from friends and family to develop an early notion into a functional prototype or proof of concept.

The primary objective is to confirm the startup's concept and show that it is feasible, which can be an important step in luring additional financing. Pre-seed money frequently helps a startup become ready for larger fundraising rounds.

Early stage

Seed funding is the first sum of money used to start a business and support its early growth. In this phase, the product or service is improved, a customer base is developed, and more market research is done.

Angel investors, venture capital firms, crowdfunding websites, or specialist seed-stage funds are some of the sources of seed money available to startups.

Seed-stage funding is intended to help startups establish a strong foundation by enhancing their products, growing their teams, and attracting their first clients.

Series A

Startups at this level should have a tested company plan and visible market traction. A company uses Series A funding to boost its operations and expand its market presence.

Institutional investors frequently join venture capital companies in leading Series A rounds. The main goal is to increase the startup's market share, frequently with a focus on raising profitability.

Series B

Startups seeking Series B funding are already profitable and looking to expand significantly. These finances are essential for expanding operations, acquiring rival businesses, and breaking into new markets.

Corporate investors and growth equity companies participate in Series B fundraising rounds in addition to venture capital firms.

Series C and later

Beyond Series B, late-stage investment focuses on rapid growth and expansion. Businesses prioritize developing new product lines, entering new markets, and making strategic acquisitions.

At this stage, capital is contributed by institutional investors, private equity companies, and occasionally strategic corporate investors. The major objective for the company is to take the lead in the market and maybe get ready for an IPO (initial public offering) or an acquisition.

Mezzanine financing

Mezzanine funding is a stage that combines aspects of debt and equity and frequently acts as a stopgap before an IPO. Although a company might not need equity capital, it may nonetheless want to raise its valuation before going public.

Private equity investors and hedge funds are frequently involved in mezzanine financing.

Exit stage

A successful move to becoming a publicly traded firm through an IPO or by being purchased by a bigger company is represented by the exit stage. The founders and early investors have an opportunity to realize their rewards during this stage.

Energy Precedes Capital

Any VC is going to have high expectations just as any other investor, such as an angel investor, will have as they look over your company and kick the tires. VCs are, after all, going to be riding with you and giving you advice about where to drive to get the smoothest trip to your next destination.

Before you can put together your pitch to proudly give to potential partners, though, you need to know what they're looking for, and we have this intelligence briefing just for you.

High potential for growth

Venture capitalists are drawn to startups with the potential to upend existing industries. They seek to support concepts that can innovate, upend established practices, and transform industries.

Scalability is crucial. VCs look for firms that can expand rapidly without needing to increase their resources linearly, which frequently necessitates a tech-driven business plan.

An outstanding founding team

VCs seek founding teams with extensive industry knowledge, a successful track record, and a wealth of experience. They look for an entrepreneurial background with examples of adding value or resolving issues.

A successful team integrates a variety of complementary abilities, including marketing, leadership, technical, business, and subject knowledge. Due of its diversity, the startup can efficiently address problems.

Validation and traction

VCs are more likely to invest in firms that have already gained some traction in the market. Key measures like customer adoption, revenue growth, client testimonials, or strategic alliances could be used to illustrate this.

What's more, VCs will look for your company's commitment to determining market fit and developing an MVP (minimum viable product) for testing and development of the product. An MVP is frequently regarded as evidence that the startup's problem-solution match is sound.

Business strategy and revenue potential

VCs want to know exactly how a firm plans to make money off of its product. It is crucial to demonstrate dependable revenue sources, such as subscription models, licensing, or freemium programs.

Investors frequently anticipate companies to present a distinct route to profitability. This could include knowledge of how to manage cash flow, expenses, pay for client acquisition, and scale while preserving profitability.

Although optimism is valued, VCs prefer financial projections based on reality as opposed to overly upbeat estimates. A cautious strategy reveals a realistic appreciation of growth possibilities.

What makes your company better

VCs choose firms with tenable competitive advantages, such as patents, exclusive alliances, proprietary technologies, network effects, or patents. These entry barriers discourage rivals.

Note attractive points of differentiation that distinguish the startup from present or potential rivals. Explaining why your answer is better is crucial.

An exit route

VCs like exit plans that are clearly laid out. This can take the form of investments made by bigger businesses, initial public offerings (IPOs), or other ways to give investors a path to liquidity. For many VCs, an IPO is a desirable exit plan.

The founders' and investors' agreement on the exit strategy is crucial. This prevents future conflicts by ensuring that both sides have the same goals.

Effective leadership and flexibility

VCs value management teams that can carry out the business plan in a cost-and time-effective manner. Startups must show they can navigate opportunities and challenges.

The VC will also gauge your growth mentality and the ability to change. Startups must consistently learn from feedback and pivot as necessary to ensure the team can adapt to changing market conditions.

Protection of intellectual property

Patents and intellectual property (IP) protection can be a major selling factor for venture capitalists when it comes to firms with a strong focus on technology and innovation. This defense can give you a competitive advantage and stop infringement.

Communication and openness

It's crucial to communicate with investors in an efficient and open manner. Regular updates are valued by VCs in both prosperous and trying times.

Companies must inform investors of significant accomplishments, difficulties, and financial results. This proactive strategy promotes a positive and fruitful interaction between investors and founders.

How to create the ideal pitch for venture capitalists

Developing a stellar pitch for venture capitalists (VCs) is essential for obtaining funding. We have some great tips from successful business entrepreneurs who have perfected their pitching techniques, and feel free to steal these ideas as you create your own pitch.

Start with a compelling narrative

Start off your presentation with a gripping tale. This draws the VC's attention and increases the recall value of your startup. Use a narrative format to emphasize the issue your company addresses, how the idea was developed, and the potential impact it could have.

Using her own health issue as an example, Sarah, the creator of a health tech business, drew investors into her quest to develop a remedy that would save lives — including her own.

Resolve a serious issue

Your startup should target a real problem. VCs are attracted to ideas that address important issues. Clearly state the issue, show its magnitude, and provide examples of how your solution is provided by your product or service.

To illustrate, John, the CEO of a cybersecurity business, highlighted the growing danger posed by online attacks. He provided data breach statistics and demonstrated how his technology might safeguard sensitive data.

Display market potential

VCs want to know that your service has a sizable market. Share market analysis and statistics that demonstrate growth potential.

For example, Mark is the creator of a firm that produces renewable energy. His pitch discussed market trends and growing environmental concerns while stressing the increased demand for sustainable energy options.

Highlight validation and traction

Demonstrate the growth of your startup. Share statistics on user adoption, revenue growth, client references, business alliances, and any accolades received from the industry.

For instance, Emily, the creator of a meal delivery service, displayed the business's explosive growth by sharing user numbers, collaborations with eateries, and raving client testimonials.

Competitive research

Thoroughly research your competitors and show how your firm exceeds them. Emphasize your defining characteristics. Then explain why your startup is more likely to succeed than your rivals.

Alex, the creator of a new e-commerce platform, described the rivals, pointing out their flaws and outlining how his platform stood out thanks to its novel features.

Large-scale business strategy

Scalable firms appeal to venture funders. Show how your company can expand quickly without seeing a linear increase in costs.

A software-as-a-service startup's founder James gave an example of how the subscription model allowed for exponential user growth without corresponding increases in infrastructure costs.

Strong team

VCs place equal value on the team and the idea. Highlight the knowledge, experience, and business plan execution skills of your team.

Laura, the creator of a biotech business, introduced her team by highlighting the members' significant expertise in biotechnology, medicine, and research.

A direct route to success

Investors must be able to perceive a long-term route to profitability. Describe your plans for increasing revenue, cutting costs, and achieving profitability.

Steve, the creator of a fintech business, presented a financial road map outlining how income would increase while costs would be kept in check.

Exit planning

Outline your plan of retreat. It demonstrates your forward-thinking nature and aids VCs in understanding how to maximize their investment.

As an illustration, Jessica, the founder of a medtech business, revealed that their exit strategy was to be purchased by a significant medical device manufacturer.

Presentation tips

Giving your potential VC the information they're looking for isn't enough. You need more to round out your presentation and make it easy for your VC to say yes.

» **Customize your pitch:** Tailor your pitch to the individual VC. Examine their financial strategy, portfolio, and hobbies. Tailored pitches demonstrate your research and sincere interest in their support.

» **Concentrate initially on the issue at hand:** Introduce your startup by outlining the issue it attempts to solve. The significance of the issue is established, which primes the VC to value your solution.

» **Show, don't just tell:** Include illustrations, mockups, or demonstrations in your proposal. VCs can better grasp your product or service by using visual assistance.

» **Share your story:** You may make an emotional connection with VCs by including a personal story that is connected to your startup. It displays your zeal and dedication.

» **Be up front:** Honesty is valued by VCs. Don't be afraid to bring up problems if you run into them. Integrity fosters trust.

» **Avoid overselling:** Enthusiasm is important, but don't oversell your startup. VCs value candor and realism when you talk about your company's problems.

>> **Consider questions:** Before the pitch, prepare responses to possible questions that VCs may ask. This illustrates your commercial acumen and leadership.

>> **Practice, practice, and yeah, practice:** This improves delivery and guarantees that you can confidently respond to the VC's questions.

>> **There's nothing wrong with being confident:** When VCs see your enthusiasm and conviction, they are more likely to invest. It's trite, but it's true: You're more confident after you've practiced a lot.

>> **Being overconfident is not recommended:** Demonstrate that you're self-aware by pointing out areas you need to improve in as a leader. If you come across as so overconfident that you're clueless about yourself, you may as well be waving a couple of big red flags in your hands as you talk.

TIP

Don't be afraid to ask for mentoring or advising assistance. A seasoned mentor can offer insightful advice and aid in pitch improvement.

Reaching out

Now that you have your pitch down cold and you can tailor it to your VC with confidence, it's time to find venture capital firms. Doing that is as easy as going on Wikipedia and typing **list of venture capital firms** in the Search box.

Figure 10-2 shows the results with lists of notable capital firms in several categories followed by lists of VC firms in geographic areas.

You should meet your VCs in person at some point. One good way to do that is to use the Meetup website to search for VC meetup groups in your area (see Figure 10-3). It can be beneficial to establish a relationship with VCs before you require their funding.

TIP

Use your network to request warm introductions to venture investors. Introductions from someone the VC trusts can frequently greatly increase your credibility. Don't have a network? Take the first step to develop one and don't be afraid to leverage other people's networks.

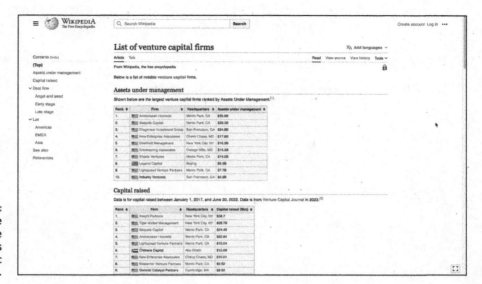

FIGURE 10-2:
Scroll down the page to view the lists of VC firms by geographic area.

FIGURE 10-3:
The Meetup page for finding where venture capitalists gather.

» Understanding the good and bad of crowdfunding

» Exploring crowdfunding platforms and models

» Creating a compelling crowdfunding campaign

Chapter **11**

Crowdfunding Made Easy

You may have opened this chapter up the moment you got your hands on this book because it's about crowdfunding! It's going to make you oodles of money because people are more willing to put in small amounts of money, and lots of them will be happy to do it because your product is going to change the world!

Whoa, simmer down there, Sparky. If you don't choose the right kind of online crowdfunding platform that will give you the best chance to reach the most people, your days of wine and roses will turn into the days of vinegar and tobacco.

That said, crowdfunding isn't panhandling, either, and this financial model is so popular because it's inclusive and these virtual marketplaces connect creators with their potential funders.

In this chapter, we start by reviewing the seven types of crowdfunding, and you'll need that information to learn what's good and not so good about each type. Then we cover several crowdfunding platforms for each of the seven types. We wrap up by telling you how to create compelling crowdfunding campaigns (how's that for some alliteration?) so you can entice backers to your glorious cause.

The Magnificent Seven

Crowdfunding comes in seven primary types, each designed to meet the unique requirements and project kinds. Read this section before you jump ahead to our discussion about platforms, because here we give you the definitions you need so you're informed when we talk about the pros and cons as well as a closer look at the platforms.

Figure 11-1 below shows a simple chart with the types of crowdfunding so you can get a quick snapshot before we drill down. (It's a good sneak preview of what's to come in this chapter, too.)

TYPES OF CROWDFUNDING

	What you give	What you get	Examples
DONATIONS	Donate to someone needy	Nothing in return	**GoFundMe Crowdrise**
REWARDS	Funds to help an entrepreneur	The product the entrepreneur develops	**Kickstarter Indiegogo**
EQUITY	An investment in a new company	An ownership stake (like stock)	**SeedInvest Wefunder**
LOANS	A loan to someone needy	Paid back over time with interest	**LendingClub Prosper**

FIGURE 11-1: The types of crowdfunding and what's involved with each.

Rewards-based crowdfunding

In order to finance their creative endeavors, artists, designers, inventors, and other creators choose the rewards-based crowdfunding approach.

In exchange for non-monetary rewards — which can include early access to the product or service, limited-edition goods, or exclusive experiences — creators pitch their ideas to backers. Well-known sites for rewards-based crowdfunding are Indiegogo and Kickstarter.

Equity crowdfunding

Startups (that's you) frequently use equity crowdfunding to generate capital and provide investors shares of the company in exchange for equity.

That is, investors buy ownership shares in the company and come along for the ride through all the twists, turns, breakdowns on the road, and the arrival at prosperous destinations. Two well-known platforms for equity crowdfunding are Crowdcube and Seedrs.

Debt crowdfunding

Under this model, borrowers commit to repay interest-bearing loans from a group of lenders in exchange for a loan from an individual or corporation.

This model is good for new businesses like yours to find startup funding, and you can find this type of crowdsourcing on peer-to-peer lending websites like LendingClub and Prosper.

Real estate crowdfunding

This type of crowdfunding enables people to pool their resources and make joint investments in residential, commercial, or industrial real estate. To buy and maintain homes, investors pool their money, frequently via Internet platforms.

By using this strategy, real estate investors can diversify their holdings without having to make direct property purchases. Rental income and possible property appreciation are the usual ways in which investors obtain returns proportionate to their capital. Top platforms for real estate crowdfunding are PeerStreet, Fundrise, and RealtyMogul.

Regulation crowdfunding

The Securities and Exchange Commission (SEC) created the regulation crowdfunding model, which the SEC calls Reg CF, to make it easier for startups and early-stage companies to raise funding.

Businesses may raise up to $5 million from accredited and non-accredited investors. Regulation crowdfunding websites include Republic, Wefunder, and StartEngine.

SAFE and KISS equity crowdfunding

This type of crowdfunding uses two standardized investment instruments known by their acronyms: SAFE, or Simple Agreements for Future Equity, and KISS, which stands for *Keep It Simple Security*. (The latter isn't the meaning that you're thinking of, but it has the same sentiment.)

For early-stage firms just like yours, these agreements provide an easy-to-understand and transparent method of equity crowdfunding. The terms of the investment are outlined in SAFE and KISS agreements, giving investors and entrepreneurs clarity.

Donation-based crowdfunding

Contributors to donation-based crowdfunding do so out of charity and support initiatives or charitable causes without anticipating financial gain. This strategy is frequently applied to charitable endeavors, helping cover huge costs of medical procedures and treatments, and community projects. Platforms for donation-based crowdfunding that rely on donations include JustGiving and GoFundMe; the latter is probably the one you know best.

The Advantages

There's a lot going for crowdfunding, but if you're trying to convince other people on your team that crowdfunding is something to consider, put a sticky flag on this page and give them a copy of your book (or better yet, buy a copy for each team member) so they can partake of the good stuff.

Access to capital

Crowdfunding gives entrepreneurs a readily available source of finance, which is particularly helpful for startups in their early stages who could find it difficult to get traditional loans or draw in venture capital. By enabling a diverse group of people to contribute to your initiative or business, it democratizes finance.

Diverse funding sources

A wide range of backers and investors are brought together on crowdfunding platforms. This diversity provides a wide base of financial support in addition to raising the total amount of monies raised.

Diverse viewpoints, backgrounds, and networks from each supporter could be advantageous to your new business because that diversity will give you insights and ideas you never considered before and get your dopamine flowing.

Market validation

One of the most effective ways to validate a market is through a crowdsourcing campaign gone well. There is a market for your product or concept when people are prepared to put their money in it. When you're trying to draw in new partners or investors, this affirmation can be very persuasive.

Customer engagement

Early adopters and ardent supporters are frequently crowdfunding backers. In addition to being investors, they may also end up becoming your first clients and brand evangelists. By including them from the start, you create a devoted clientele and nurture word-of-mouth advertising.

Decreased risk

Because crowdfunding doesn't require taking on debt or giving up ownership in your business, it reduces financial risk. It's a more economical way to raise money because you're not giving up ownership or paying interest.

Marketing and promotion

Crowdfunding initiatives make great tools for marketing. They raise interest in and publicity for your company. You're interacting with prospective clients and promoting your idea or product through your campaign. This may have a long-term effect on the awareness and familiarity of your brand.

Flexibility

With a variety of models to select from, crowdfunding provides flexibility. You can choose the model that best suits your business needs and customize your campaign to meet your unique financial goals and objectives.

The Challenges

We like to be positive even when we're talking about bad stuff, so let's talk about the challenges of crowdfunding. The skeptics on your team will point to these obstacles that you'll find on the road to glory, but that's just an opportunity for you to come up with confident comebacks.

Competition

Thousands of campaigns are hosted on crowdfunding platforms, which leads to fierce competition for funds and attention. To stand out in this crowded market, you need a distinctive value proposition, well-thought-out marketing, and an engaging story.

It's time-consuming

Starting and running a crowdsourcing project can take a lot of time. It frequently requires a large amount of your time and energy, taking you away from other crucial facets of your company, like operations or product development.

It costs money

The amount of time you invest in your crowdfunding project will probably cost you some amount of money. What's more, crowdfunding companies charge fixed fees and then a percentage of the money you raise. So, make sure you know what your preferred platform charges before you craft your budget.

Risk of failure

Not all crowdfunding initiatives are successful. Should you fall short of your financing target during the campaign's timeline, your efforts can be in vain and you might not receive any money at all. This can be depressing and force you to reconsider your financing plans, if not your entire business model.

Lack of control

Depending on the crowdfunding model you select, you might have to give backers some control or split your profits. Giving up a piece of your company's ownership through equity-based crowdfunding, for instance, may result in shared decision-making.

Transparency

Detailed financial and corporate transparency is required for several crowdsourcing types, most notably equity-based crowdfunding. You might not want to disclose this information if you would rather keep some parts of your company private.

Client expectations

Backers of crowdfunding campaigns may have high standards for your product or service. It may be difficult to live up to these expectations, particularly if there are delays or other problems in the development or delivery process. It's critical to control these expectations and keep lines of communication open.

What's Your Best Fit?

Still feeling good about crowdfunding? What we just talked about are the overall benefits and challenges no matter what platform you use. Different crowdfunding types have their own pros and cons, and we're here to give them to you in a format that will help you select what crowd you want to help fund your business.

We offer two or three pros and cons for each crowdfunding type, so you'll be in and out just as quickly as when you're in the express lane in the supermarket (at least in theory). We cover the specific platforms later in this chapter.

Rewards-based crowdfunding

Seed crowdfunding, better known as rewards-based crowdfunding, is a campaign where entrepreneurs and small businesses ask for monetary donations in exchange for rewards, such as a product or service. You may also want to provide different products or services for different donation levels, such as early access to a cookbook app with the purchase of a cookbook.

Pros

Rewards-based crowdfunding helps you build not only money, but also gives your company credibility:

>> **Pre-sales strategy:** By allowing entrepreneurs to sell their products and/or services before they are fully developed, rewards-based crowdfunding

enables them to make early profits that can go a long way toward funding their initial operations.

>> **Market validation:** A campaign that is successful proves the concept and shows that there is a market for what you're selling.

>> **Customer engagement:** Developing a rapport with early adopters can result in a long-term commitment from them, and their input can be very helpful for improving your product or service.

Cons

Now it's time to take off the proverbial rose-colored glasses, because rewards-based crowdfunding brings some challenges:

>> **Fulfillment challenges:** It might be difficult to meet delivery obligations. This can lead to unanticipated delays or higher expenses, which could damage your business's brand and cause clients to go away using whatever tired cliché they prefer.

>> **You don't get all the money:** When you crowdfund using a platform like Kickstarter, be aware that platforms charge a percentage from 5 to 13 percent, and they may also charge additional processing fees.

>> **Competition:** Because rewards-based crowdfunding platforms are home to many projects, standing out from the crowd is not always easy.

Equity crowdfunding

Equity crowdfunding is straightforward: You raise money from investors in exchange for equity ownership in your business. Selling shares of your company is one alternative to a business loan, but read the following pros and cons before you dig deeper. (Chin rubbing is optional.)

Pros

Bringing in more people with different ideas can help you accelerate your business further down the road in three ways:

>> **Access to capital:** Your shiny new startup can finance growth, product development, and market expansion, which provides a sizable source of cash without requiring them to take on debt.

>> **Diverse investors:** Drawing in a range of investors with different specialties and backgrounds can open up important networks and offer opportunities

for mentorship and a range of viewpoints about how you can (hopefully) make your startup go faster.

>> **Expertise and mentorship:** In addition to their financial contributions, some equity investors — especially those making larger investments may provide advice and mentorship, which can significantly boost your startup's value.

Cons

Now it's time to pump the brakes because bringing in equity investors brings a lot of new responsibilities:

>> **Ownership dilution:** Founders may face problems with shared decision-making and governance when they offer equity, which dilutes their ownership and control over the business.

>> **Regulatory requirements:** Due to securities legislation governing equity crowdfunding, it's vital to manage the intricate legal and compliance requirements involved, so plan on adding legal expenses to your project budget.

>> **Disclosure requirements:** The legal structure governing equity crowdfunding frequently requires investors to receive thorough financial and business disclosures, some of which may include sensitive data that you may not want to share.

Debt crowdfunding

Crowdlending, better known as debt crowdfunding, is a form of crowdfunding where you can raise money from a large number of investors on online platforms that we'll talk about later in this chapter.

Pros

Debt crowdfunding has several features that make it attractive to startup business owners like you:

>> **No stock sacrifice:** Debt crowdfunding helps founders keep control and decision-making by enabling firms to raise capital without giving up ownership or stock in the business.

>> **Fixed interest rates:** In order to provide predictability for financial planning and debt management, borrowers and lenders usually agree on fixed interest rates and repayment terms.

>> **Credit accessibility:** Debt crowdfunding can fill financial shortages for companies that would have trouble securing conventional loans or luring venture capital.

Cons

The inclusion of the word debt in debt crowdfunding means there are financial responsibilities that you and your team need to abide by:

>> **Interest payments:** Interest payments are a requirement for borrowers, and they can have an impact on the cash flow of the business, especially in recessionary times or when earnings aren't high enough to support repayment.

>> **Regulatory compliance:** Adherence to regulatory compliance is required by certain platforms, which complicates the fundraising process and may bring administrative and legal expenses you have to plan for.

>> **Credit risk:** Repaying debt to investors is a top concern in times of financial troubles, and it can put pressure on the company's credit standing and stability.

Real estate crowdfunding

If you're looking to get office space or if you have a brick-and-mortar business, real estate crowdfunding is straightforward: You raise money from many investors to buy land to develop a new office building or buy an existing building and upgrade it inside and out as needed.

Pros

There are several attractive features of real estate crowdfunding for both you and investors:

>> **Diversification:** By exposing investors to a previously elite asset class and lowering risk, real estate crowdfunding enables investors to diversify their portfolios with very little capital.

>> **Accessibility:** It makes real estate investments that were previously only available to institutional investors accessible, democratizing the market and opening doors for a wider spectrum of investors.

>> **Low entry barriers:** Real estate investing is more democratic because it is available to people who might not otherwise be able to own real estate properties on their own.

Cons

We're talking about real estate, so you've probably guessed that this form of funding brings its own set of issues:

>> **Complexity:** Real estate investments can be complex, and assessing the risks associated with various projects calls for a level of knowledge that inexperienced investors might not possess, which could result in poor investment decisions.

>> **Market fluctuations:** Investments in real estate can be impacted by a variety of events, including variations in rental demand, property value fluctuations, and market downturns. Real estate markets are also vulnerable to economic volatility.

>> **Risk management:** In order to reduce possible losses from real estate investments, effective risk management and due diligence are crucial. It frequently necessitates a thorough comprehension of market dynamics and real estate dynamics.

Regulation crowdfunding (Reg CF)

Reg CF was introduced with the JOBS Act of 2016 that helps democratize the investment industry by making it possible for anyone to invest in privately-held securities.

Pros

Reg CF brings both money and regulatory advantages to the table:

>> **A broader investor pool:** Reg CF increases access to capital from a wide array of supporters by expanding the investor pool to include non-accredited investors, improving startup funding opportunities.

>> **Not-too-shabby capital raising:** You can obtain up to $5 million from that broad investor pool to give you an ample source of funding for your development, expansion into new markets, and company growth.

>> **Simplified regulatory requirements:** Although there are regulatory considerations, they are typically less onerous than in other equity crowdfunding models, which simplifies the process and may cut down on complexity and legal fees.

Cons

>> **Annual limitation:** Companies with higher capital requirements, particularly those in capital-intensive industries, may find fewer funding options available due to the $5 million limitation.

>> **Regulatory compliance:** Despite the simplification of legislation, compliance remains necessary, which complicates the fundraising procedure and may incur legal expenses.

>> **Investor limitations:** The maximum amount that an individual investor may give is limited. This could have an effect on fundraising efforts, particularly for businesses looking to raise more than $5 million.

SAFE and KISS equity crowdfunding

The word *simple* is in both acronyms *SAFE* and *KISS* when it comes to equity crowd-funding, and that's what attracts startups like yours to this funding method like the proverbial moths to a light bulb.

Pros

SAFE and KISS streamline the equity crowdfunding process in three ways:

>> **Simplified terminology:** The terminology used in both SAFE and KISS devices is intended to be clear and uniform. This makes investing easier to understand, especially for people who are not familiar with intricate legal contracts.

>> **Ease of implementation:** Making, modifying, and implementing SAFE and KISS agreements is simple. As a result, establishing investment terms takes less time and incurs fewer legal fees.

>> **Transparency:** Detailed documentation outlining the rights of investors and the requirements for conversion into equity is provided to them. Trust is fostered between investors and startups by this transparency.

Cons

SAFE and KISS funding aren't all wine and roses, and both you and potential investors have to be aware of the drawbacks:

>> **Restricted investor rights:** Compared to traditional stock investors, investors that use SAFE and KISS agreements may have fewer rights or influence, despite the fact that openness is a benefit. They might not be involved in decision-making or have a voice in company governance.

>> **Non-debt structure:** Because SAFE and KISS agreements do not have a set repayment timeline or interest payments, investors might not get paid until the following funding round or liquidity event.

>> **Complicated valuation:** It can be difficult to grasp the discount rate and valuation cap, which could cause misunderstandings between investors and founders. So, it's a very good idea to get financial advice as you explore this route, and you need to budget accordingly.

Donation-based crowdfunding

Asking for donations to build your business has its charms, especially if you're trying to work on projects that you think may turn into a business.

Pros

Aside from connecting with customers to potentially build your business around an idea, there are several other good things that come with crowdfunding through donations:

>> **Low risk:** Donation-based crowdfunding doesn't need delivering rewards, shares, or debt in return.

>> **Supporting causes:** Because contributors frequently value the chance to have a good influence and support worthwhile projects, it works especially well for social causes, charitable endeavors, and community projects.

>> **Funding personal projects:** Because this approach doesn't require repayment or financial returns, it's perfect for creative people, artists, and entrepreneurs pursuing personal projects and creative efforts.

Cons

Now stop and take a moment to consider the following drawbacks to donation-based funding:

>> **Limited funding potential:** Compared to other methods, donation-based crowdfunding usually yields lesser amounts of money, which makes it inappropriate for firms with significant capital requirements.

>> **Niches are best:** Donation-based crowdfunding is less adaptable for strictly commercial ventures and is best suited for enterprises with a strong emotional or social appeal.

>> **Regulatory considerations:** Legal and tax obligations must be paid attention to even when there are no rewards or equity granted. In certain circumstances, regulatory and tax issues may still apply.

Kicking the Tires on Each Platform

If you're still not sure about a crowdfunding type and want to find out what the options are, we're here to show you the platforms for all seven types, just like the brochures you get at a car dealership showing you all the models available in each category.

TIP

If you're reading the online version, you can click on the links to go to their websites.

Rewards-based crowdfunding

When you search online for rewards-based crowdfunding platforms, you'll see three of the most popular ones, and each one is geared toward a specific audience with different requirements.

Kickstarter

One of the first platforms, Kickstarter (https://www.kickstarter.com/) features a wide variety of artistic endeavors, ranging from tech devices to art installations. Kickstarter uses an all-or-nothing fundraising strategy that requires a project to meet its financial target in order to get any funds.

Indiegogo

Indiegogo (https://www.indiegogo.com/) allows for versatility with your funding; you may opt for a keep-what-you-raise model or an all-or-nothing funding plan. It's perfect for a wide range of funding campaigns.

Patreon

Dedicated to continuous artistic endeavors, Patreon (https://www.patreon.com/) enables authors to obtain regular donations from their admirers. For musicians, content producers, and artists, it's a reliable source of money.

Equity crowdfunding

Equity crowdfunding is a global enterprise, and there are two leading platforms in the European sphere that are also available to startups in North America.

Crowdcube

With a solid track record across multiple industries, Crowdcube (https://www.crowdcube.com/) is a well-known equity crowdfunding platform established in the U.K., or Great Britain if you prefer. Investors can purchase shares in early-stage and startup businesses in order to split any possible earnings.

Seedrs

Another prominent platform based in the U.K., Seedrs (https://www.seedrs.com/) focuses on investments in the early stages. It offers a secondary market where investors can exchange shares and chances to invest in a variety of startups.

Debt-based crowdsourcing

If you're looking at debt-based crowdsourcing platforms, your search will bring up two of the leading platforms available as of this writing.

Prosper

One well-known peer-to-peer lending website in the United States is Prosper (https://www.prosper.com/). By facilitating the connection between lenders and individual borrowers, it allows lenders to earn interest on their investment while borrowers can obtain personal loans.

LendingClub

LendingClub (https://www.lendingclub.com/) offers personal loans, much like Prosper. A portion of loans to a group of borrowers can be funded by investors so as to distribute risk and potential profit to members of the entire group.

Real estate crowdfunding

If you're looking into real estate crowdfunding but don't know where to start, we have two leading platforms for you to research.

Fundrise

Fundrise (https://fundrise.com/) provides a novel method for investing in real estate. It provides varied portfolios and permits investors to take part in commercial real estate projects.

RealtyMogul

Offering opportunities in a range of property types and investment structures, RealtyMogul (https://www.realtymogul.com/) concentrates on real estate debt and equity investments.

Regulation crowdfunding

If Reg CF is something that may work for you, then visit one of these two websites to continue your exploration and see if one or both is a good fit.

Wefunder

Wefunder (https://wefunder.com/) aims to match investors with startups and small companies in need of funding. It provides a wide range of investing options.

StartEngine

StartEngine (https://www.startengine.com/) gives users access to a variety of startup investments, such as possibilities for revenue sharing and equity. It is renowned for its approachability.

SAFE and KISS equity crowdfunding

When you search for SAFE and KISS equity crowdfunding, two sites will likely come up in the results page. But one of them has experienced changes as we were writing this book.

SeedInvest

You may see SeedInvest in your crowdfunding search online, but at the end of 2022 StartEngine acquired SeedInvest, and you can read more about the acquisition at https://www.startengine.com/seedinvest. This webpage touts that the combined company has 1.7 million prospective investors and has raised $1.1 billion in capital.

MicroVentures

MicroVentures (https://microventures.com/) stands out for its secondary market, which links investors with companies looking for funding. It's a platform that pools capital for early-stage and startup businesses.

Donation-based crowdfunding

If you're seeking donations to fund your startup, or an idea that could develop into a startup, you'll find one of the following three platforms are worth looking into.

GoFundMe

Well-known for facilitating personal fundraising, GoFundMe (`https://www.gofundme.com/`) contributes to a range of causes, including artistic endeavors, disaster relief, and medical costs.

Kickstarter

Despite being primarily a rewards-based platform, Kickstarter (`https://www.kickstarter.com/`) also features projects that seek donations under headings like theater and dance.

JustGiving

The main purpose of JustGiving (`https://www.justgiving.com/`) is to facilitate nonprofit and philanthropic fundraising. It enables people to set up fundraising pages for many types of philanthropic purposes.

Creating a Compelling Crowdfunding Campaign

Crowdfunding is all about telling people your story and creating an emotional connection with them, because we're all hardwired for storytelling. And people want to listen to your story if you tell them what they want to hear.

Different audiences need different messages, so let's craft your story in this section. You may want to fire up your favorite note-taking app as you read along so you can catch the ideas that will pop into your head as you read this section.

We have some platform-specific recommendations at the end of this section, too, but we start with a road map that will work with any platform(s) you choose.

Rewards-based crowdfunding

Put a lot of work into creating an emotionally charged and captivating tale for your enterprise. Talk about your motivations, struggles, and path. Make use of eye-catching visuals, such as crisp photos and videos. Describe the impact your project will have locally, regionally, nationally, and even globally.

Create a wide variety of reward tiers to accommodate backers of different financial capacities. Make sure every layer presents a different value proposition.

TIP

To increase interest, think about offering early access, personalized options, and limited-edition rewards.

Prior to launch, establish a robust community surrounding your product. Use online forums, newsletters, and social media to interact with possible backers. Build anticipation and excitement prior to the launch of your campaign.

Equity crowdfunding

When it comes to equity crowdfunding, transparency is essential. Provide comprehensive financials that include profit margins, cost structures, and revenue models. Make sure to explain the potential return on investment and how the cash will be used.

Be aware that a large number of equity crowdfunding participants can be novice investors. To aid in their understanding of the investment process, provide them with educational resources like webinars, frequently asked questions (FAQs), or in-person Q&A sessions.

Debt crowdfunding

Make sure your profile is flawless. Emphasize the reason for the loan, your past financial history, and your creditworthiness. Clearly state the advantages of contributing to your cause.

You also need to stay in constant contact with your lenders to reinforce that you're trustworthy. Answer inquiries right away and give regular updates on the status and utilization of the loans.

Real estate crowdfunding

Give as much information as possible about your real estate venture. Add the project's location, objectives, projected returns, and information on previous, well-executed initiatives. Provide a comprehensive overview of the investment's possibilities to investors.

Update investors on a regular basis on the status of the project, industry trends, and any modifications. Regular updates promote confidence and trust.

Regulation crowdfunding (Reg CF)

We're going to put our Captain Obvious hats on: You need to describe in detail how the money will be used. Demonstrate that you have thought through different financial situations and have a successful plan.

Respond to investor questions, have virtual and/or in-person Q&A meetings, and send out regular updates to make your campaign interactive. Include your supporters in the adventure.

SAFE and KISS equity crowdfunding

When you create your budget for your crowdfunding campaign, set amounts for each of the milestones in your campaign. To illustrate your development, highlight the accomplishments you've made at each level.

Organize virtual meetings or live webinars for prospective investors. Seeing everyone's faces helps you make personal connections, answer inquiries, and share your vision.

Provide funders with exclusive access to behind-the-scenes updates through private updates. Talk about your struggles, victories, and lessons gained to increase their level of engagement. You can also ask your funders for their feedback and adopt good ideas that propel your business even faster toward the next milestone.

Donation-based crowdfunding

Construct an endearing and genuine story that strikes an emotional chord with possible benefactors. Tell personal tales, relate your experiences, and explain the strong motivations behind your idea. Yes, you guessed it, you need more than just your story. You should get testimonials from your early adopters and combine them with photos and videos to help drive your message home.

Don't keep your presentation a one-way conversation. Create a feeling of community and involvement around your cause by getting people involved. Urge contributors to interact with one another, tell their own tales, and take an active role in the fundraising process.

Platform-specific advice for crowdfunding

We have more specific advice for four different crowdfunding platforms based on our experiences. If you're thinking about another platform than the ones we've listed, we're sure you'll get a spark of inspiration to apply to your platform of choice.

Kickstarter

Take an active part in the community by lending support to other projects and interacting with backers via updates, live chats, and comments. Work together on related initiatives to promote each other's work.

Indiegogo

After your campaign ends, you can still take donations by using InDemand. Send out thank-you notes and newsletters on a regular basis to interact with your supporters.

StartEngine

Conduct educational webinars that offer comprehensive details about your business, goals, and potential investors. Give thoughtful answers to inquiries and consistent updates on your investments.

Wefunder

Build a strong community around your campaign. Provide interesting content about your background, your company's core principles, and the impact you hope to make. Motivate investors to provide input and take an active role.

Chapter **12**

Leveraging Incubators and Accelerators

ncubators aren't just for keeping chick eggs warm until they hatch or to keep a baby from getting hypothermia as their organs develop. They're also great for businesses and combined with incubators, they provide developing companies with crucial resources, assistance, and mentoring.

Although incubators and accelerators are closely related, they each have a unique function and are suited to different phases of a startup's growth. We explain the differences between incubators and accelerators to start this chapter. We also talk about how they work and what their roles are.

After you know what incubators and accelerators are and which one is best for your new business, we give you a road map to find them as we close this chapter.

Incubators Help You Push Through the Soil

You've probably already guessed what a business incubator does: It provides early-stage enterprises with a helpful ecosystem, frequently from the very beginning of conception, to help the business grow. The ecosystem is what comes included in the box and boy howdy, do you get a lot.

Early-stage support

For an incubator, you need a controlled environment to thrive, and business incubators provide a range of tools such as real office spaces, networking opportunities, and access to industry experts.

Mentoring and guidance

Speaking of those experts, incubators come with mentors and advisors in the package, and they mentor you through obstacles, crucial decision-making procedures, and help you with your strategic planning.

Access to resources

But wait, there's more! Incubators include access to priceless resources including accountancy services, legal advice, and investor networks. These materials are essential for creating a solid operational base.

Peer learning

Sharing space with other startups creates a cooperative atmosphere that promotes learning from one another. Founders can share experiences, gain insight from one another's paths, and build valuable connections that will help grow your business from a seed into a giant and vibrant philodendron.

The not-so-fine print

Usually lasting from a few months to a few years, incubator programs are longer in length. This extended involvement enables businesses to focus on honing their ideas and approaches before pursuing quick growth.

Unlike accelerators, incubators usually take a smaller equity portion in the firms they sponsor. However, incubators may still take stock holdings. This strategy protects the founding team's larger ownership interest.

Upgrade to Turbo

Accelerators act like turbochargers for your car. In a car, the turbocharger is powered by the flow of exhaust gases that forces more intake air into the air to make it go faster. Your business accelerator can see that your engine already makes your business go down the road faster and that you can go even faster.

A bigger piece of the pie

Before you shop for an accelerator, you need to be comfortable with the fact that they usually accept a larger ownership share in the company in exchange for their participation in the accelerator program. This mutual interest highlights how dedicated the accelerator is to your startup's growth.

Feel the burn

Business accelerators are brief, intensely concentrated courses that usually last a few months. These initiatives are designed to help startups expand quickly and scale.

Accelerator programs are recognized for their fast-paced and competitive cultures, which force companies to hit important milestones quickly and develop a sense of urgency and discipline in their operations.

To reach these goals, accelerator programs adhere to a clearly laid out curriculum that is focused on important topics including market expansion, product development, and funding.

Plugged in

Accelerators also provide access to a wide range of seasoned mentors and business leaders who can provide mentorship and strategic advice.

Your accelerator will also frequently arrange carefully chosen networking events so you can connect with investors, industry experts, and prospective customers.

On with the show

The last event in accelerator programs is frequently a "demo day," and it's not like what you think of on HGTV shows, though the day is just as exciting. On this demo day, entrepreneurs present their ideas to an audience of possible investors that can lead to deals, and we can hear you shouting out the name of the CNBC show this reminds you of.

When you graduate, your business will not only be running faster, but you'll also be ready to get even more fuel from outside funders to get to your ultimate destination.

The Mechanics of Incubators

If you've come to this stage, you want to read the spec sheet to see if your business qualifies for an incubator before you even start shopping for one later in this chapter. So, let's go down the list.

>> **You're still working on it:** You may not have a finished product or company plan.

>> **Available for many:** From consumer goods and social enterprises to technology and healthcare, incubators frequently support a broad range of industries. They can support a wide range of startup concepts because of their adaptability.

>> **You're in it for the long haul:** Incubator programs typically last for several years, sometimes even up to six months. With greater time to develop, you can work more deliberately and improve your ideas and products over time.

>> **You want to be taught:** Business incubators provide a structured curriculum that covers a range of topics including finance, product development, marketing, and market research.

>> **You can be flexible:** The incubator calendar is more flexible so you can go through the curriculum at your own speed.

>> **You can work on site:** Many incubators offer shared office or coworking spaces so you can collaborate with other startups.

If you're not willing to work in a coworking space, the incubator may not think you're a good fit.

REMEMBER

>> **You want to be a sponge:** Mentors offer one-on-one counseling and advice customized to your unique requirements and problems.

>> **You want help:** Incubators offer resources including accounting services, legal counsel, marketing assistance, and industry-specific knowledge. They also help your business hone your pitch decks and business plans so you can get ready for the dog and pony show.

Accelerators under the Hood

Yes, you can pass go and collect $200, because you guessed that accelerators are for businesses that have a minimum viable product (MVP) or service that people love and can't wait to get more of. Accelerators target entrepreneurs who are prepared to grow their companies and penetrate new markets.

Is working with an accelerator a good fit, you ask? We're here with a list for you to check and see:

>> **Specific focus areas:** Accelerators frequently concentrate on particular markets or fields, such as technology, medicine, or social impact. They can provide startups in such niches with specialized help because of their specialty.

>> **Not as much investment:** In exchange for stock, usually a small portion of the company, accelerators frequently give firms seed money. This investment is meant to help enterprises accelerate their development and acts as a catalyst for growth.

>> **Short and intense:** Accelerator courses usually have a duration of three to four months. Startups go through an accelerated curriculum with set targets and milestones to meet during this time.

>> **Can you stand the heat?** Accelerators are known for frantic, competitive settings. The initiatives put firms under pressure to hit ambitious targets and expand quickly.

>> **Speaking in public is required:** The culmination of most accelerator programs is a demo event where entrepreneurs present their ventures to a room full of angel and venture capitalists, among other possible investors. This is a chance for entrepreneurs to obtain further funding.

>> **You need to connect:** Accelerators have connections with a large number of mentors, business leaders, investors, and successful entrepreneurs. Using this network is essential to get what you want out of your accelerator program and your business as a whole.

>> **Trust and verify:** Accelerators concentrate on rapidly verifying a startup's product-market fit and business model. Gaining more funding, collaborations, and growth prospects depends on this validation.

Where Do You Sign Up?

Go put this book down for a minute and splash your face with cold water, because before you scour the web for an incubator or an accelerator, know before you go!

Do your research, Sparky

Begin by carrying out extensive research to find possible accelerator or incubator programs that complement the objectives of your firm. Seek courses that are tailored to your sector, development stage, and region.

To find pertinent programs, use startup databases, industry-specific platforms, and Internet directories. Consult with mentors, advisors, and other business owners for recommendations.

A bespoke solution

Life is a lot about finding the right match. So, take into account elements including the program's success stories, track record, target areas, and alumni network.

Review the resources, office space, funding options, and mentorship that the program offers. Make sure the program's goals complement the vision and mission of your startup.

Apply carefully and well

When you've found programs that fit your needs (don't worry, we've almost arrived at that section), it's time to get your application ready. Usually, this entails filling out an online application and giving pertinent information about your firm.

Write a clear and appealing application that emphasizes the team's qualifications, market potential, and distinctive value offer for your startup. Make sure you respond to any particular queries or prompts that the program gives you in a timely manner.

Comply with each program's application requirements and deadlines including any additional materials such as your business strategy, pitch deck, and/or video presentation.

Make sure your application conveys your enthusiasm, commitment, and willingness to take advantage of the mentorship and resources offered by the program.

Throw your pitch

You might be asked to present your company to the program's judging panel or selection committee if your application is selected for further consideration. You have the chance to highlight the potential of your startup during your pitch.

Craft an engaging and convincing pitch that touches on all the important facets of your company, including the problem you're trying to solve, your solution, market validation, revenue projections, and your team's experience.

Do your due

Anticipate interviews and processes related to due diligence as programs assess your startup more thoroughly. Financial evaluations, reference checks, and background checks could be part of this review.

Throughout this stage, be open and accommodating, giving the needed information as soon as it is asked for. You can increase your chances of getting accepted by showcasing your professionalism and moral character.

Get out your magnifying glass

Carefully read over the terms and conditions of the program if you receive an acceptance offer. This covers the terms of the program, the equity or investment, and any obligations you may have.

If required, seek legal counsel or assistance to properly comprehend the ramifications and obligations related to program participation.

Bring your Trapper Keeper

After being approved, begin getting ready for the course. This could entail making logistical arrangements, including moving to the program's location or making sure you have access to the tools you need.

Establish clear expectations and goals for the things you hope to accomplish during the program. What's more, make sure you have a well-defined plan in place for utilizing the program's resources.

Assimilate everything

Participate actively in interactions with advisors, mentors, and other program participants. Participate in the program's workshops, seminars, and networking opportunities.

Make the most of the mentorship and advice that are at your disposal. Ask for guidance on developing your product, your marketing plan, generating money, and other important business-related issues.

Break through on demo day

Your pitch, better known as demo day, is like a thesis defense on graduate day for your accelerator program. That is, it's the end of the program and now you get to dazzle a room full of possible investors, corporate partners, and stakeholders.

You can't do that without leaving a lasting impression, so prepare a professional and persuasive pitch with the mentors and advisors that your accelerator has provided for you for this purpose.

Toss your caps

With the fresh contacts, information, and resources you obtained during the program, keep developing your startup after your graduation. For continued assistance, we recommend remaining active in the program's alumni network.

Let's go shopping

The time has finally come to review the incubators and accelerators that you can find around the world. Though we can't play the role of matchmaker, we give you our top ten companies you can look at to find out if it's worth the equivalent of swiping right.

We include screenshots of their webpages so you can get a better idea of who they are, and if you have the digital version of the book (or go to our book page on Dummies.com), you can get the links to all the sites.

500 Global

500 Global (https://500.co) is an accelerator program and venture capital firm based in Silicon Valley, California, that offers access to a large network of investors and entrepreneurs as well as financial support and mentoring (see Figure 12-1).

FIGURE 12-1:
500 Global has locations in North America, Europe, the Middle East, and Asia.

AngelPad

Renowned for its rigorous mentoring and support, AngelPad (https://angelpad.com) in Silicon Valley is a startup accelerator shown in Figure 12-2. It has aided in the founding of many prosperous businesses, such as Postmates and Periscope.

FIGURE 12-2:
AngelPad notes MIT has named them the number one U.S. accelerator since 2015.

Antler

Antler (`https://www.antler.co`), which is shown in Figure 12-3, is an international program for early-stage venture capital and accelerators that assists creators in creating technology firms from the bottom up. Antler is active on all continents except Antarctica.

FIGURE 12-3:
Start working
with Antler by
clicking or
tapping the Apply
Now button.

Founders Factory

Founders Factory (`https://foundersfactory.com`) is located in London, the capital city of the United Kingdom; they're an accelerator program supported by corporations that connects entrepreneurs with investors and corporate partners in a range of industries (see Figure 12-4).

HAX

HAX (`https://hax.co`) is located in San Francisco and Shenzhen, China (see Figure 12-5). It's a hardware accelerator that supports startups in robotics and hardware. HAX offers capital, production resources, and market access in Asia.

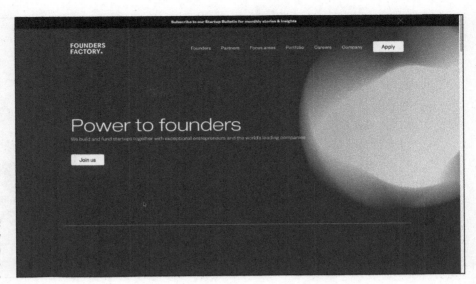

FIGURE 12-4: Founders Factory works with fintech, climate, media, and more.

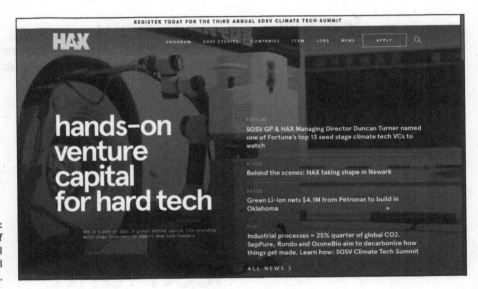

FIGURE 12-5: HAX is part of SOSV, a global venture capital firm.

Plug and Play

Plug and Play (https://www.plugandplaytechcenter.com), which is shown in Figure 12-6, is an international platform for innovation that manages accelerator programs across a range of sectors, such as mobility, health, and financial technologies, better known by its portmanteau *fintech*.

FIGURE 12-6:
Plug and Play works with corporations and startups.

Seedcamp

Seedcamp (`https://seedcamp.com`) is an accelerator program centered in Europe that provides capital, guidance, and access to a network of investors and business owners for early-stage firms (see Figure 12-7).

FIGURE 12-7:
If you're in Europe, check out Seedcamp.

Station F

One of the biggest startup campuses globally, Station F (`https://stationf.co`) is located in Paris — yes, the one in France. Station F accommodates multiple accelerator programs and offers tools to entrepreneurs operating in diverse industries (see Figure 12-8).

FIGURE 12-8: The Station F website touts that it's the world's largest startup campus.

Techstars

Techstars (`https://www.techstars.com`) is a global business accelerator program that provides resources, funding, and mentorship to aspiring entrepreneurs (see Figure 12-9). It focuses on a number of areas including technology, healthcare, and fintech.

Y Combinator (YC)

Y Combinator or YC, which you can find at `https://www.ycombinator.com`, is among the world's most renowned startup accelerators and it's located in Silicon Valley, California (see Figure 12-10). Two times a year, it offers resources, money, and mentorship to early-stage companies. Notable graduates include Coinbase and Dropbox.

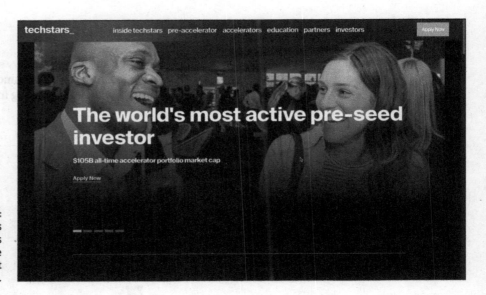

FIGURE 12-9:
The Techstars
website asserts
that it's the
world's largest
pre-seed investor.

FIGURE 12-10:
The Y Combinator
website answers
the why question.

4

Negotiating and Closing the Deal

Understand term sheets and investment agreements.

Prepare for your investors' due diligence examination.

Learn how to close the funding round and seal the deal.

Chapter **13**

Understanding Term Sheets and Investment Agreements

ongratulations on finding the right fuel and the right engine that will help your new business speed down the road toward the milestones that you have on your map. Time to just sit back and enjoy the ride, right?

You may not have noticed that your business is the size of an RV, and your investors are joining you and your team for the journey. And everyone's going to have an opinion about how your RV is going to be fueled and what the rules of the trip are.

That's where term sheets and investment agreements come in. Now it's time to put on your dress shirt and fancy shoes and come to your negotiations with your investors ready to talk . . . that is, after you read this chapter, take notes as you read, talk with your attorney, and then confidently take your notes and your knowledge into the room for a successful negotiation.

We start by telling you what term sheets are all about. Then we tell you about the ins and outs of investment agreements, followed up by reviewing the common clauses in those agreements that you need to focus on. Finally, we tell you how everyone wins just like that meme where Oprah is giving away a free something to all the members of her excited audience. (We presume they're not bees.)

The Terms of Term Sheets

A term sheet is similar to an investment plan for the future. It's a document that lists the important financial and legal conditions that must be met by an investor who wants to fund a new company. Figure 13-1 below shows an example of what a form term sheet looks like.

Although a term sheet is largely non-binding, it still marks a key milestone in the negotiation process because it shows the parties' initial understanding regarding the parameters of the investment.

So why make a term sheet?

Wait, we hear you saying — what do you mean by non-binding? A term sheet's main goal is to make sure all parties are in agreement on the essentials of the deal before paying the hefty legal bills that come with forming legally binding agreements such as an investors' rights agreement, stock purchase agreement, and other ancillary agreements.

Think of a term sheet as a defined framework that you saw in Figure 10-1. The term sheet outlines the responsibilities, rights, and preferences of the founders and investors. In other words, they streamline the negotiations that are to come by getting the most crucial elements of the deal worked out first.

REMEMBER

You don't like stress, right? Term sheets help manage expectations and lower stress during the negotiations by outlining the terms up front. And when everyone agrees on the rules, it can also mean faster negotiations.

The essential elements of term sheets

There are eight essential elements of term sheets that fall into two categories: financial requirements and management provisions:

>> **Valuation:** Establishes the investment's price per share based on the company's pre-money valuation.

TERM SHEET

Company:	[ ], a Delaware corporation.
Securities:	Series A Preferred Stock of the Company (**"Series A"**).
Investment Amounts:	$[ ] million from [ ] (**"Lead Investor"**) $[ ] million from other investors
	Convertible notes and safes (**"Convertibles"**) convert on their terms into shadow series of preferred stock (together with the Series A, the **"Preferred Stock"**).
Valuation:	$[ ] million **post-money** valuation, including an available option pool equal to [ ]% of the post-Closing fully-diluted capitalization.
Liquidation Preference:	1x non-participating preference. A sale of all or substantially all of the Company's assets, or a merger (collectively, a **"Company Sale"**), will be treated as a liquidation.
Dividends:	6% noncumulative, payable if and when declared by the Board of Directors.
Conversion to Common Stock:	At holder's option and automatically on (i) IPO or (ii) approval of a majority of Preferred Stock (on an as-converted basis) (the **"Preferred Majority"**). Conversion ratio initially 1-to-1, subject to standard adjustments.
Voting Rights:	Approval of the Preferred Majority required to (i) change rights, preferences or privileges of the Preferred Stock; (ii) change the authorized number of shares; (iii) create securities senior or pari passu to the existing Preferred Stock; (iv) redeem or repurchase any shares (except for purchases at cost upon termination of services or exercises of contractual rights of first refusal); (v) declare or pay any dividend; (vi) change the authorized number of directors; or (vii) liquidate or dissolve, including a Company Sale. Otherwise votes with Common Stock on an as-converted basis.
Drag-Along:	Founders, investors and 1% stockholders required to vote for a Company Sale approved by (i) the Board, (ii) the Preferred Majority and (iii) a majority of Common Stock [(excluding shares of Common Stock issuable or issued upon conversion of the Preferred Stock)] (the **"Common Majority"**), subject to standard exceptions.
Other Rights & Matters:	The Preferred Stock will have standard broad-based weighted average anti-dilution rights, first refusal and co-sale rights over founder stock transfers, registration rights, pro rata rights and information rights. Company counsel drafts documents. Company pays Lead Investor's legal fees, capped at $30,000.
Board:	[Lead Investor designates 1 director. Common Majority designates 2 directors.]
Founder and Employee Vesting:	Founders: [ ]. Employees: 4-year monthly vesting with 1-year cliff.
No Shop:	For 30 days, the Company will not solicit, encourage or accept any offers for the acquisition of Company capital stock (other than equity compensation for service providers), or of all or any substantial portion of Company assets.

FIGURE 13-1:
A term sheet includes information about investment amounts, dividends, and voting rights.

>> **Type of security:** Indicates what will be used for the investment, such as convertible notes, preferred stock, or common stock.

>> **Board composition:** Defines the number and make-up of the board of directors for the company, frequently providing investors with a voice at the discussion.

- » **Protective provisions:** Describes specific steps that, in order to safeguard the interests of the investors, the corporation cannot conduct without their consent.

- » **Liquidation preferences:** Indicates how money will be distributed in the event of a sale, merger, or shutdown — in other words, a liquidation event.

- » **Anti-dilution provisions:** Protection against future dilution in the event that the corporation issues new shares at a lower price than investors previously paid is provided by the anti-dilution provisions.

- » **Conversion rights:** Describes the circumstances in which convertible securities, frequently tied to particular triggers or events, might be converted into equity.

- » **Dividend rights:** Refers to an investor's ability to receive dividends and, if so, details the amount and order of priority over other shareholders.

What does it all mean, Basil?

With all this said, what's the significance of term sheets for future negotiations? They do three things.

First, they prepare investors for due diligence, which includes checking the company's finances, legal position, and other important details.

Term sheets also serve as an official declaration of intent, allowing the startup to move forward with assurance and even use the terms to negotiate better conditions or collaborations between your team members and the investors.

Finally, they help set clear expectations for the partnership by aligning the company's and investors' ideas. (Yes, it's important.)

WARNING

Entrepreneurs occasionally misunderstand the term sheet as a funding guarantee, failing to realize that extensive due research and negotiation must come after it is signed. What's more, be on alert about features that appear insignificant but could subsequently have a big impact, like pro rata rights or option pools.

Getting it right

In order to avoid expensive misunderstandings and guarantee that the contract is reasonable and compliant with industry standards, both you and the investors need to use the services of knowledgeable legal counsel throughout the term sheet process.

REMEMBER

That sound counsel will help you navigate changes to the term sheets, as they are wont to do during the negotiation. When you have changes, handle them proactively with your investor(s) because no one likes being blindsided.

Investment Agreements and You

Investment agreements are detailed contracts that specify the parameters in which funds are given to your startup.

These legal papers, which serve to conclude many facets of the investment and shareholder relationships, include Stock Purchase Agreements (SPAs), Shareholders' Agreements, and Subscription Agreements.

Investment agreements are binding legal documents, not just a formality. They have three crucial roles:

>> They establish a structure that is legally binding and controls the investment transaction.

>> To make sure that everyone is aware of the precise terms of the investment, including any terms, rights, and responsibilities.

>> They provide a framework for the post-investment management of the business and the handling of upcoming events, such as exits or new funding rounds.

That's why we're here to guide you, young Padawan, about the force of investor agreements. To give you an idea of what's involved, and what we talk about in this section, Figure 13-2 has an example of the first page of an investment agreement.

In Figure 13-2, you saw some of the features of an investment agreement, but you guessed right that there's a lot more to it than just a couple more pages. Ensure you have these sections in your agreement as you put it together.

REMEMBER

Creating an investment agreement is not a situation where you buy a legal book from a bookstore and fill in the blanks. To guarantee the agreement is thorough and enforceable, a legal expert must be involved in the meticulous drafting process.

Due diligence is an essential part of the process, where investors carefully review the legal, financial, and operational aspects of the firm to make sure the guarantees and representations made in the agreement are true.

INVESTMENT AGREEMENT

This Investment Agreement (the Agreement) is made and effective [DATE].

BETWEEN: **[YOUR COMPANY NAME]** a Company (the "COMPANY") organized and existing under the laws of [STATE/PROVINCE], with its head office located at:

[COMPLETE ADDRESS]

AND: **[YOUR NAME]** the principal members of the Company (the "Company Principals") collectively referred to in this Agreement as the "Company Parties." and existing under the laws of [STATE/PROVINCE], located at:

[COMPLETE ADDRESS]

AND: **[YOUR COMPANY NAME]** a Company (the "COMPANY") organized and existing under the laws of [STATE/PROVINCE], with its head office located at:

[COMPLETE ADDRESS]

WHEREAS the Company was formed for the purpose of further developing, commercializing, and operating the business concept identified and includes any subsequent iteration of the business concept developed by the Company Parties (the "Business");

WHEREAS the Investor is desirous of making an investment (the "Investment") in the amount of [TOTAL INVESTMENT AMOUNT] into the Company to facilitate such Business.

NOW THEREFORE, in consideration of the mutual covenants and agreements herein contains, the parties hereto intending to be legally bound agree as follows:

1.   **THE INVESTMENT**

1.1   The Investor will make the Investment in the Company in consideration for the rights and privileges set forth in this Agreement.

2.   **FUTURE ISSUANCES OF SECURITIES**

2.1   From and after the date of this Agreement, the parties agree to take such further action and to execute, acknowledge and deliver all such further documents as are reasonably requested by the otherparty for carrying out the purposes of this Agreement.

2.2   If at any time in the future, the Company proposes to sell and issue any debt or equity securities, or any other securities or instruments entitling the holder thereof to receive any profits, capital, assets or property of the Company (collectively, "Securities"), in a single transaction or series of related transactions that results in gross proceeds to the Company of at least [STATE AMOUNT] (a "Qualified Financing"), the Company shall deliver written notice to the Investor stating (i) its bona fide intention to offer such Securities, (ii) the amount and type of Securities to be offered and (iii) the

---

Investment Agreement   Page 1 of 3

As part of that work, here are the sections of the agreement that you need to focus on and get right.

>> **Preamble and recitals:** In this section of the agreement, the parties are introduced, the agreement's background is given, and the fundamental goals of the investment are outlined.

- » **Define and interpret:** To facilitate mutual understanding and prevent misunderstanding, every technical word used in the agreement is explained in detail.

- » **The agreement structure:** This section covers the kind and quantity of securities being bought, the investment's cost, and the assessment of the firm used to support the investment.

- » **Representations and warranties:** Extensive declarations made by the business about its current position, encompassing its financial standing, obligations, intellectual property, legal compliance, and potential hazards.

- » **Covenants:** Covenants are legal commitments made by the corporation to carry out specific actions (like filing reports on time) or abstain from specific actions (like entering into particular commercial ventures).

- » **Conditions prior to funding:** This section details the particular requirements that must be met before money is released; these requirements may include receiving regulatory clearances, obtaining third parties' cooperation, or reaching predetermined business milestones.

- » **Closing conditions and procedures:** This section contains a comprehensive set of instructions covering all aspects of exchanging investment funds for securities, including delivering any necessary paperwork and finishing any outstanding tasks at closing.

- » **Corporate governance:** This section contains terminology about post-investment governance of the corporation, encompassing voting rights, board composition, and investor vetoes.

- » **Economic rights:** These are conditions governing distributions, dividends, and liquidation preferences that establish the terms of the business's financial arrangement with its investors.

- » **Protective provisions:** This section has requirements that the business gets investors' approval before taking certain activities in order to protect investors' interests.

- » **Conversion rights and anti-dilution protections:** These are mechanisms that specify when and how convertible securities can be converted into equity, as well as safeguard investors against dilution in future financings.

- » **Information rights:** These are rights granted to investors by the company to receive regular financial statements and other important business information.

- » **Rights of first offer/refusal and co-sale agreements:** These clauses enable current investors to purchase shares ahead of time before the business makes them available to third parties or to sell shares with other investors.

>> **Non-compete, non-solicit, and confidentiality agreements:** These contain provisions that limit the founders' and employees' ability to do certain things in order to safeguard the company's commercial interests.

>> **Dispute resolution:** Specifying the procedures that will be followed in the event that a dispute arises regarding the agreement. These procedures may include arbitration or litigation.

Common Clauses

Now that you know what sections you need in an investment agreement, you need to think about the clauses within that agreement so you can not only prepare for the short term to travel to the next destination on your itinerary, but also to get to all the other destinations you have on your map.

So, this section helps you better understand clauses in an investment agreement so you can protect your interests and your company's long-term viability. There are a lot of clauses, so we resort to the web approach of chunking — that is, we give you each clause in bullet form (except when there's only one clause) separated by topic.

TIP

Grab a tall glass filled with your favorite beverage, settle into your comfy chair, and write down notes and questions on a separate piece of paper (or your favorite notepad app). When you're done, you can bring your notes to your legal counsel so you can get all your questions answered before you begin work on your investment agreement.

Clauses on equity and valuation

Understanding the nuances of equity and valuation is fundamental for both entrepreneurs and investors. This section delves into the key clauses that govern equity ownership and valuation in investment agreements.

>> **Pre-money valuation:** This describes the worth of the business prior to the addition of fresh funding. It is imperative that founders comprehend how investors evaluate the company and how this influences their stake in the business.

>> **Post-money valuation:** This calculates the company's value after the investment and has a direct bearing on the dilution of current shareholders' equity. It is done by adding the new capital to the pre-money valuation.

>> **Option pool expansion:** To encourage potential employees, the term sheet might mandate the establishment or growth of an option pool. It is frequently anticipated to be established prior to the new investment, impacting the founders' ownership, and is typically expressed as a percentage of the post-money capitalization.

Terms of Investment

As you venture into the realm of funding your startup, it's important to understand the terms and conditions that your investors will talk about:

>> **Amount being raised:** The entire amount of money the firm hopes to raise in the round, which will determine how much control it gives up to new investors and how long it may operate on.

>> **Price per share:** An important number that establishes the price at which new shares are issued and establishes the number of shares that investors will receive in exchange for their capital.

Governance

Just like driving a car with a bunch of passengers, you need to know who's going to drive, who's going to be your navigator, and who else in your business is in a governance role by defining the roles in two areas:

>> **Board composition:** Determines who sits at the board meetings' table. This provision is essential to preserving the company's strategic control.

>> **Voting rights and thresholds:** Specifies the proportion of board or shareholder votes required to support a particular action, which may have an effect on the strategic choices made by the company.

Financial rights

Navigating the landscape of startup funding involves more than just securing capital; it also entails understanding the financial rights associated with investments in two provisions within an investor agreement:

>> **Dividend provisions:** These clauses specify which class of shares will receive dividends and when they will be paid. They can have an impact on investor returns and the financial reserves of the company.

>> **Liquidation preference:** An important provision that determines the payout sequence in the event of a company sale or dissolution. It frequently comprises a multiple of the investment and has a big influence on how much money each shareholder gets paid in these kinds of situations.

Protective provisions

Protective provisions play a crucial role in safeguarding the interests of both investors and founders in two ways:

>> **Anti-dilution protections:** Prevents investors' share value from declining as a result of subsequent investment rounds at a reduced price. Generally speaking, the "weighted average" provision is more equitable and frequent than the "full ratchet."

>> **Pro rata rights:** Enables investors to preserve their ownership share by contributing more money in subsequent rounds.

Rights of conversion and redemption

In the dynamic arena of startup financing, the rights of conversion and redemption are pivotal elements that can significantly influence the future trajectory of your startup in three areas:

>> **Conversion rights:** These rights effect control and financial rewards upon a departure by defining the conditions under which preferred shares may be converted to common shares.

>> **Mandatory conversion:** A provision that, in certain situations, such as an IPO (initial public offering) or acquisition, may compel the conversion of preferred shares.

>> **Redemption rights:** A less frequent provision that enables investors to return their shares to the corporation at a discount, albeit at a considerable financial cost to the enterprise.

Regulatory and legal

You can't forge a successful investment agreement unless you deftly navigate the regulatory and legal aspects of your startup, so you need to pay particular care to these two areas:

>> **Representations and warranties:** Entrepreneurs should exercise caution when making these claims regarding the legal and financial standing of the business, because errors may result in agreement violations.

>> **Covenants:** These might restrict operational freedom. They include affirmative covenants, which the company agrees to perform, and negative covenants, which the company agrees not to perform.

Exit-related clauses

Crafting a strategy for an eventual exit is as crucial as securing initial funding. So, make sure that your investor agreement includes these three things before you sign on the dotted line:

>> **Right of first refusal (ROFR):** This allows the firm or current investors to buy shares before they are sold to a third party, giving them control over who can acquire shares.

>> **Co-sale agreement (also known as the *right of co-sale* or *tag-along*):** Enables shareholders to participate in the share sales made by other shareholders, guaranteeing their exit concurrently.

>> **Drag-along agreement:** This type of agreement allows the majority to compel minority shareholders to participate in the company's sale, thereby removing any obstacles from the minority and enabling the majority to sell the business.

Investor reporting

Reporting requirements describes the operational and financial data that the business must consistently give investors. This data may include audited financial statements, annual budgets, and monthly or quarterly financial reports.

Confidentiality, non-compete, and non-solicit provisions

Safeguarding your intellectual property and maintaining your strategic advantages are not negotiable. So, your investor agreement must have the following details without question:

>> **Confidentiality provisions:** Prevent investors from learning about the company's proprietary information.

>> **Non-compete and non-solicit clauses:** Prevent founders and, occasionally, investors from launching or taking part in rival companies, as well as from taking clients or employees in the future at another company.

Other provisions

The following clauses don't fit neatly into any of the previous categories, but they're still important inclusions to ensure you have a fair and equitable agreement with investors:

>> **Assignment:** Describes the transferability of an interest in an agreement to another party, which may have an effect on the agreement's control.

>> **Governing law:** Indicates which legal jurisdiction will apply to the agreement; this can have an impact on potential legal conflicts.

>> **Dispute resolution:** Specifies the procedures that have been agreed upon to settle any disagreements pertaining to the agreement, which may involve litigation or arbitration.

Nobody Wins Unless Everybody Wins

Now you know all the terms, and it's time to negotiate. Finding common ground needs preparation, knowledge, and a willingness to create the proverbial win-win.

If you don't know your business before you start negotiations, and you don't understand your investors' needs, then you'll report to your company team much like Obi-Wan told Qui-Gon: The negotiations were short.

Like Qui-Gon and his master Yoda, we're your guides to tell you exactly what you need to know to prepare you and your team for a successful (and longer) negotiation.

Know the details

Be ready to go into great detail about your growth strategy, market potential, competitive landscape, and business model. Investors will anticipate that you are well-versed in your industry.

You also need to have a thorough understanding of your important company metrics, including burn rate, runway, lifetime value (LTV), and customer acquisition cost (CAC). These numbers will frequently serve as the foundation for both the investment terms and your valuation.

Know your audience

Seek out investors who share your objectives. Have they previously been in committed relationships, or would they rather end things more quickly?

If you think your investor(s) are a potential match, review the conditions of the investors' prior agreements to gain insight into their norms and expectations.

Focus on developing relationships

Make contact with possible investors long before you require the money. Early relationship building can result in more advantageous negotiations.

What's more, establish a personal connection. Mutual networks or shared interests can foster rapport and trust.

Look for fair and balanced terms

Seek conditions that are reasonable and in line with industry norms. Use of language that is too combative can damage relationships and erode trust.

Also construct the agreement to offer rewards for sustained expansion and achievement. Make sure the performance of the company is linked to the success of investors.

Use strategic bargaining techniques

As with any negotiation, arrange your offerings ahead of time. Understand what you must fight for and what you can afford to give up.

Then put your thinking cap on and produce innovative ideas that satisfy investors' requirements without sacrificing your own. This could entail many kinds of payment, such as royalties or warrants.

Plan for the long term

See the discussion as the start of a collaboration rather than merely a business deal, because you might have to return to these investors for additional rounds of funding. Later on, the conditions and dynamics you establish now will help set expectations for more funding and make that funding come more quickly.

Navigate exit strategy conversations carefully

Make sure that any expectations about possible liquidity events and exit timings are communicated clearly. Conflict may arise later if there is misalignment here.

Although having a well-defined exit strategy is important, remain receptive to investor feedback. They might offer insightful information that could result in a better end result.

Closing the deal

To close the deal, you need to do **three** things:

>> **Move quickly:** In order to maintain the momentum of discussions, give prompt attention to both proposals and counterproposals.

>> **Keep good documentation:** To prevent future problems, keep thorough records of all areas of negotiation and terms that were agreed upon.

>> **Set closing conditions:** To prevent last-minute obstacles, be aware of and agree upon the closing conditions in advance. This is something to talk with your legal counsel about to fit your specific negotiation and agreement.

Chapter **14**

Preparing for Due Diligence

A s an adult, it's very likely that you've encountered the term due diligence. In terms of the law, Merriam-Webster defines due diligence as the care that a reasonable person exercises to avoid harm to other persons or their property. (We hope you haven't had to learn this term the hard way.)

The other use of due diligence is in the world of business. Specifically, it's a process that investors use to find good investment opportunities, reduce risks, and safeguard their money. It's a painstaking process that closely examines your business to see if it's feasible as a going concern, any possible hazards that could threaten your business, and a worthy investment overall.

We're going to get you ready for the bright lights of due diligence in this chapter by talking about what's involved with the process. Then we talk about the documents you need to prepare and present to your investors. Finally, we talk about the dreaded red flags and show that as in the Stoic form of philosophy, the obstacle is the way.

Put On Your Deerstalker Cap

Due diligence requires your investors to assign or hire their own Sherlock Holmes clones to put your company under their magnifying glasses to get answers in three areas:

» **Risk assessment:** This is the process of locating and assessing possible risks related to the investment, such as those pertaining to money, law, operations, and reputation.

» **Investment thesis validation:** The investors check to make sure the business fits the investor's risk tolerance, industry focus, and investment requirements.

» **Making an informed decision:** Giving potential investors a thorough grasp of the company's advantages, disadvantages, and possibilities so they can decide which investment to make.

Though this process isn't just going down a checklist, it's likely that the investor examination team will have an overall checklist such as a spreadsheet to ensure that every task is completed as you can see in Figure 14-1.

Due Diligence List for Startups
1. Company Structure and Background
- Articles of Incorporation/Organization
- Bylaws or Operating Agreement
- Shareholder Agreements
- Cap Table (list of equity ownership)
- History of the company
- Organizational chart
2. Financial Information
- Audited financial statements (if available)
- Recent unaudited financial statements
- Projections and business plan
- Capitalization table
- Details of debt, equity, and convertible instruments
- Tax returns and compliance
3. Product or Service
- Detailed description of products or services
- Information on development stage
- Roadmap for future development
- Intellectual property (patents, trademarks, copyrights)
- R&D activities and expenditures
4. Market and Industry Analysis
- Market size and growth prospects

FIGURE 14-1:
A sample due diligence task list spreadsheet.

The process of due diligence

The investor's team of experts will have a variety of specialties, including financial analysts, attorneys, intellectual property specialists, and market researchers, who work together throughout the multi-stage process of due diligence. Generally, the procedure is in this order.

Term sheet and first screening

Taking into account variables like sector emphasis, investment stage, and possible return, investors determine how well the investment opportunity fits into their overall set of requirements.

To obtain a high-level understanding of the firm and spot any potential red flags, investors perform a preliminary examination of the company's financial statements, executive summary, and business strategy.

Following a positive first assessment, investors work on a non-binding term sheet that outlines the salient features of the proposed investment, such as funding amount, valuation, and equity share.

The microscopes come out

Investors put together a due diligence team that includes specialists in financial analysis, legal issues, intellectual property, and market research, among other fields. They may also hire other specialists to confirm particular facets of the business, including intellectual property evaluations or financial audits.

The due diligence team obtains comprehensive data from the business, such as financial statements, contracts, court records, employee agreements, and anything pertaining to intellectual property.

What's more, investors occasionally go on site visits to the business's locations to watch operations, speak with important staff members, and get a clear idea of how the company functions on a daily basis.

The thesis presentation

The team conducting the due diligence generates a thorough report that includes a summary of the risks, liabilities, and areas that need more information.

Investors decide whether and under what conditions to move forward with the investment based on the due diligence report and their overall evaluation of the investment opportunity presented by your business.

The due diligence table of the elements

There are several components that investors are going to review, and you should know what they're looking for as you prepare to give them unequivocal cooperation.

Finances

Investors examine the company's financial accounts in great detail, including:

>> **Financial statements:** A detailed examination of the income, balance, and cash flow statements from your company's past.

>> **Revenue projections:** An analysis of your estimated revenue, taking into account the methodology, underlying market trends, and assumptions.

>> **Where your cash is:** An assessment of your cash flow management procedures, encompassing debt commitments, capital expenditure plans, and working capital management.

>> **Financial ratios:** An evaluation of your financial performance and health using important financial ratios like debt-to-equity, gross profit margin, and EBITDA margin.

WARNING

If you don't know basic financial information such as EBITDA (which stands for *earnings before interest, taxes, depreciation, and amortization*), become expert as soon as you can or your investors may well use your company in their marketing as an example of what not to do.

But that's not all! Investors conduct legal due diligence by examining the business's legal framework, rights to intellectual property, contractual responsibilities, regulatory compliance, and likelihood of litigation.

Following the law

The examiners are going to look at five areas of both legal compliance and legal risk:

>> **Corporate structure:** An examination of the ownership, legal structure, and adherence to corporate governance guidelines of your company's corporate structure.

>> **Intellectual property:** An evaluation of your company's portfolio of protected works, such as trade secrets, copyrights, patents, and trademarks.

>> **Contractual obligations:** Examining all significant contracts that your business has, such as those with suppliers, customers, employees, and lenders.

- **Regulatory compliance:** Assessment of your company's adherence to pertinent laws and rules, such as labor laws, environmental regulations, and rules particular to its industry.
- **Litigation and legal risks:** Evaluation of the possible legal risks that your business may face, such as ongoing legal disputes, ongoing regulatory inquiries, and possible liabilities.

The market you serve

Investors evaluate how your company is performing and can perform in your market by looking at four departments:

- **The industry in which you operate:** This comprehensive examination includes market dimensions, expansion patterns, rivalry, and significant industry influences.
- **Competitive positioning:** An analysis of the market share, competitive advantages, factors of differentiation, and competitive threats that your company faces.
- **Customer base:** An analysis of your company's clientele that takes into account customer retention rates, customer acquisition tactics, and customer segmentation.
- **Market growth potential:** Finally, the examination team looks at your prospects for expansion within its sector, taking into account variables such as market trends, new product developments, and growth prospects.

Your team and your culture

Your internal management team and key people are vital to the success of the business as well as your relationship with the investors on your ride to glory. So, your investors will take a deep dive into four pools:

- **Experience and expertise:** Expect to answer questions about the management team's background, credentials, and performance history of the organization.
- **Leadership inspection:** Your management team will be evaluated for its capacity for decision-making, leadership, and strategy execution.
- **Recommendations and compensation:** The investor team will examine the executive compensation plan of the organization and coordinating incentives with its long-range objectives.
- **Team dynamics and culture:** Evaluation of the organization's culture, team dynamics, and capacity to draw and hold on top talent.

The fork in the offramp

After your prospective investors review the results of their due diligence, there will be three paths before you. The first, and the one you obviously want, is to get on the freeway — that is, the investors agree to work with you using the terms you negotiated before the investigation.

The second path is moving into a roundabout where you and the investors renegotiate the conditions, including changes to the value, the equity stake, or risk mitigation strategies. Then you decide where you exit after you make a few O-turns.

The final option is the exit ramp where the investigation reveals material risks or concerns, but don't let that daunt you. You may end up thanking your lucky stars that the report exposed risks that caused you to pull over, fix your business, and get it back on the road with better prospects for growth.

REMEMBER

After your business gets back on the road again, you may not only attract more investors, but also the investors who turned you down may come calling again.

Channel Your Inner Marie Kondo

We can hear you breathing hard after reading all that, but wait a second — can you feel the good vibes radiating into your hands as you read this? That's because we have a list of everything you need to get ready for the due diligence examination.

No, we can't give you a cheat sheet because every business is different, but this exhaustive checklist is what you need to ensure you impress your investors with your foresight and organization.

Give a warm welcome

It's likely your investors will want to learn more about your company in a formal, in-depth presentation. So, take the initiative and schedule a meeting with your investors to kick off the due diligence examination and get the process off on the right foot.

That presentation needs to include:

>> An executive summary that provides investors with a succinct synopsis of your company's goals, target market, offerings, and competitive environment.

>> The history, goals, strategy, and finances of your business.

>> Your company's financial estimates, market analysis, business model, and growth strategy.

TIP

Don't forget to rehearse your presentation with your team before the big day! (If your eyes are rolling like a teenager's, our job is done.)

Of course, the examiners will be excited to look into your business in even greater detail after your stellar presentation. Here's what you need to know in all areas of your business.

REMEMBER

Have a notepad or your notepad-taking app at the ready to help you write down where everything is. What's more, include all relevant team members in this exercise so they can help you find where everything is.

Financial records

Investors will ask for your financial records straight away, so have the following documents prepped and ready to share:

>> **Historical financial statements:** Statements of cash flow, balance sheets, and income over the last three years or since your company's founding, no matter whether they are audited.

>> **Financial projections:** Comprehensive financial forecasts include revenue, expenses, cash flow, and profitability parameters spanning the next three to five years.

>> **Tax returns:** Copies of the tax returns filed by your business for the last three years or ever since it was founded.

>> **Cap (or capitalization) table:** This table shows the ownership structure of your business and includes information on investors, ownership percentages, and the number of shares issued.

Legal records

Get all your ducks in a row (or use your favorite cliché) as you prepare the following legal records to show to your inspection team:

>> **Articles of incorporation:** The original or certified copy of the articles of incorporation that govern your business.

>> **Bylaws:** A copy of the rules that regulate your business's internal operations.

- >> **Stock certificates:** Shareholders are provided with copies of stock certificates.

- >> **Relevant contracts:** Contracts pertaining to suppliers, customers, employment, and financing should be kept on file.

- >> **Intellectual property:** Images of any patents, trademarks, copyrights, or other intellectual property that your business has.

Documents for regulatory compliance

The following three regulatory compliance documents can vary based on your jurisdiction and your industry:

- >> **Licenses and permits:** You need to show certified copies of all licenses and permits needed for your business to function within your sector and legal jurisdiction.

- >> **Regulatory filings:** Show the inspectors regulatory filings made with the appropriate government offices.

- >> **Documentation of environmental compliance:** If you need to adhere to federal, state, or local environmental laws, you need to show records that your compliance is up to date.

Institutional records

These records summarize the important elements of your organization:

- >> **Org (or organizational) chart:** This chart is a visual representation of the important persons, departments, and reporting lines inside your corporation.

- >> **Key employee agreements:** Provide copies of contracts for employment with important executives and staff members.

- >> **Board of directors minutes:** These are copies of the most recent board meeting minutes.

Play it straight

Making a good impression on potential investors during due diligence requires that you present your important documentation. When you keep your important documents in order, investors will find it easier to get the information they require for due diligence.

Get it together

We see you nodding your head in agreement, but your documents may not be as orderly as they should be. But we have your back, and here's what you need to do to ensure you have good documents not only for potential investors, but also for anyone else who may come calling like, say, government regulators.

>> **Make a document index:** Create an extensive index that enumerates every document you have and the file locations that go with it.

>> **Create a filing system:** Put in place a sensible filing system that sorts papers into subcategories as needed and according to their kind (financial, legal, and so on.).

>> **Use consistent naming conventions:** To make document identification and retrieval easier, use consistent naming conventions for your documents.

>> **Digitize papers:** To facilitate sharing and simple access, turn hard copy papers into digital formats using tools such as scanning documents with a multi-function printer.

TIP

Many of these options are available in document management software, and there are different packages for general and industry-specific companies such as accountants. All you have to do is search online for *document management software* to start reviewing potential solutions for your new business.

Sharing properly is caring

If you're so proud about your documentation that you'd bring a stranger off the street to show it off, then you're ready to share that information with your investors. Here's what to do to make it easy for your inspectors to review your documents:

>> **Create a virtual data room (VDR):** A VDR is also known as a deal room used during the due diligence process so that investors may securely access and review your documents online.

>> **Make documentation easy to access:** Ensure investors can easily obtain the documentation they require, and give them clear guidance on how to use the VDR.

>> **Customize your presentation for the investor:** When choosing and presenting documents, take into account the unique requirements and interests of each investor. For example, if there are related documents to one that an investor has asked for, include those in your presentation.

>> **Answer any and all questions:** Be ready to respond to inquiries regarding your documents and offer more details if required.

Look Both Ways

Red lights are going to flash during the due diligence examination. (If they don't, consider buying a lottery ticket.) So, here are the areas where your examiners may see red and how you can answer their questions with confident comebacks.

Financial warning signs

Investors place a high value on financial performance and stability, because logically money has a direct bearing on the long-term survival and possible profits of your business. Here are the areas where the green lights could switch to flashing red.

>> **Unsustainable revenue growth:** In the absence of a clear route to profitability, fast revenue growth, even though it's sometimes a positive sign of market traction, raises concerns about your company's capacity to sustain its growth trajectory and produce long-term profitability, especially if your expansion is mostly the result of unsustainable practices or one-time events.

>> **Inadequate cash flow management:** In order to pay bills, finance operations, and make investments in expansion prospects, investors want confidence that you're managing your cash flow effectively. Excessive expenditures, a lack of working capital, or irregular cash flow patterns are all warning signs in cash flow management. These problems may indicate impending financial trouble and trouble paying short-term debts.

>> **High debt levels:** A company with too much debt may find it more difficult to make ends meet, be less able to invest in expansion plans, and be more vulnerable to changes in interest rates. A highly leveraged balance sheet can raise questions about your company's financial risk profile and ability to manage debt commitments, even though certain debt funding is allowed.

>> **Inadequate accounting procedures:** Accurate and trustworthy financial information for investors depends on sound accounting procedures. Inconsistent accounting procedures, improper accounting recordkeeping, and a failure to produce audited financial statements will cause your inspectors' forehead veins to pop out.

>> **Uncertain revenue recognition practices:** The timing and method of recording revenue in your company's financial statements are determined by its revenue recognition practices. Unusual or aggressive methods of revenue recognition, like manipulating sales or recognizing revenue early, can inflate a company's earnings and cast doubt on the accuracy of its financial reporting.

Red flags in law and regulations

Any company that wants to legally safeguard its assets and stay out of trouble must adhere to all legal and regulatory obligations. Red flags in this area may point to underlying legal issues that have the potential to affect the operations and financial performance of your organization going forward:

>> **Pending litigation or regulatory investigations:** Prolonged legal battles or regulatory inquiries may indicate future legal troubles, harm to the company's image, and diversions from its main commercial activities. Your investors will quickly figure out that a company that is subject to severe legal battles or regulatory investigation, and your severe stress that's keeping you from focusing on the business, is not a sound investment decision.

>> **Problems with intellectual property:** A company's distinctive goods, services, or innovations can be protected and given a competitive edge by using intellectual property (IP), which is a valuable asset. Concerns in this domain include unclear IP ownership, inadequate IP protection, or possible IP infringement lawsuits. These problems could make the business less competitive and put it in danger of legal trouble.

>> **Non-compliance with rules and regulations:** Violating the relevant rules and regulations in your country, state, region, and/or industry may result in fines, penalties, harm to one's reputation, and possibly even legal action against your company. Investors don't want that. No one wants that.

Trouble with your market and competition

Comprehending the competitive environment and market landscape is essential to a startup's success. Concerns in this domain may point to deeper issues with gaining market share, fending off rivals, and attaining sustained expansion:

>> **Lack of market differentiation:** In order to draw in and keep clients, startups need to set themselves apart from rivals. Red flags in this area include a lack of distinctive features for the product, an inability to satisfactorily answer the needs of the consumer, or a poor communication of the value proposition of the company. You'll need to explain how your new business can carve out a solid niche for itself in the industry and see long-term success.

>> **Weak competitive posture:** To stand out in the market and draw clients, startups must have a strong competitive posture. A lack of a distinct competitive advantage, poor brand recognition, or an inability to gain market share despite considerable efforts are warning signs in this domain. If the inspectors find those signs, you'll need to explain how your company will compete successfully and meet its growth goals in the absence of a strong competitive position.

>> **Unrealistic market estimates:** Accurate market estimates are crucial for investors to evaluate a company's development prospects and the viability of its business plan. In this context, excessively optimistic or unrealistic market estimates, a dearth of corroborating information or presumptions, or a disregard for potential risks and uncertainties in the market are warning signs. Impractical forecasts may give rise to doubts about your company's comprehension of the market and capacity to carry out your grand expansion plans.

>> **Disruptive innovations or a changing industry landscape:** As the business environment is always changing, startups need to be ready to adjust to new developments in their sector as well as shifting consumer preferences. Red flags in this zone include incapacity to use disruptive technology to obtain a competitive edge, incapacity to recognize or address new risks, or incapacity to adjust quickly to changes in the market. You'll need to assuage the investors' concerns by telling them how you and your team will innovate and adapt.

Ominous operational signs

Your due diligence examiners will take a tour of your facilities and they will take copious notes about what they see . . . and don't see. Here are four issues they may come up with in their report.

>> **Inadequate operational infrastructure:** Your company has some outdated technology, ineffective procedures, or a lack of scalability that can impede your company's capacity to grow and satisfy client expectations. Frequent system breakdowns, an inability to handle an increase in the amount of customers, or a lack of investment in technology and operational upgrades are warning signs in this area.

>> **Ineffective supply-chain management:** Getting supplies and services in a timely and economical manner depends on having an effective supply chain. Unreliable vendors, expensive inventories, or frequent supply chain interruptions are problems that investors will want fixed, and they'll want to know how you'll fix them. What will you tell them?

>> **Inadequate quality control and manufacturing standards:** Creating a reputation for a brand and winning over customers depend on maintaining high standards of quality. Frequent product problems, a lack of quality control methods, or non-compliance with industry norms will get your inspectors' red cards out.

>> **Inadequate risk-management practices:** Inadequate contingency plans for handling hazards, a formal risk-management procedure lacking, or a failure to recognize and evaluate critical risks are what your investors would define as a hazard. You'd better have a risk-management plan to hand to your inspectors

so they know your team will keep your business driving on the pavement and not into a cow pasture.

Bad management omens

Your investors are going to see how you work with your team and how your team interacts with your employees (if you have any at this stage). When the inspectors follow you around like hungry dogs, they could take you aside to point out your shortcomings in four areas:

>> **Absence of transparency and communication:** Stakeholder alignment and trust-building depend on open and honest communication not only with their employees but also with investors.

Red lights flashing in this intersection include failing to swiftly address investor concerns, providing inconsistent or misleading information, or not communicating with investors on a regular basis. Investors may decide to bail out during the due diligence process or at any time during their deliberations without transparency.

>> **Ineffective decision-making and strategy execution:** Reaching the objectives of the organization depends on making effective decisions and carrying out strategies. A history of making poor decisions, a vague or poorly defined plan, or ineffective strategy execution are warning signs in this area. Without effective decision-making and plan execution skills, the business can find it difficult to meet its goals and adjust to shifting market conditions.

>> **Unrealistic growth plans:** If you have growth plans that are excessively ambitious or unrealistic and, worse, you lack a well-defined plan for attainment, then don't be surprised that your investors are apprehensive about the company's capacity to effectively oversee and control its expansion. (Unless you really are that self-unaware.)

The inspectors will raise and wave red flags if you have one or more of the following afflictions: You're failing to take into account potential risks and obstacles, you don't have enough data or assumptions to support development estimates, or you aren't able to draw in the resources required to support growth.

>> **Weak corporate culture and values:** Innovation, a healthy work environment, and the ability to draw and keep top personnel all depend on a strong corporate culture and shared values.

High staff churn, a toxic workplace, and/or a misalignment between the company's principles and its executives' behavior are all bad juju signs in your business. Bad culture is a poison pill not only for your prospects of getting investors but also for your company itself.

Poor technology connections

You can't succeed in business without the right technologies implemented the right way, or as Scotty said, "The right tools for the right job!"

Your due diligence investigators will channel their inner Scotty and look closely at how you implement the technologies in your business. If they find something, they'll look in one of the following five areas, and be ready to ask you questions with an eyebrow arched.

>> **Insufficient technology infrastructure:** The expansion and operations of the business depend on a strong and scalable technology infrastructure. Outdated technology, a lack of investment in infrastructure updates, or an incapacity to manage growing demands are flashing red alert signs in this sector.

>> **Unreliable technology and regular outages:** Recurrent system failures, security flaws, or data breaches can cause business disruptions, erode customer confidence, and result in bleeding money your company can't afford to lose. Investors don't like to lose money.

>> **Inadequate technology integration and data management:** Simplifying processes, obtaining knowledge from data, and coming to wise conclusions all depend on efficient technology integration and data management.

Data silos, a lack of system integration, or the inability to get actionable insights from data are what inspectors will look for and call out if they find those problems can reduce the effectiveness of your operations.

>> **Excessive dependence on proprietary technology:** The saying is trite and it was drilled into you from a young age: Don't put all your eggs in one basket. If you've done that with a single source of technology to get your daily work done, expect your inspectors to ask you why you haven't diversified — especially because your key systems are controlled by one company's solution.

They'll have concerns about your proprietary technology's high maintenance and upgrade costs, its inability to integrate with third-party systems, and its lack of interoperability with industry standards. If you don't have an explanation about why you don't use industry-standard software and (maybe) open-source solutions, that could nix the deal.

>> **Inadequate technology talent and skills:** Developing, maintaining, and upgrading your company's technology infrastructure and products require a strong workforce with the needed skills. Are you proud of your team's tech abilities?

If you are, your investors may not be. They may tell you that you have inexperienced technical leadership, challenges in luring and keeping top personnel, and a high rate of turnover within the technology department. They'll expect that you'll have a good comeback.

Chapter **15**

Sealing the Deal: Closing the Funding Round

We know, we know — you came right to this chapter because you think you've done everything you had to do to seal the deal with your investors no matter if you read the previous chapters or not. All you have to do is go through this chapter and you're all good, right?

Yes, this chapter serves as a reminder checklist for what you need to do and ensure that you're ready for your investors' final exam. But if you haven't read about this information in detail and talked with both your team and the investors on a regular basis to know how to make this deal work, you're not ready for outside investment in your business. Full stop.

If you're waving your hand furiously in protest, then it's time to see how much you know, some ideas you may not have thought of, and how much you need to review. What's more, we include information about what to do after you get funding so you have a healthy relationship with your investors as everyone profits from the ride.

We present this list in bullet form so it's easy to take a pen and put a check mark next to each one in this book. (Go all out — we won't report you!)

What You Need to Finalize Funding Deals

Before we start, if you haven't reviewed Chapter 13 about understanding the term sheet and Chapter 14 about due diligence, bookmark this page and read those chapters. You'll be glad you did, and so will your investors because they'll expect that you know what you're doing.

Consult a lawyer

Your first step is to find qualified legal help by doing three things:

>> Hire a lawyer or legal office with venture capital financing experience.

>> Make sure they are knowledgeable about the particular funding stage and sector.

>> To prevent surprises, go over fee schedules and agreements in advance.

Review the term sheet

After you have your term sheet, it's time to do your homework:

>> Go over the term sheet in detail with your legal advisors and strongly consider following their advice.

>> Pay close attention to investor rights, ownership percentages, and valuation.

>> Work out any terms that could significantly affect your control of your business or are not in line with the mission of your organization.

Get ready for due diligence

Now it's time to get ready for the due diligence phase:

>> Establish a thorough due diligence data room with well-organized paperwork.

>> Answer questions from investors promptly and transparently.

>> Anticipate a thorough examination of contracts, intellectual property (better known as IP), financial records, and litigation history.

Aim for a win-win agreement

Your agreement needs to be a positive experience wherever possible, and here's how to approach it:

>> Have the right mindset going in to have constructive negotiations where you address concerns cooperatively. Your mindset is your greatest asset.

>> If you think you're going to have difficult conversations, think about using an experienced negotiator to help you. That experience could be money you recoup when the investor finances your business.

>> To build a solid partnership, keep your eyes on your ultimate destination rather than merely short-term profits at the next milestone.

Keep your contractual discipline

Discipline is essential for success not only in life, but also when you're finalizing a funding agreement:

>> Never sign anything without first having a lawyer analyze it, even if it seems simple.

>> Clean up any unclear or ambiguous legal terminology. (Just like this *For Dummies* book!)

>> Verify that agreements correspond to the terms that were negotiated.

Respect the law

Funding agreements come with plenty of legal requirements, so never forget to do these three things:

>> Navigate securities rules and regulations with the assistance of legal professionals who specialize in this area.

>> Verify investor accreditation, if required.

>> Send any necessary notices or disclosures about securities to the relevant regulatory agencies, which your legal team will help you with.

Adopt sound board governance practices

Should the investment result in board positions for the investors, you need to ensure that three things happen:

>> Revise your company governance framework accordingly.

>> Make certain that the addition and integration of new board members goes seamlessly.

>> Clearly define roles and responsibilities for everyone on the board who will stay and who will come on board to prevent any misunderstandings.

Communication between you, stakeholders, and employees

Completing a funding agreement isn't a state secret, so here's how to spread the news:

>> Inform staff members and important parties about the successful funding round.

>> Quickly respond to any queries or concerns from your investors, employees, and partners.

>> Retain openness about any modifications or effects on your company's operations.

Integration following funding

After you bring your investors on board, you need to bring them into your company's fold in three ways:

>> Arrange for frequent reporting or meeting times with investors to keep them informed and involved.

>> Leverage their experience to reach strategic goals and accelerate growth.

>> Encourage cooperation by including them in important decisions.

Record everything

Your funding agreement and any other supporting documents may need to be reviewed from time to time, especially by new team members who join your company. So, here's how to ensure you have those documents safe and available:

» Keep thorough records of all correspondence, agreements, and money exchanges.

» Use digital archiving options for storing records safely.

» Keep any hard copy records in a safe location that's protected as much as possible from theft, fire, water, or physical destruction of the location.

» Assure accessibility for audits and future reference.

Remain persistent and patient

As Napoleon Hill said, "Patience, persistence, and perspiration make an unbeatable combination for success." In terms of the funding process, keep these three tips in mind:

» Have patience throughout the process and be prepared for delays or unforeseen obstacles.

» Keep the lines of communication open with all parties involved.

» Be persistent in resolving problems because giving up means that you've wasted not only your time, but also everyone else's time — and likely made it harder to get funding the next time around (if there is one).

Plan for the next round

Your first successful funding round doesn't mean you can just sit on your laurels, because you won't reach your ultimate destination without more fuel. So, follow these three tips to keep moving like Speed Racer:

» Make use of the money and momentum you've obtained to fortify your company.

» Create a plan for reaching benchmarks that will draw in more funding.

» Continue to be aggressive in seeking out potential investors and partners for upcoming funding cycles.

Don't forget to celebrate!

Your successful funding round does mean that you should take a little time to enjoy the win by bringing in everyone to the party:

>> Celebrate with your team and investors the completion of your investment round.

>> Thank them for their support and confidence throughout the process.

>> Recognize and honor important participants who were instrumental in closing the deal.

Avoid bad habits

When you're trying to seal the funding deal, be self-aware and work with your team to ensure that no one engages in the following bad behaviors during the negotiation:

>> **Poor communication:** Refrain from being evasive or hiding important information when conducting due diligence. Transparency fosters investor trust and helps avert issues down the road.

Never be worried about "bothering" people with information. Bother them. Overcommunicate. If you forget to communicate, it may look to others that you're hiding information, which is a no good, very bad thing. So, set up a regular reporting schedule and ask for feedback about what is and should be reported.

>> **Overinflating your value:** Potential investors may be turned off if an inflated valuation is set. Take a realistic view of your company's value in light of the state of the market and its financial results.

>> **Disregarding legal advice:** Never disregard legal advice or work with untrained attorneys. Legal professionals are essential for managing intricate contracts and adhering to regulations. (Unless you don't want the money after all.)

>> **Hastily entering into negotiations:** Hastily proceeding with discussions may result in disadvantageous terms or miscommunications. Spend the necessary time making sure that everyone is happy with the final agreement.

>> **Disregarding regulatory compliance:** Legal issues may arise from breaking securities laws or other rules. Throughout the funding process, make sure all applicable laws and regulations are followed.

>> **Unrealistic expectations:** Steer clear of giving investors implausible returns or assurances. Be open and honest about the risks and uncertainty that come with making startup investments.

>> **Insufficient communication with investors:** Relationships can be harmed by not keeping lines of communication open with investors. Update investors on a regular basis about your business accomplishments, obstacles, and advancements. (Having them call you for an update is a textbook definition of bad juju.)

>> **Lack of adaptability:** Refusing to budge during talks can turn off possible investors. Be willing to make concessions and adjust to new situations.

>> **Disregarding cultural fit:** Failure to evaluate the cultural fit with investors may result in disputes down the road. Talk with your investors often to reassure you and them that your expectations, goals, and values are in line.

>> **Observing post-funding scheduling:** Inefficiencies may result from a lack of a defined plan for using the infusion of cash from your investors. Create a plan to optimize the investment's effects.

>> **Taking your eye off the ball:** Overemphasis on fundraising may take attention away from important business functions. Strike a balance between expanding and managing the company and fundraising.

>> **Inadequate or careless recordkeeping:** Check the accuracy and completeness of all contracts and agreements carefully, and then fix any documentation that is erroneous, disorganized, or incomplete.

REMEMBER

Don't cheap out on hiring an administration professional. If you think that you can run a business and manage administration at the same time, good luck with that.

>> **Ignoring investor due diligence:** Unwanted partnerships may arise from failing to thoroughly investigate possible investors. Analyze investors' histories, standing, and degree of agreement with your objectives.

>> **Thinking financing alone will bring instant success:** Securing finance is only one stage; it does not ensure success. Keep a realistic outlook and carry on with your hard work on your company.

>> **Mismanagement of burn rate:** Misusing or overspending money can result in problems that you could have avoided. So, establish stringent financial controls and budgeting to prevent high burn rates.

>> **Not prepared for a worst-case scenario:** Not every discussion results in a capital round that is successful. Be ready for your investor to say no and ensure you have a backup plan in place, be it to find another investor or keep going as you have been without outside funding.

Addressing Legal and Compliance Concerns

When completing funding arrangements for your business, you'll be better prepared to negotiate the complex legal and compliance landscape if you dig into these nuances and consult with knowledgeable legal counsel. By taking the wheel, you may keep your business from running off the road, which naturally boosts investor trust and creates the conditions for a successful fundraising round.

Choosing the correct lawyer

Be sure to carefully consider and choose a lawyer or legal practice that has a solid reputation in corporate law and startup finance. To identify the ideal fit for your needs, ask around for recommendations from reliable people and think about scheduling interviews with a few different applicants.

TIP

Your local chamber of commerce can be a good resource for finding the right lawyer. Another option is to search your social media networks, especially LinkedIn because it's the largest platform for professionals including attorneys — and we bet dollars to donuts that you already have a LinkedIn account, so log in and start sleuthing.

Due diligence documentation

Begin by putting together an all-inclusive package of due diligence. Contracts with important clients and partners, employment agreements, intellectual property documents (patents, trademarks, copyrights), audited financial accounts, and any ongoing or past legal issues are all examples of this. Then make sure that all documentation is well-organized and readily available. (Here's another friendly reminder to bookmark this page and go back to Chapter 14 for a refresher.)

Legal due diligence

Have a thorough legal due diligence study conducted by legal counsel. This includes the review of:

>> Contracts

>> Intellectual property

>> Legal history

- » Term sheets
- » Subscription agreements
- » Investor rights agreements
- » Any other investment-related documents
- » All pertinent laws and regulations

REMEMBER

It's critical to spot any legal red lights early on and take appropriate action. Don't move ahead with an investor funding agreement until your legal team gives you green lights across the board.

Regulatory compliance

Find out about and comprehend the particular regulations that apply to your sector and mode of fundraising. For instance, become familiar with the guidelines set forth by the Jumpstart Our Business Startups (JOBS) Act in the United States if you plan to raise money through equity crowdfunding. Requirements specific to a given industry may exist; for example, HIPAA requirements apply to companies in the healthcare sector. (HIPAA stands for Health Insurance Portability and Accountability Act.)

TIP

You can read an overview of the JOBS Act at https://www.investopedia.com/terms/j/jumpstart-our-business-startups-act-jobs.asp.

Securities regulations

You will probably have to abide by securities regulations when you issue debt or equity securities to investors. If that's so, hire a securities law expert attorney to help you navigate the process. Make sure your offering meets the requirements for an exemption or is registered with the relevant regulatory organization.

Investor agreements

Draft agreements with investors that precisely specify the terms and circumstances of the investment. These agreements must outline the kind and quantity of securities being offered, the company's valuation, any safeguards, and each party's rights and obligations. Take into account elements such as founders' equity vesting schedules and anti-dilution clauses.

Protection of intellectual property

To protect the intellectual property of your business, collaborate with intellectual property lawyers. Make sure your IP portfolio is safe and current by conducting routine audits. Deal with any possible violations or disagreements right away.

Tax considerations

Work with professionals who specialize in taxation for startups. For your investment round, consider tax-efficient structures like SAFEs (*simple agreements for future equity*) or convertible notes. Recognize the effects of capital gains taxes on investors as well as any tax breaks or incentives that may be applicable to your sector.

Labor and employment laws

You should do what any upstanding company does when it comes to your employees, including:

>> Comply with all applicable state and federal laws.

>> Keep respectful and safe working conditions.

>> Comply with pay and hour laws.

>> Classify workers and contractors appropriately.

If you don't have employment law attorneys working with you, get one now. Their advice will be invaluable now and as your business grows.

Updates on compliance

Be aware of any modifications to laws and rules that can have an impact on your startup. Legal advice can advise you on any necessary adjustments to preserve compliance as well as give you updates on regulatory developments.

Ongoing legal assistance

After the fundraising round, the need for legal assistance will continue for the life of your business. As your startup grows, your attorneys can help with post-closing changes, negotiating conditions, and handling any legal issues that may come up.

Aligning Expectations for a Smooth Transition

You may have jumped to this section because you want to know how to put together an action plan. If we pegged you, we invite you to look at other sections of this chapter so you can get a more thorough explanation of why you need to do these things to sign on the dotted line.

Form an investor relations team

If at all possible, you shouldn't be managing your investor relations yourself. Instead, you should put together a team of people with a clear leader:

>> Designate an experienced investor relations specialist with strong communication skills.

>> Make sure this specialist understands the finances and operations of your startup.

>> Provide a direct channel of contact between investors and the investor relations representative.

Clear and honest communication

We mentioned you need to communicate early and often earlier in this chapter, and here are three guidelines for keeping everyone involved in the loop:

>> Create regular avenues for communication, including progress reports or meetings held every month or every quarter.

>> Discuss the triumphs and difficulties your startup is encountering.

>> Give updates on industry developments, competitive conditions, and market conditions that could have an impact on your company.

Have reasonable aspirations

The thought of coming into a large amount of money makes people lovesick no matter if they're in business or not, but you have to stay grounded by following these principles:

>> Create a thorough budget and business strategy outlining the allocation of cash.

>> Be truthful about any dangers and unknowns in your business plan.

>> Steer clear of hyperbolic or overstated assertions regarding the potential of your startup.

Give realistic financial projections

If you're confident that you don't have on rose-colored glasses, then you need to apply your sobriety to your financial projections:

>> Develop a thorough financial model with cash flow, balance sheet, and income statement components.

>> Make sure your financial estimates are stress-tested for a range of scenarios by using conservative assumptions.

>> Provide investors with thorough budgets and projections to demonstrate your financial plan.

Key performance indicators

Neither you nor your investors will know how well your business is doing and how well the financial infusion is helping your business, so here's what to do to measure your progress:

>> Establish precise key performance indicators (KPIs) that correspond with the goals of your startup.

>> Monitor and evaluate KPIs regularly to measure how well your business is moving down the road.

>> Put in place instruments or dashboards that provide investors access to performance data.

Create plans for mitigating risks

There are going to be roadblocks and sudden turns along the road, so you need to be ready for them as best you can:

>> Determine possible hazards such as shifts in the market, obstacles to regulations, or disruptions from technology.

>> Create action plans that address resource allocation and contingency planning in order to mitigate these risks.

>> To show investors that you are ready to roll, share these risk evaluations and mitigation strategies with them.

Give frequent updates

Here's another reminder that you need to communicate early and often with investors to make sure everyone's on the same page by following three guidelines:

>> Keep investor updates and meetings on a regular basis.

>> Establish a specific website or platform where investors can obtain information and updates.

>> Promote two-way dialogue by inviting inquiries and comments from potential investors.

Prioritize the law and compliance

It's also worth repeating that you need to stay compliant with all rules and regulations so you can keep your stress as low as possible. Here are three things to know:

>> Hire legal counsel with experience in startup fundraising transactions to make sure agreements are followed.

>> Keep meticulous records of all agreements and papers pertaining to the funding round.

>> Review and update compliance processes on a regular basis to adjust to evolving regulatory requirements.

Effectively resolve conflict

Conflict resolution is a skill that you can learn online and keep updating, but in terms of your investor agreements, here are three guidelines to follow:

>> Include a defined procedure in your investor agreements for resolving disputes.

>> Talk with your investors about incorporating a provision for arbitration or mediation as a quick and effective way to settle disputes.

>> Promote honest communication and compromise in order to arrive at win-win solutions.

Have an exit plan

You don't have control over what happens in your business, but in case you need to take the offramp, you'd better know what to do by following these steps:

>> Develop several exit scenarios, including possible dates, expected valuations, and the possibility of incapacitation or death of key people.

>> Clearly state the circumstances and triggers that would cause an exit.

>> Collaborate with investors on the development of the exit strategy.

Protect intellectual property

Intellectual property, better known as IP, is one of the most valuable things your business owns, and its protection is a responsibility on par with that of protecting your family. So, adhere to these requirements:

>> Constantly keep an eye on and protect the intellectual property of your startup with the help of your IP lawyer. (You are, right?)

>> Work with data security and access control experts to establish procedures if you don't have them already. (You do, right?)

>> Hire people who will train your stakeholders and staff on the value of intellectual property protection. (You have, right?)

Create a framework for governance

Just like a car needs a framework for it to go, your business needs a framework for how you will govern it with all the members of your board and management team. Here's a framework to describe how to build your framework:

>> Specify the obligations and roles of investors, board members, and founders.

>> Define voting procedures and decision-making rights.

>> Discuss the difference between ownership-level (board) decisions and business-level (management) decisions in detail with your team.

>> Create procedures for resolving conflicts or changes in leadership, because both will happen.

Provide comprehensive financial reports

Sure, you say, producing comprehensive financial reports is self-evident, but how do you do it? Here are four things you have to do:

>> Create thorough financial statements, such as cash flow statements, balance sheets, and profit and loss statements.

>> Hire experts to help you shop for, implement, and manage accounting platforms to guarantee accuracy and openness.

>> To ensure transparency, provide investors with thorough financial disclosures.

>> Be prepared for in-depth inquiries about your finances from your investors, because they'll expect that you'll have all the answers they're looking for.

5

Managing Finances and Growing Your Startup

Understand the basics of financial management for new businesses.

Learn about budgeting and cash flow.

Analyze financial reports to make sound decisions.

Know how to create and employ funding strategies to grow your business.

management

» **Establishing strong financial controls**

» **Finding technology solutions that work for you**

Chapter 16

Financial Management 101

E ven if your business hasn't embarked on the road yet, you need to understand finances. After all, you can't figure out what's happening with your
fancy vehicle without knowing the meaning of things like the fuel gauge and
how your speed affects the amount of fuel in your tank.

Yeah, we know, it's more complicated than that. And we know that many of your
investors work in finance or have plenty of experience in it. Before your vein pops
out of your forehead, no one expects you to be a financial expert.

However, and you saw this coming, you need to know the fundamentals if you're
going to succeed, and we're here to help fill you in. Even if you think you know
everything, we challenge you to at least skim through this chapter and see if you
know everything we cover here.

Reading the Scorecard

Understanding your financial statements is like reading a scorecard from your
favorite sport. If you haven't looked at the score information about your team's
game in too much detail, the numbers may not make a lot of sense unless you take
the time to understand (and Google) what various numbers and acronyms mean.

This section talks not only about the basics of your financial statements, but also about how to budget your money and forecast what's going to happen so it makes sense to the investors you want to be on your team.

TIP

If you're not sure you have sound financial judgment and you have a social learning style, think about employing a fractional CFO (chief financial officer) or accountant who has experience working with investors and startups. As you may have guessed, a fractional CFO is a term for part-time or contract CFO who can not only help you get off the ground, but also help train you and your relevant team members.

Leading off with financial statements

We cover three statements first because they're the ones your potential investors will examine right off the bat.

Income statement, aka the profit and loss statement

This financial statement gives you a thorough overview of the income and costs of your business for a given time frame, which is often a month, quarter, or year. It helps you monitor the profitability of your company's activities. Sales are included in revenues, whereas costs like rent, payroll, and utilities are included in expenses.

When expenses are deducted from revenues, the net profit or loss is what remains. By examining this statement, you may determine which aspects of your company are profitable and which might benefit from cost cutting or outright elimination from the tourney.

Check out Figure 16-1 below for an example of what an income statement looks like.

The balance sheet

Usually produced at the conclusion of a fiscal year (such as year-end), a balance sheet provides an instantaneous view of your company's financial situation. It's divided into three primary sections: equity, liabilities, and assets. All of the items that your company possesses, including money, stock, machinery, and accounts receivable, are considered assets.

	A	B	C	D	E	F
1	**[Company Name]**				**Income Statement**	
2	Address: 123 Street Avenue, Cityville, State, 12333					
3						
4	**Date Created:**	**Date Issued:**				
5	11 Jan, 2020	11 Jan, 2020				
6						
7						
8	**Income Statement**					
9	**Revenue**			Year 1	Year 2	Year 3
10	Sales			$78,000.00	$78,000.00	$78,000.00
11	*Less:* Sales Return			$3,000.00	$3,000.00	$3,000.00
12	*Less:* Discounts and Allowances			$1,000.00	$1,000.00	$1,000.00
13	**Net Sales**			**$74,000.00**	**$74,000.00**	**$74,000.00**
14	**Cost of Goods Sold**					
15	Materials			$8,000.00	$8,000.00	$8,000.00
16	Labor			$9,000.00	$9,000.00	$9,000.00
17	Overhead			$2,000.00	$2,000.00	$2,000.00
18	**Total Cost of Goods Sold**			**$19,000.00**	**$19,000.00**	**$19,000.00**
19	**Gross Profit**			**$55,000.00**	**$55,000.00**	**$55,000.00**
20	**Operating Expenses**					
21	Wages			$10,000.00	$10,000.00	$10,000.00
22	Advertising			$500.00	$500.00	$500.00
23	Repairs & Maintenance			$100.00	$100.00	$100.00
24	Travel			$50.00	$50.00	$50.00
25	Rent/Lease			$5,000.00	$5,000.00	$5,000.00
26	Delivery/Freight Expense			$1,000.00	$1,000.00	$1,000.00
27	Utilities/Telephone Expenses			$1,000.00	$1,000.00	$1,000.00
28	Insurance			$500.00	$500.00	$500.00
29	Mileage			$1,500.00	$1,500.00	$1,500.00
30	Office Supplies			$1,000.00	$1,000.00	$1,000.00
31	Depreciation			$8,000.00	$8,000.00	$8,000.00
32	Interest			$2,000.00	$2,000.00	$2,000.00
33	Other Expenses			$100.00	$100.00	$100.00
34	**Total Operating Expenses**			**$30,750.00**	**$30,750.00**	**$30,750.00**
35	**Operating Profit (Loss)**			**$24,250.00**	**$24,250.00**	**$24,250.00**
36	*Add: Other Income*					
37	Interest Income			$2,000.00	$2,000.00	$2,000.00
38	Other Income			$1,000.00	$1,000.00	$1,000.00
39	**Profit (Loss) Before Taxes**			**$27,250.00**	**$27,250.00**	**$27,250.00**
40	*Less:* Tax Expense			$4,000.00	$4,000.00	$4,000.00
41	**Net Profit (Loss)**			**$23,250.00**	**$23,250.00**	**$23,250.00**

FIGURE 16-1: A spreadsheet with all the features of an income statement.

Liabilities are all of the bills and commitments that your business has, such as loans and accounts payable. Equity is the remaining stake you have in your assets after subtracting your liabilities. Your assets should always exceed your liabilities on a well-managed balance sheet, of which an example is shown in Figure 16-2, as this shows your potential investors that you have positive equity and sound financial standing.

	Year 1	Year 2	Year 3
[Company Name]			**Balance Sheet**
Address: 123 Street Avenue, Cityville, State, 12333			
Date Created: **Date Issued:**			
11 Jan, 2020 11 Jan, 2020			
Pro Forma Balance Sheet			
Assets	**Year 1**	**Year 2**	**Year 3**
Current Assets			
Cash	$78,000.00	$36,000.00	$78,000.00
Accounts Receivable	$36,000.00	$45,000.00	$36,000.00
Other Current Assets	$0.00	$0.00	$0.00
Total Current Assets	**$114,000.00**	**$81,000.00**	**$114,000.00**
Fixed Assets			
Property, Plant, and Equipment	$36,000.00	$36,000.00	$36,000.00
Accumulated Depreciation	$36,000.00	$36,000.00	$36,000.00
Total Fixed Assets	**$0.00**	**$0.00**	**$0.00**
Total Assets	**$114,000.00**	**$81,000.00**	**$114,000.00**
Liabilities and Equity	**Year 1**	**Year 2**	**Year 3**
Current Liabilities			
Accounts Payable	$1,800.00	$1,800.00	$1,800.00
Credit Cards	$1,800.00	$1,800.00	$1,800.00
Customer Credit	$1,800.00	$1,800.00	$1,800.00
Taxes Payable	$1,800.00	$1,800.00	$1,800.00
Unearned Revenue	$1,800.00	$1,800.00	$1,800.00
Other Current Liabilities	$1,800.00	$1,800.00	$1,800.00
Total Current Liabilities	**$10,800.00**	**$10,800.00**	**$10,800.00**
Long Term Liabilities			
Long Term Liabilities	$36,000.00	$36,000.00	$36,000.00
Total Long Term Liabilities	**$36,000.00**	**$36,000.00**	**$36,000.00**
Total Liabilities	**$46,800.00**	**$46,800.00**	**$46,800.00**
Equity			
Net Profit (Loss)	$36,000.00	$36,000.00	$36,000.00
Retained Earnings - Opening Balance	$36,000.00	$36,000.00	$36,000.00
Owner's Deposits (Withdrawals)	$36,000.00	$36,000.00	$36,000.00
Total Equity	**$108,000.00**	**$108,000.00**	**$108,000.00**
Total Liabilities and Equity	**$154,800.00**	**$154,800.00**	**$154,800.00**

FIGURE 16-2:
A spreadsheet that shows all the parts of a balance sheet.

Cash flow statement

This document shows how much money comes into and goes out of your company over a specific time frame, such as one month or one quarter. Operating activities, investing activities, and financing activities make up its three components. Your operating activities includes cash generated from your main business operations.

Financial flows associated with purchasing or disposing of assets are referred to as investing activities, whereas borrowing, loan repayment, and share issuance or repurchasing are considered financing activities. This statement helps you determine that you have enough cash on hand to pay bills, make investments, and cover other obligations for your business.

Charting budgets and forecasts

To create a budget, you must first identify projected income and expenses for a given time frame, usually a fiscal year, as well as set financial goals.

Budgets act as road maps for your trip where you make wise financial decisions and allocate your resources efficiently. They support your budgeting efforts for both variable and fixed expenses (such as rent, salary, and marketing). By routinely comparing your budgeted statistics with actual financial performance, you can spot differences and fix problems straightaway.

Forecasting is the process of estimating future financial performance with a high degree of accuracy by using market trends, historical data, and other pertinent information.

Forecasting is a common tool used so you can project your future cash flow, costs, and revenues. By taking a forward-looking strategy, you can make proactive decisions by anticipating financial opportunities and obstacles. Precise data analysis and an acute awareness of industry changes are prerequisites for effective forecasting.

That all sounds good, you say, but how do you actually budget and forecast? Here are the best practices you should check to ensure that you're actually doing them and implement the practices that you may not have thought of before.

Create a detailed budget

Make a thorough budget that accounts for all of your company's costs, including capital expenditures, revenues, and expenses. Take into account both variable and fixed costs such as marketing, suppliers, and rent or salary.

Be realistic

Make reasonable assumptions for your projections and budget. For guidance on your forecasts, consult market research, historical financial data, and industry benchmarks. If you don't, your investors will and they'll call you on your lack of research.

Be conservative

It is advisable to estimate income conservatively. It's tempting to inflate numbers when you're full of excitement, but if real sales fall short of highly optimistic revenue estimates, everyone involved in your company is going to be in a world of hurt.

Observe, assess, and adjust

Keep a close eye on your financial performance in relation to your forecasts and budget. Frequent evaluations enable you to quickly detect deviations, pull over on the side of the road to fix the trouble, and get back on the road again with all deliberate speed.

Make a contingency plan

Leave room in your budget for a contingency reserve to cover unforeseen costs or shifts in the market. Having a safety net can help your startup overcome unanticipated obstacles and helps you sleep better at night.

Make cash flow a priority

When creating a budget, give careful consideration to cash flow before you approach investors. Make sure that your estimates, especially for the starting and expansion phases, indicate positive cash flow. Don't bother to read the rest of this book until the flow is on.

Include others

Include pertinent stakeholders and team members in the forecasting and budgeting process. You may also want to hire a fractional CFO who we talked about earlier in this chapter. Everyone's knowledge and experience can put together the best financial strategies for your company.

Plan scenarios

Create several scenarios in your projections to evaluate the effects of various factors, like adjustments to production costs, market demand, or price. This enables you to make sound decisions in a variety of situations without the stress.

Share your financial goals

To ensure that everyone on the team is aware of the company's financial goals and objectives, share your budget and financial predictions with them. A sense of accountability and ownership is fostered by transparency.

Think long term

Create long-term financial plans that specify your startup's financial goals and tactics for a number of years ahead, going beyond short-term budgets. If you don't, prospective investors will ask you why that is. And investors don't like to ask many basic questions.

Money management

Ensuring liquidity and fulfilling immediate financial obligations depend on effective working capital management. This means you and your trusted financial team members need to keep an eye on your money and your payables and receivables. Even in times of erratic cash flow, effective working capital management guarantees you have enough cash on hand to pay for your regular operating expenses.

REMEMBER

It's wise to establish and keep an emergency fund, sometimes known as a cash reserve. This reserve offers a cushion of money in case of unforeseen costs, recessions, or urgent business needs. It guarantees that in hard times, you won't have to rely entirely on outside funding sources. If you don't have one, your potential investors may pointedly ask you why that is.

Financial ratios

There are three types of financial ratios that will tell you and your prospective investors how profitable your business can be, your company's ability to pay short-term debts, and the financial risk to your company.

Profitability ratios

These measures determine how profitable your business can be in relation to its income. Gross profit margin, or gross profit divided by revenue, and net profit margin, or net profit divided by revenue, are typical profitability measures.

Liquidity ratios

These ratios assess your company's capacity to pay short-term debts. Examples of these ratios are the current ratio, which is calculated by dividing current assets by current liabilities, and the quick ratio, which calculates the difference between quick assets and current liabilities. They show the liquidity and short-term solvency of your business. (Investors like that.)

Debt ratios

These ratios assess the leverage and financial risk of your company. An example of a debt ratio is the debt-to-equity ratio, which is calculated by dividing total debt by total equity. If you have lower debt ratios, that means your company has greater financial stability and lower financial risk. (Investors like those, too.)

Managing expenses

When you manage your daily expenses, you need to control your costs from the get-go so you don't waste money on expenditures that don't benefit your company. (So many companies get this wrong, and we don't want that for you.)

Cost control

It's critical to put cost-effective techniques into place to reduce costs without sacrificing quality. Because if you don't, your customers will call you out on it and, worse, tell their colleagues, family, and friends to avoid you like the proverbial plague.

So, regularly assess your cost structure to find places where you may cut costs or increase efficiency. This could entail revising agreements with suppliers, streamlining production procedures, or implementing technological solutions to improve operations.

Cost allocation

In your business, you're the mother bird to a lot of baby birds in your company. These babies are various divisions inside your company that provide the products and services your customers want as well as the internal company support your employees need to serve your customers. And money is the food.

You need to work with your team to find out where that money goes so all your birds are happy and working together to grow the nest. When you have precise cost distribution guarantees, that helps improve your company's profitability.

Tax considerations

It should go without saying that you should have a certified tax professional on retainer, and not keeping tax information in a shoebox using TurboTax.

A human tax professional will help you reduce your tax burden by using all available credits, deductions, and incentives. They'll make sure you're still adhering to all of the tax laws and regulations in your country and state, because we suspect you aren't even aware of many of them.

Insurance assessment

Another area where a human professional is needed is with insurance. You've probably already taken into account your insurance needs, but now is a good reminder to talk with your insurance agent about your property, professional, and/or general liability insurance.

Investors will want to know that you're shielding your company from unanticipated risks through your insurance coverage. During their examination, they may also suggest that you take on additional coverage that you may be missing and/or may need as your business gets bigger.

Contingency planning

Create backup plans in case of unexpected financial events, such as market turbulence, supply chain interruptions, or economic downturns. Your team and your investors are good people to talk about here as you consider scenarios that Hollywood scriptwriters would think would make a great film.

These plans specify actions to follow in response to particular difficulties, assisting your company in adapting and prospering in challenging circumstances. And if you have these plans in place, you and your investors will sleep better at night knowing that you have the "in emergency break glass" documents ready to go. (You can still buy those cases online if you really want to impressively remind your team that you're on top of things.)

Setting budget goals

For your startup, establish attainable financial targets, with attainable being the key word here. Establish short- and long-term goals for cost control, cash flow, profitability, and revenue growth.

Before you start approaching investors with your grand plans, review these objectives' progress with your team. Then review them regularly with your team as your prospective investors look closely at your budget and tweak them as necessary. And, you guessed it, you'll need to review your budget goals even after you have funding. Your investors will expect nothing less.

Establishing financial controls

If you've made it this far in the chapter, you already know the message we're sending you: You need frameworks for your finances much like highways have the rumble strips on the edges of the road to keep you in your lane. Let's start by understanding how financial controls help you keep control of your daily business life, and then we talk about how to implement them.

Risk mitigation

To maintain your company's long-term and stable financial health, financial controls assist in identifying, evaluating, and mitigating financial risks. These hazards may consist of credit concerns, operational uncertainty, and changes in the market.

Fraud prevention and detection

Internal controls serve as both a preventative and a detective measure for fraudulent activity. By reducing the possibility of fraud and assisting in the discovery of any irregularities or wrongdoing, they protect your company's assets.

Regulation compliance

It (probably) goes without saying that businesses need to follow tax laws, accounting standards, reporting requirements, and other legal and regulatory requirements. Financial controls lower your stress by lowering the possibility of fines, legal problems, or reputational harm by assisting in ensuring that the business complies with these requirements. Oh, and investors don't want to be involved with any company that's sketchy with regulations.

Operational efficiency

By streamlining financial procedures, controls save operating expenses and increase process efficiency. That frees you and your team to focus on growth possibilities and manage resources more efficiently.

How to implement financial controls

We can hear you asking how to do this, and we're here for you. Here's your checklist for implementing the financial controls you need for your startup.

Build your package

Determine which financial procedures, such as budgeting, cost approvals, invoicing, and cash management, are essential to your company. If you don't have one or more procedures your investors think you need to cover, they'll tell you to add those controls if you want their money.

Design control procedures

Create comprehensive written protocols outlining the proper way to carry out each financial process. These protocols should have distinct roles, stages, and directives. To secure important stakeholders' support and knowledge, think about incorporating them in the design process.

Assign responsibility

Clearly identify the people or groups in charge of carrying out and keeping an eye on each control procedure. Make sure that duties and responsibilities are clearly stated to avoid misunderstandings or supervision gaps.

Apply technology

Whenever feasible, automate and simplify control processes by using software and even hardware tools where necessary, such as using iPads to document and cross-check inventory. Automation boosts productivity, lowers the possibility of human error, and offers real-time financial data insights.

Document, document, document

Keep thorough records of all financial transactions, approvals, and actions taken in accordance with regulations. Accurate documentation is essential for accountability, transparency, and auditing. Install a safe document management system that people can access and update securely.

Monitor and review frequently

To make sure your financial controls are relevant and effective, ensure that you and your team keep a close eye on them. Frequent evaluations aid in identifying areas of weakness or room for development. Make sure that your team knows to communicate early and often about any control weaknesses so you can fix them on the fly and keep moving down the road.

Types of financial controls

Startups should think about constructing a variety of financial controls. Software programs can frequently be useful in keeping an eye on these restrictions and in assisting new business owners in more efficiently growing their enterprises.

Budgetary controls

These controls are all about developing and keeping an eye on your budget to make sure that spending is in line with both your projected income and your financial objectives. What's more, budgetary control integrates frequent budget reviews so you and your team will know if there are any issues in a specific area, such as with a particular product, so you can figure out what to do about it.

Authorization controls

Before some financial transactions may take place, managers or other specific personnel must authorize them. Purchase order authorizations, credit limit authorizations, and spending approvals are a few examples.

REMEMBER

Be sure to have a list of people who are authorized to approve financial purchases documented, and communicate this information to the appropriate employees clearly to ensure that everyone follows procedure and no one is caught unaware.

Segregation of duties

This essential control entails dividing up the financial responsibilities of several team members, because when you do, the chance of fraud or mistakes goes way down. For example, the individual who authorizes spending and the one who handles payments ought to be distinct.

Audit trails

Put in place procedures that keep thorough records of all financial transactions. It is simpler to find and look into any anomalies, illegal access, or questionable activity thanks to these logs. Who started the transaction, who approved it, and when it happened should all be recorded in an efficient audit trail. (This process is better known as "covering your behinds.")

Control your inventories

Set up procedures to track and manage inventories if your firm sells tangible goods. This involves cycle counting, precise recordkeeping, and security precautions to lower the possibility of theft or spoiling.

Financial reporting controls

Establish protocols for producing timely and accurate financial reports and statements on a regular basis, such as once every two weeks or at the end of the calendar month. Controls over financial reporting guarantee openness and adherence to accounting rules. They also aid in preventing inaccurate or false financial statements.

Data security restrictions

Use encryption, access restrictions, and cybersecurity measures to prevent unauthorized access to sensitive financial data. It's a good idea to hire a technology services company to keep on retainer, because they'll not only put in a security system but also update security procedures often to handle new threats and weaknesses that never stop coming.

Finding Technology Solutions

There are plenty of software solutions out there to help your new business organize your finances and manage your employees' time, and each one has its own set of features, good things, and not-so-good things. You may have already started looking but if you're overwhelmed about where to start, this section is a good place to get your bearings.

We talk briefly about many of the popular software packages available today for managing your finances, payroll, and time management from B to Z. In each section, we give you a brief description of what the software does, the pros and cons, and then provide the company's website URL for you to access if you think one or more of these solutions are worth more research.

TIP

If you have the online version of the book, feel free to click on each URL to open it in your browser.

Budgyt

Budgyt is as advertised: It's financial forecasting and budgeting software for thorough planning of your budget.

» **Pros:** Beneficial for startups on a tight budget.

» **Cons:** Budgyt may be too specialized when your business in the startup phase.

» **Website:** https://budgyt.com/

Expensify

Expensify tracks and reports expenses through the use of automation and integrations.

>> **Pros:** Easily manages expenses and connects with accounting software.

>> **Cons:** High transaction volumes may not be suitable for the pricing.

>> **Website:** https://www.expensify.com/

FreshBooks

Designed with small businesses in mind, FreshBooks shines at time tracking, expenditure management, and invoicing.

>> **Pros:** Easy to use, excellent for managing expenses and invoicing.

>> **Cons:** Doesn't have sophisticated accounting functions for bigger startups.

>> **Website:** https://www.freshbooks.com/

Gusto

Gusto provides HR and payroll software to make tax compliance and employee-related activities easier.

>> **Pros:** Simplifies HR and payroll procedures.

>> **Cons:** Gusto is only payroll and HR-related, so you need to use it along with an accounting solution.

>> **Website:** https://gusto.com/

Microsoft Excel

Spreadsheet program with great flexibility for data analysis, modeling, and financial applications.

>> **Pros:** Adaptable, widely accessible, and reasonably priced.

>> **Cons:** Doesn't have the real-time features and automation of specialized accounting software.

>> **Website:** https://www.microsoft.com/en-us/microsoft-365/excel

QuickBooks

QuickBooks is the most popular software package out there. It's all-inclusive with financial reporting, tracking expenses, invoicing, time tracking, and more.

» **Pros:** Pretty easy to use and extensively supported by accountants and tax professionals.

» **Cons:** You may find that the price of advanced versions is somewhat costly.

» **Website:** https://quickbooks.intuit.com/

Sage Intacct

Advanced reporting and automation available through cloud-based financial management for larger startups.

» **Pros:** Strong financial reporting and automation.

» **Cons:** Expensive and possibly too complicated for smaller firms.

» **Website:** https://www.sage.com/en-us/sage-business-cloud/intacct/

Swell

Free accounting software with all the necessary functions, such as scanning receipts and creating invoices.

» **Pros:** Free version available, and it can scan receipts.

» **Cons:** Swell doesn't have all sophisticated features and the free version contains advertisements.

» **Website:** https://swellsystem.com/features/accounting/

Xero

Xero offers strong bank reconciliation and integrations and is also easy to use.

» **Pros:** Comprehensive third-party app integrations, strong reporting, and ease of use.

>> **Cons:** You may find the cost of advanced features to be a bit steep.

>> **Website:** https://www.xero.com/us/

Zoho Books

Zoho app connectors and a feature-rich accounting program with an easy-to-use interface.

>> **Pros:** Easy to use and compatible with other Zoho apps.

>> **Cons:** If you're looking for advanced accounting features now or in the future, you may find Zoho Books unable to meet your needs.

>> **Website:** https://www.zoho.com/us/books/

» **Understanding how to optimize cash flow and manage working capital**

» **Leveraging professional expertise**

Chapter **17**

Budgeting and Cash Flow: Keeping Your Startup Running

Y ou may have arrived at this chapter in something approaching crisis mode, because effective cash flow management and budgeting are the two main pillars supporting your startup's financial stability, and you may find those pillars look more like the game of Jenga than pieces of cut marble.

That's why we're here to help you make yourself and your team expert with managing your finances, and we start by telling you about best practices for both budgeting and managing your cash flow so you can better avoid roadblocks or get over the current roadblock you're facing now.

So, this chapter is set up for you both as a review of what you need to know and a checklist of what you need to do. Sit around with your team members with your books in hand (you did buy copies for everyone, right?) and talk about these issues to make sure you're all in agreement about what's been done, what needs to be done, and who needs to do each task.

A great starting point is the Small Business Budget Template and Planning Guide shown in Figure 17-1. You can find and download this Excel template from our book page on the Dummies.com website so you can fill it in with your team.

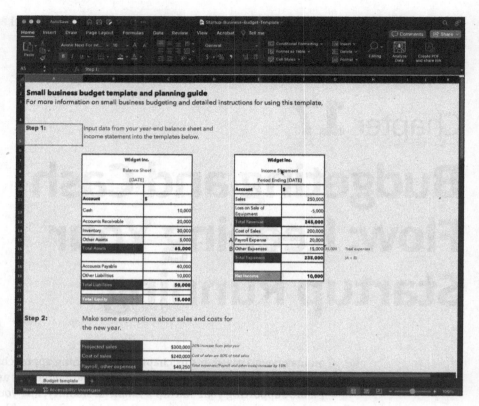

FIGURE 17-1:
A glimpse of the
Small Business
Budget Template
and Planning
Guide.

Five-by-Five Budgeting

When you're working out your budget for various lengths of time, such as every month, every six months, and every calendar year, you need to have command in five areas for your money to communicate clearly to you and your team.

» **Strategic planning:** An effective budget is a strategic instrument that charts the financial trajectory of your firm, not just a means of monitoring revenue and outlays.

Start by establishing precise, well-defined financial targets that are in line with your company's objectives. Establish your financial objectives, including your desired profit margins, cost reduction targets, and revenue targets. Then you can do what you do best and make good, informed decisions.

>> **Expense control:** Budgeting gives you command over the costs associated with your startup. It entails dividing costs into fixed (rent, salary) and variable (marketing, office supplies) categories and establishing spending caps for each. Keep a close eye on your actual expenditure in comparison to your planned spending to spot areas where you can make savings or reallocate resources.

TIP

Book time in your calendar regularly (for example, once a month) to review your expenses and take notes before and after each review about what you're looking for — especially red flags.

>> **Risk reduction:** You should account for unanticipated expenses in your budget. Set aside a certain amount of money each month for an emergency fund that will help with unforeseen costs and revenue shortages. This planning lowers risk and insulates your startup from unexpected financial blows.

>> **Prioritizing investing in your business:** A carefully thought-out budget aids in asset prioritization. Evaluate the effect of each proposed expense on revenue growth and overall company expansion. Invest resources on projects that will yield the best *return on investment,* a term that's far better known by its acronym *ROI*. This guarantees that your startup makes the most of its funding.

>> **Practical estimates:** Realistic estimates are necessary for budgeting. Your budget should be based on precise data and market analysis. Steer clear of overly optimistic estimates because they may cause financial burden and disappointment. A realistic prediction gives you attainable goals and a solid foundation on which to assess the financial performance of your startup.

REMEMBER

Goals and targets should be considered adjustable based on new circumstances. Always feel good about going back to your budget and adjusting it as you learn more. There's always a bit of guessing, even if it's educated guessing.

The Best Ways to Manage Cash Flow

Your investors will run away like the gallant king and knights from the rabbit in *Monty Python and the Holy Grail* if they even get a hint that you can't handle your company money. After all, they'll figure you won't be around for much longer, anyway.

So, you only get one shot to show that you can not only manage your cash flow to keep the lights on and people paid, but that you've also used that money to keep your business growing. Here are six areas to cover with your investors to assuage any concerns they have about working with you.

>> **Assurance of solvency:** Regularly evaluate the liquidity of your startup to ensure solvency. Keep track of your cash inflows and outflows to make sure you always have enough to pay your bills. Make a cash flow statement that shows you where your money is going to be in the next few days, weeks, or months.

>> **On-time payments:** Potential investors will want you to show that you give priority to paying creditors, suppliers, and staff on time. If paying people is one of the ten other hats you wear upon your head, set aside regular time blocks to pay bills so you never lose track of them.

Showing investors that you use cash flow forecasting and that your past forecasts show that you've had enough money on hand will keep your investors talking with you.

Not making payments on time might strain your relationships inside and outside the company and result in fines or interest.

>> **Making the most of chances:** A healthy cash flow puts your startup in a position to take advantage of growth prospects. Having cash on hand allows you to take quick decisions when it comes to investing in research and development (R&D), acquiring assets, or entering new markets. To take advantage of these chances, make sure you show your investors that your cash flow is constantly positive. If it's not, be prepared to explain why those negative numbers happened and why they don't mean you'll have those issues again.

>> **Debt control:** Good cash flow management is essential to debt repayment. Cash flow is necessary in order to pay interest on a regular basis and, if at all possible, to reduce principal. If you don't, you risk damaging your credit and getting into debt, and nobody wants that.

>> **Planning short and long:** Cash flow management takes into account both immediate requirements and long-term viability, and investors will want to see that you're paying attention to both realms. As you prioritize paying your bills on time, don't forget to set aside funds for longer-term goals like increasing your cash reserves, growing your business, or introducing new goods and services.

>> **Building self-belief:** A well-managed cash flow gives lenders, investors, and members of your staff confidence in your startup. Building confidence and credibility goes hand-in-glove with proving your ability to manage daily financial operations effectively and stay in a positive cash position.

Additional Cash Flow and Budgeting Considerations

Startup founders may improve their ability to handle their finances and successfully negotiate the opportunities and problems that present themselves in this area by keeping these extra factors in mind.

>> **Adaptability in planning:** Although making a budget is necessary, it's also critical to maintain flexibility because we live in real life and things change. Rapid changes might happen because of market conditions, client needs, and unforeseen events. Be ready to reallocate funds to address new issues or priorities when needed, adjusting your budget as needed. What's more, if you've ever had to adapt because of just such an shock, show your investors what you did, what you learned, and how you've applied your experience to your "in emergency break glass" plans.

>> **Track KPIs:** Include key performance indicators (KPIs) in the cash flow and budgeting processes. If you're not sure what those are, they include gross margin, churn rate, client lifetime value, and acquisition cost. These KPIs offer insightful information about your startup's sustainability and financial health, and your investors will look at them closely.

>> **Leverage cash flow forecasting tools:** If you don't have software you're using for cash flow forecasting, that will likely make your investors' faces look like a child's when they get a food they hate. With the use of these tools, you may model numerous situations, evaluate the effects of different choices, and obtain a more precise image of your cash position going forward.

>> **Emergency preparedness:** Investors will check to see if you've budgeted for contingencies to ensure you're ready for anything unforeseen. Determine possible hazards and put plans in place to lessen their effect on your money. This can entail opening credit lines or keeping a bigger cash reserve.

>> **Strategies for managing debt:** Here's another area your investor's investigative team will expect to see: a well-defined debt management plan. Consider if it makes sense to take on debt in order to take advantage of growth prospects or if paying off debt should come first. Be aware of the conditions of your loans, such as interest rates and payback dates, because your investors will ask about those.

>> **Frequent evaluation of finances:** Arrange for frequent financial assessments to evaluate the performance and trends of your cash flow. Determine whether there are any differences between your expected and actual outcomes. This continuous evaluation helps you to make wise corrections and improvements, and potential investors will expect those assessments as starting points for a question and answer session with you and your team.

>> **Expert counsel:** Take into account getting expert financial counsel. Their knowledge can assist you in making wise financial choices, and will help put prospective investors' minds at ease with the knowledge that you're humble. We talk more about leveraging professional expertise later in this chapter.

>> **Streamlined processes:** Adopt lean operations, because you don't want to show potential investors that you've had to cut back large expenses like headcount because you grew too fast. Always be on the lookout for methods to streamline your startup's operations and cut costs without (and here's the trick) burning people and yourself out. Your cash flow and overall financial health can be positively impacted by operational efficiency.

>> **Terms of invoices and payments:** Be mindful of your invoice and the terms of payment that you have with suppliers and consumers, because your investors certainly will when they come calling for your books. When at all possible, negotiate advantageous terms. To enhance your cash flow, think about providing incentives to clients that pay early.

>> **Tax guidance:** Work with an experienced tax professional to put tax planning techniques into practice to reduce the tax liabilities of your startup. Examine the tax breaks and credits accessible to small companies, because effective tax planning might release funds for expansion. Oh, and by the way, if you're working with a tax pro, investors will not only demand that you get one, they'll also be even more rigorous in their review of your past tax returns.

TIP

Set aside taxes you need to pay in a separate bank account so you don't think the money is available for spending.

>> **Statements of cash flow:** Construct and maintain cash flow statements on a monthly or quarterly basis; we recommend monthly in the beginning. Take into account projected expenses such as rent, salary, and supplier payments, together with anticipated revenue from loans, investments, and sales.

These statements help you make wise decisions and lower your stress. You'll definitely start breathing faster when your investors ask for your cash flow statements and you don't have one. (Accounting software that we covered in Chapter 16 makes this easy.)

>> **Train your brains:** Train your employees so they know about cash flow management and budgeting either by hiring an experienced trainer or by taking online courses. Even if employees don't directly interact with budgets and forecasting, they need to know how finances work so any team member can identify financial issues that come up in their line of work and let others know.

A financially accountable culture will help you keep your business lean, help your business grow, and help attract investors like bears to honey or whatever trite metaphor you prefer.

Stay in the Flow

Just as monitoring your exercise and diet routine is the best way to ensure you are doing what you need to get the results you want, you need to do the same with your business finances to keep it in top shape. And just like your personal trainers who tell you to keep going for ten more reps (without the garish training outfits), we have our plan to build on what we told you earlier in this chapter to keep your ledger fit.

TIP

>> **Managing invoices:** To create invoices fast and precisely, use specialized invoicing software. Indicate in detail the conditions of payment (net 30 or net 60, for example) and add late fines for unpaid invoices.

Make sure your invoicing software has an automated reminder system to increase the frequency of reminders, which can greatly increase your timely cash flow.

>> **Negotiate payment terms where you can:** Ask suppliers for longer payment periods; this is especially important for non-essential products and services. Try to find net payment conditions, like Net 60, which indicates that money must be paid within 60 days of receiving the products or services.

>> **Control the receivables:** Use an accounts receivable aging report to find invoices that are past due. To encourage timely payments, send polite reminders and follow up with calls or emails.

>> **Manage your inventory wisely:** To cut carrying expenses, use just-in-time (JIT) inventory management. To get rid of extra inventory, identify slow-moving items and think about offering discounts or promotions.

>> **Control the payroll:** Agree on supplier contracts that match your cash flow cycles with the periods of payment. Refrain from making early payments unless there are considerable savings.

>> **Cushion for cash flow:** Regularly set aside a percentage of profits in a money market or separate company savings account. Develop a cash reserve that can cover operational costs for at least three to six months.

TIP

>> **Cost management:** Examine monthly spending carefully. Sort them into important and non-essential categories. Think about cutting back on unnecessary spending or renegotiating contracts.

>> **Turnover of inventory:** Divide the cost of goods sold (COGS) by the average inventory value to find the inventory turnover ratio. Aim to accelerate the sale of inventories in order to raise this ratio.

If you're not familiar with COGS or other financing terms, the Investopedia website has a good glossary to become expert here: https://www.investopedia.com/financial-term-dictionary-4769738.

>> **Options for short-term financing:** Look into business credit cards, invoice finance, and revolving credit from respectable lenders. (Respectable is the key term here, because there are plenty of disreputable ones who will try to make your acquaintance.) Ensure you comprehend the conditions, interest rates, and costs related to these choices.

>> **Client advancements:** Offer special discounts or perks to entice clients to make deposits or advance payments. To promote this habit, make sure that the benefits of prepayment are made clear.

>> **Supplier agreements:** Build trusting connections with suppliers to secure volume-based pricing, early payment reductions, or preferential terms for payments.

>> **Simplify your processes:** Review the process to find any inefficiencies. If at all possible, automate tasks to cut down on errors and manual labor.

>> **Analyze capital investments:** Conduct a thorough cost-benefit analysis before making a purchase of new machinery or technology. To save money, think about financing or leasing if the company offers those options.

>> **Debt control:** Keep an accurate record of interest rates and loan payment schedules. If refinancing becomes an option and lowers loan rates or improves cash flow management, it's time to drill down and see if you can find a better deal.

>> **Projections of cash flow:** Update your cash flow estimates frequently in light of current information. Forecasts should be adjusted as necessary to account for seasonality and market fluctuations.

>> **Fund for emergencies:** Set aside a certain amount of your financial reserves as an emergency fund, intended only for unforeseen events like equipment failures or downturns in the economy.

>> **Planning scenarios:** Create thorough backup plans for different budgetary situations. For instance, budget for a 20 percent drop in sales or an unexpected increase in costs. Having these plans in place will enable you to respond quickly when things are unclear.

Leveraging Professional Expertise

Beyond merely ensuring compliance, and little things like maybe staying out of prison, hiring experts in the financial and legal facets of startup funding gives you the edge in earning the right investors:

>> **Compliance and financial accuracy:** Accountants make sure that all of your financial records are up to date, error-free, and clearly kept so that you can see the financial picture with confidence. They make sure your financial statements comply with all legal standards and keep up with financial legislation.

>> **Financial strategy and planning:** Financial advisors collaborate with you to create a customized financial plan that supports the objectives and expansion strategies of your startup. They assist you in allocating resources effectively and in making well-informed financial, investment, and spending decisions.

>> **Tax efficiency:** To reduce your tax bill, tax specialists find opportunities for tax savings and deductions that are unique to your startup. By making sure your startup complies with tax regulations, they help you avoid fines and legal problems.

>> **Legal knowledge:** Lawyers safeguard your rights and make sure agreements are enforced by drafting, reviewing, and negotiating contracts. They guarantee that your legal documents and finance transactions comply with all applicable laws and regulations.

>> **Investor self-assurance:** Investors are reassured that their money will be managed appropriately by a group of professionals who demonstrate a commitment to financial transparency. Startups that exhibit a dedication to sound financial and legal procedures are more likely to win over investors.

>> **Saving time:** You can concentrate on core business operations, such as product development and sales, by assigning financial and legal chores to others. Because of their experience, professionals can finish work more quickly, which saves you the one thing you can never get back: your time.

>> **Network access:** You can broaden your network by utilizing the established contacts that financial advisors and attorneys may have with possible investors or funding sources. They have the ability to recommend you to other experts or service providers who can help your startup even more.

>> **Mitigation of risk:** By assisting in the identification of possible legal and financial issues, professionals enable proactive risk-management techniques. By following their advice, there is a lower chance of expensive errors, legal action, or monetary losses.

>> **Monetary education:** Dealing with experts can be instructive because they can help you understand legal and financial issues and enable you to make wise judgments. Your knowledge will continue to be useful long after this financing round ends.

>> **Peace of mind:** Having peace of mind and less worry and anxiety comes from knowing that professionals are managing your financial and legal affairs. It frees you from the burden of worrying about intricate legal or financial matters so you can concentrate on expanding your startup.

Leveraging Potential Expertise

We have our Captain Obvious hats on again: Be sure to carefully screen possible advisors before interacting with them. This includes examining references, confirming qualifications, going over terms and costs, and evaluating their experience working with businesses.

All good, you say, but where? You know we have your back, and the following is a comprehensive list of locations where you can obtain expert assistance from financial advisors, attorneys, accountants, and tax specialists with experience working with startups:

>> **Conferences and networking events:** Participate in industry-specific conferences, meetups, and events where experts with an emphasis on startups are frequently present. Start by checking the Meetup website (https://www.meetup.com/) to find events in your area if you haven't done so already as you search for investors.

>> **Accelerators and incubators for startups:** Enroll in startup incubator or accelerator programs. These initiatives frequently include professional networks that offer advice and assistance to firms enrolled in them.

>> **Internet-based listings:** Look for experts with startup-related experience by using professional networking websites such as Crunchbase, AngelList, and LinkedIn. Sort based on experience and region.

>> **Expert associations:** Search online for organizations like the Certified Financial Planner Board of Standards (CFP Board), American Bar Association (ABA), and American Institute of CPAs (AICPA). CFPs are also in 27 countries and territories around the world. These groups frequently have directories of their members that include information on their specializations.

- >> **Connect with attorney sites:** Check out websites like LegalMatch (https://www.legalmatch.com/) and UpCounsel (https://www.upcounsel.com/), which can help you find seasoned attorneys. When you explain your needs, attorneys will come up with suggestions.

- >> **Networks of financial advisors:** To connect with financial advisors who specialize in startups, take into consideration networks such as the XY Planning Network and NAPFA (National Association of Personal Financial Advisors). Financial advisors are also in other countries, such as the Financial Planning Association of Canada.

- >> **Suggestions from other entrepreneurs:** When you build up your network of startup founders online and/or in person, ask them for referrals. They can have insightful knowledge about experts who delivered top-notch services.

- >> **Collaborative spaces and startup hubs:** Investigate innovation centers, coworking spaces, and startup hubs. Many of these places are home to experts or businesses that specialize in providing startup services.

- >> **Platforms for online freelancing:** Make use of Internet freelance marketplaces such as Upwork (https://www.upwork.com/) and Freelancer (https://www.freelancer.com/) to locate experts, such as financial advisors, attorneys, and accountants. These sites also allow you to examine their past work and biographies.

- >> **Forums and associations for business:** Participate in online startup communities, forums, or communities on sites like Quora or Reddit's r/startups forum. Proficient entrepreneurs frequently recommend professional services to one another.

- >> **Connect with universities and law schools in your area:** Get in touch with local legal schools and universities. Certain organizations provide clinics or initiatives that give entrepreneurs free or inexpensive legal and financial guidance.

- >> **Investors in angels and venture capital:** Ask about their network of specialists who work with startups when you speak with venture capitalists or angel investors. They might know useful people.

- >> **Websites dedicated to startups:** Go to websites like Gust (https://gust.com/), which provide access to expert services and act as a bridge between investors and companies.

- >> **New venture advisory services:** Research advice companies that focus on helping startups such as Freelancer as we talked about a few bullets ago. Some of these companies match upstarts with experts suited to their requirements.

>> **CPA societies and bar associations:** Look for directories of certified attorneys and accountants with startup experience by contacting your local bar association or CPA society.

>> **Suggestion-based websites:** Check out directories and referral websites tailored for professionals in startup environments. Reputable advisors in the startup scene are listed on these networks.

>> **Organizations that support startups:** Make contact with groups like SCORE or Small Business Development Centers (SBDCs), which are devoted to helping entrepreneurs. They frequently have the means to put companies in touch with experts in their field.

Chapter 18

Analyzing Financial Reports and Making Informed Decisions

When you're reading financial statements on your road to prosperity, it can often feel like traveling in a foreign country and being unable to speak the language. But you're reading this chapter because you bought it or you're thinking of buying it (we'd like that) and you want to translate these documents into words you can understand.

Come with us as we delve into the three fundamental pillars of financial reporting: the balance sheet, income statement, and cash flow statement. We expose their secrets and reveal the stories they tell about your business. And we know that you want to stay in the express lane, so we tell you what the statements are and what you and your team need to understand and show to potential investors.

After we finish your checklist, you'll need to set up your financial metrics so you and your team know what's going on and make sound decisions. Yes, that dinging sound means you guessed right — potential investors will expect to see this information when they're kicking the tires on your business.

Making Your List, Checking It Twice

Your mindset is your greatest advantage, and when it comes to financial statements you should view them in your mind as a tool for storytelling, not just a collection of numbers. The narrative you reveal can be used to communicate your company's progress, attract investors, and motivate your team. So, this section outlines the script for your story to get your team in the right mindset and get prospective investors excited to work with you.

REMEMBER

As you move down the road, transparency and open communication about your financial performance with stakeholders is critical. Regular reporting and clear explanations will build trust and foster a culture of financial responsibility early in the life of your business.

The big three statements

It's very simple: You have to know your startup's financial health. You need to know where it stands at all times in order to get to the next milestone, the milestone after that, and eventually your final destination. To do this, you have to pay particular attention to three statements on your financial dashboard: the balance sheet, income statement, and cash flow statement.

The balance sheet

The balance sheet is a snapshot of your startup's financial standing at a specific point in time, and when you review it with your potential investors, you'll need to cover these four things:

>> Dive into specific line items like current assets (cash, inventory), non-current assets (equipment), current liabilities (accounts payable), non-current liabilities (loans).

>> Explain the concept of working capital and its importance for short-term liquidity.

>> Discuss the difference between book value and market value, and how it affects the balance sheet.

>> Illustrate the balance sheet equation and its implications for financial health.

The income statement

The income statement, often referred to as the profit and loss statement, reveals how effectively your startup is converting its operations into profits. Your potential investors will want to do three things when you sit down with them to look over your income statement:

>> Break down revenue categories (product sales, service fees) and expense categories (cost of goods sold, operating expenses).

>> Explain key profit margins like gross margin, operating margin, and net income margin.

>> Analyze the impact of different costs on profitability and identify areas for cost reduction.

The cash flow statement

The cash flow statement is a crucial financial tool that's key to understanding your startup's liquidity, solvency, and overall financial health. When you sit down with your potential investors and present your cash flow statement, do these four things:

>> Explain the difference between cash flow from operations, investing activities, and financing activities.

>> Illustrate how the cash flow statement links to the balance sheet and income statement.

>> Analyze the cash conversion cycle and its impact on cash flow management.

>> Discuss the importance of maintaining a positive cash flow for ongoing operations and growth.

Diving deeper: Key metrics and ratios

In the fast-paced world of startup business, keeping a keen eye on key financial metrics is vital for steering your venture towards success. Understanding and effectively tracking the five metrics we talk about in this section will empower you to communicate your startup's performance to stakeholders and potential investors.

Profit margin

Profit margin gives you and your potential investors a clear perspective on your business's ability to manage costs and generate earnings. To illustrate these perspectives during your presentation to investors, focus on these three things:

>> Explain how profit margin varies across industries and stages of growth.

>> Discuss the relationship between profit margin and pricing strategy, cost management, and efficiency.

>> Provide examples of how to improve profit margin through various strategies.

Revenue growth rate

Revenue growth rate helps you gauge your startup's financial trajectory, assess the effectiveness of growth strategies, and provides a benchmark for future projections and investor expectations. Your potential investors will expect you to cover the following three revenue growth rate topics:

>> Analyze sustainable versus unsustainable growth rates and potential risks associated with rapid growth.

>> Discuss the importance of understanding the drivers of revenue growth (customer acquisition, retention, and so on).

>> Provide examples of how to track and measure revenue growth trends effectively.

Burn rate

Burn rate is a crucial metric for startups, particularly in their early stages, as it provides insights into how long a startup can sustain its operations before needing additional funding. When you review how long your startup can keep going, do the following:

>> Discuss the impact of burn rate on your runway (time until cash depletion) and fundraising needs.

>> Provide strategies for extending your runway and managing cash flow effectively.

Debt-to-equity ratio

The debt-to-equity ratio provides valuable insights into how a company is leveraging debt versus equity to finance its operations and growth. Your potential investors will want you to show those insights by doing the following three things:

>> Explain the relationship between debt financing and financial risk.

>> Discuss industry benchmarks for debt-to-equity ratios and their implications for investors.

>> Show understanding of how to manage your startup's debt levels and maintain a healthy financial structure.

Current ratio

The current ratio measures your startup's ability to cover short-term liabilities with current assets. Focus on the following three topics to show potential investors that you have a solid understanding of the current ratio and what it means:

>> Explain the importance of having sufficient short-term assets to cover short-term liabilities.

>> Discuss the relationship between current ratio and operational liquidity.

>> Provide strategies for improving your current ratio and ensuring short-term financial stability.

Context matters: Compare and contrast

In the intricate world of startup finance, understanding your company's performance in isolation is not enough; context is key. This section delves into the critical practice of benchmarking your startup against various yardsticks.

Industry benchmarks

Industry benchmarks serve as vital signposts for startups; they provide a framework to gauge performance against standardized metrics within your industry. Potential investors want to know how you fit within your industry, so do these three things:

>> Explain the importance of benchmarking your financial performance against industry standards.

>> Provide resources for accessing industry benchmarks and reports.

>> Discuss the limitations of relying solely on benchmarks and the need for individual analysis.

Competitor analysis

Competitor analysis is a strategic tool that allows your startups to gain critical insights into their rivals' operations, strategies, and performance. When your potential investors ask you how you'll stake out your unique position in the market, talk about these three things:

>> Explain how to compare your financial performance to your competitors.

>> Discuss the importance of understanding competitor strengths and weaknesses.

>> Provide strategies for using competitor analysis to inform your own financial decisions.

Historical performance

If you don't know how your startup has performed over time, you won't understand its growth trajectory. What's more, you can't identify patterns and trends over time. That shows potential investors that you can't plan, can't set goals, and can't make adjustments. You think investors will put down their hard-earned money for that? Instead, during your presentation, show them you know what's going on:

>> Explain the importance of tracking your own historical financial trends.

>> Discuss the use of financial ratios and metrics to monitor progress toward goals.

>> Provide tips for creating effective financial dashboards and tracking progress over time.

From analysis to decisions

You've heard about the term *paralysis by analysis*, and we've written this section to help you tell potential investors how you actually make decisions in four key areas.

Resource allocation

You need to tell investors that you can allocate resources effectively so your business runs smoothly and can reach its milestones. To do that, do these three things in your investor presentation:

>> Explain how to allocate resources based on profitability, growth potential, and financial constraints.

>> Provide examples of using financial data to inform investment decisions and budget allocation.

>> Discuss the importance of setting clear financial goals and metrics to track progress.

Pricing strategy

Pricing your product or service correctly is a crucial element of your business model, because if you don't get it right you could have trouble making money and gaining traction in the market. These are the things you need to talk about with your investors to give them confidence that the price is right:

>> Explain how to use profit margins and cost analysis to inform pricing decisions.

>> Discuss the impact of competitive pricing and customer value perception on pricing strategies.

>> Provide examples of using financial data to optimize pricing for profitability and market competitiveness.

Cost control

You can't get your business to your next milestone, let alone all the way to glory, unless you control costs. Potential investors want to make sure that you're making the best use of your money and not spending it on what they see (and hopefully you see) as frivolous things, so in your presentation, key in on these three topics:

>> Explain different methods for identifying and reducing unnecessary expenses.

>> Discuss the importance of cost-benefit analysis and prioritizing value creation.

>> Provide examples of implementing cost-saving measures based on financial analysis.

Growth strategy

Growth strategy is the road map that guides your startup's efforts to do all the cool things: Expand its operations, increase market share, and achieve long-term success. Potential investors want your company to grow, too, or they won't finance you. So, here's what to talk about during your investor presentation:

>> Explain how to align your growth strategy with your financial resources and market opportunities.

>> Discuss the importance of considering funding options, cash flow needs, and return on investment when making growth decisions.

>> Provide examples of using financial data to inform expansion plans, new product development, and market entry strategies.

>> Emphasize the importance of financial agility and the ability to adapt your strategy based on market changes and performance data.

Even more important reports

If you thought that was all, you have even more homework to do. Your potential investors will ask you to prepare more reports. From showing that you understand how long cash reserves last to keeping your board up to date, this section tells you everything you need. (And here's a bonus: They'll help you keep track of your business performance, so you'll sleep better at night.)

Cash flow projections and runway analysis

These reports help you understand how long your current cash reserves can sustain your operations. Knowing your runway allows you to plan for future funding needs and make informed decisions about growth and expansion.

By analyzing different funding scenarios, you can prepare for potential fundraising rounds and negotiate terms more effectively.

Unit economics

Understanding the cost and revenue associated with each unit reveals areas for potential cost reduction and pricing optimization. This can improve profitability and make your business more attractive to investors.

Unit economics also helps you identify and scale profitable product features or services, leading to more efficient resource allocation.

Break-even analysis

Knowing your break-even point helps you set realistic growth targets and understand your minimum revenue requirement for sustainability. This allows you to make strategic decisions about pricing, marketing, and cost control.

Burn rate by expense category

This report reveals which expenses are driving your burn rate, enabling you to identify areas for potential cost reduction. Prioritizing high-impact expenses can extend your runway and improve overall financial health.

Competitive intelligence reports

Understanding your competitors' financial performance and strategies can help you identify potential threats and opportunities. Benchmarking your metrics against your competitors can reveal areas where you need to improve.

Competitive intelligence also helps you develop a differentiated strategy, avoid making the same mistakes as your rivals, and move quickly to win the big customer.

Scenario planning and sensitivity analysis

These exercises prepare you for potential risks and unforeseen circumstances. By modeling different economic scenarios and strategic decisions, you can make informed choices in the face of uncertainty.

Scenario planning can help you identify potential triggers for fundraising, develop contingency plans, and build resilience into your business model.

Board of directors reports and quarterly updates

Keeping your board informed about your financial progress builds trust and transparency. Regular reports demonstrate accountability and showcase your commitment to achieving your goals.

You should also use board reports to highlight key achievements, address challenges honestly, and seek guidance to help your business overcome roadblocks.

Metrics, KPIs, and You

You may have seen the acronym KPI and been left scratching your head, but key performance indicators (KPIs) are just like the dashboard on your car that tells you what's happening in your business. Not all KPIs are necessary and will depend on your specific business model and goals.

By carefully selecting and tracking the right metrics, you can gain valuable insights into your startup's performance, make informed decisions, and optimize your path to success.

You can use KPI dashboards in spreadsheet software like Microsoft Excel or using tools like HubSpot or ClickUp. Figure 18-1 shows a sample of what a KPI dashboard looks like.

Your KPI dashboard should have the ability to choose different periods of time for viewing your KPIs to inform you about how to adjust your KPIs as your business evolves and your priorities change (see Figure 18-2).

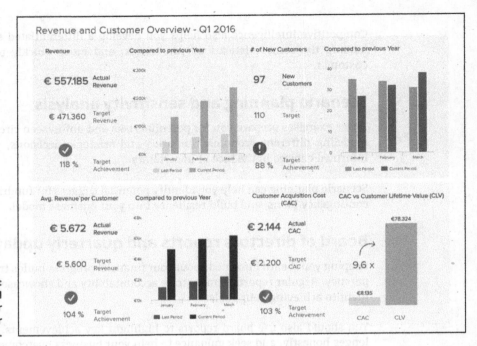

FIGURE 18-1:
A sample KPI dashboard for the first quarter of 2016.

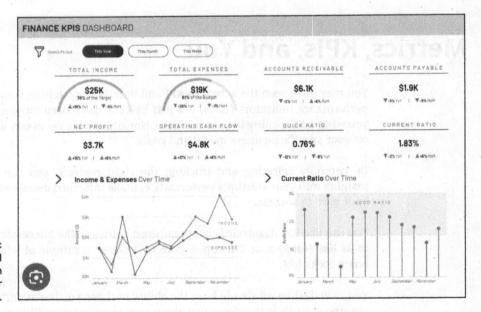

FIGURE 18-2:
A sample KPI dashboard with data shown for the current year.

Key performance indicators (KPIs)

So now that you know how to track KPIs using software tools, what exactly do you have to track? Here's an exhaustive list of KPIs in a variety of categories so you can put a check mark next to each KPI that you should track. (If you need permission to write in your own book, we give our seal of approval.)

REMEMBER

Be mindful that your investors are likely to have KPIs that they view as important that you will have to measure and report on.

Financial performance

The first area to measure with KPIs is (you guessed it) financial performance. Specifically, you need to measure five areas:

>> **Gross margin:** Monitor the percentage of revenue remaining after covering direct costs to assess profitability and cost-efficiency.

>> **Net burn rate:** Track the rate at which your cash reserves are depleting to understand your runway and potential funding needs.

>> **Customer lifetime value to customer acquisition cost (CLTV/CAC) ratio:** This ratio compares the value of your customers to the cost of acquiring them to assess the sustainability of your business model.

>> **Free cash flow:** The cash remaining after all operating expenses and investments are paid to gauge your financial health and ability to generate sustainable cash flow. Give yourself a well-deserved treat if you realized that this is what investors will look at closely.

>> **Monthly recurring revenue (MRR):** MRR provides predictable revenue and valuable insights into customer churn and growth. Tracking MRR helps you forecast future cash flow and assess the stability of your business model.

Customer acquisition and engagement

Customer acquisition and engagement KPIs are pivotal metrics that you'll rely on to assess their ability to attract, retain, and nurture customers. Here are the most common ones that potential investors will pay attention to:

>> **Customer acquisition cost (CAC):** Understanding your CAC helps you optimize marketing spend and allocate resources effectively. Tracking CAC over time can reveal if your acquisition strategies are becoming more efficient or more costly over time.

>> **Customer lifetime value (CLTV):** CLTV helps you assess the long-term profitability of your customers. High CLTV indicates strong customer relationships and potential for recurring revenue. Knowing your CLTV allows you to tailor retention strategies and prioritize high-value customers.

>> **Net promoter score (NPS):** NPS reveals customer loyalty and satisfaction, providing crucial feedback for improving your product and service offerings. High NPS can boost brand reputation and attract new customers through word-of-mouth marketing.

>> **Customer acquisition channel effectiveness:** Track the performance of different acquisition channels such as paid advertising, organic traffic, and referrals to optimize your marketing spend.

>> **Conversion rate:** Monitor the percentage of visitors who convert into customers at various stages of your funnel, such as when a visitor signs up and purchases your product or service, to identify areas for improvement.

>> **Customer churn rate:** Measure the percentage of customers who cancel or stop using your product/service over a period. Analyzing reasons for churn can inform retention strategies.

>> **Customer engagement metrics:** Track metrics like session duration, feature usage, and repeat visits to understand how engaged your customers are and identify opportunities for deeper interaction.

Product and service performance

You need to set up the following KPIs to evaluate the effectiveness, quality, and reception of your products and/or services. Without them, you don't know how you're meeting your customer needs and change your offerings to give you a competitive advantage. So, potential investors will want to see that you've implemented the following KPIs:

>> **Active users:** Monitor the number of users actively engaging with your product/service to gauge its overall adoption and user base growth.

>> **Average revenue per user (ARPU):** Track the average revenue generated from each user to assess pricing strategies and monetization effectiveness.

>> **Product features usage:** Analyze which features are most popular and least used to inform product and/or service road map decisions and prioritize development efforts.

>> **Customer satisfaction score (CSAT):** Gather feedback through surveys or direct interactions to measure customer satisfaction and identify areas for improving your product and/or service as well as your relationships with customers.

Operational efficiency

Startups use operational efficiency KPIs to assess and streamline their internal processes. Not only do potential investors want to see numbers that show you're doing well, we bet you do, too. So, here are the KPIs to use:

>> **Customer support cost per ticket:** Track the average cost of resolving customer support tickets to measure efficiency and identify potential cost-saving opportunities.

>> **Employee productivity metrics:** Monitor key performance indicators for different roles such as sales calls made, and support tickets resolved to ensure efficient resource allocation and team productivity.

>> **Inventory turnover rate:** Measure how quickly your inventory is sold and replaced to optimize inventory management and avoid unnecessary holding costs.

>> **Marketing ROI:** Track the return on investment for your marketing efforts to ensure they are driving profitable customer acquisition.

Technology-related KPIs

For tech startups, success hinges not only on financial performance but also on the effectiveness of their technology and its impact on users. By tracking the technology-related KPIs and metrics here just for you in this section, you can gain valuable insights into the performance, user experience, and growth potential of your startup.

REMEMBER

The specific KPIs you choose will depend on your unique technology and business model. Don't hesitate to adapt and refine your metrics as your startup evolves and your technology matures.

Website and app performance

You already know that a website and apps are required to sell your stuff, but if you don't have KPIs for those online assets, how will you know how well they convert engagements into buyers? Potential investors will want to know, too, so here are the KPIs and the data you need to share with your investors during your meetings:

>> **Page load speed:** Monitor how quickly your website or app loads for users, as slow loading times can lead to frustration and abandonment. Aim for consistent, sub-second load times across different devices and network conditions.

- » **Uptime and availability:** Track the percentage of time your website or app is accessible to users. Strive for high uptime (ideally above 99 percent) to ensure reliable service and user trust.

- » **User interface (UI) and user experience (UX) metrics:** Analyze metrics like click-through rates, session duration, and conversion rates to understand how users interact with your platform and identify areas for UI/UX improvements.

- » **Error rates and bug tracking:** Monitor the frequency and severity of errors encountered by users. Implement bug tracking systems to prioritize and fix issues promptly to ensure a smooth user experience and reduce stress for everyone.

- » **Active users and sessions:** Track the number of users actively engaging with your platform and the frequency of their sessions. Analyze trends to identify periods of high engagement and areas for user retention strategies.

- » **Feature adoption and usage:** Monitor how different features within your platform are being used. Identify underused features and consider optimizing them or removing them to improve both the user experience and your company's resource allocation.

- » **Network traffic and bandwidth usage:** Analyze network traffic patterns to understand user activity and resource consumption. Optimize your infrastructure to handle peak traffic and avoid performance bottlenecks.

- » **Social media engagement and sentiment analysis:** Track social media mentions and analyze sentiment to understand user perception of your technology and identify potential areas for improvement.

Software development and innovation

If your company produces software, then there's no question that you have to have KPIs to assess your software efficiency and quality. What's more, you need to track your software projects including the innovative undertaking you may know as skunkworks. So, have the following KPIs set up so you can provide the data to your potential investors:

- » **Development velocity and release cycles:** Monitor the speed and frequency of your development cycles to ensure you're delivering new features and updates regularly. Balance rapid iteration with stability and quality control.

- » **Code coverage and quality metrics:** Analyze code coverage and metrics like bugs per thousand lines of code to assess code quality and identify areas for improvement in development practices.

- » **Technology adoption and trends:** Stay informed about emerging technologies and trends relevant to your industry. Consider incorporating innovative solutions into your platform to maintain a competitive edge.

- » **Experimentation and A/B testing:** Implement A/B testing to compare different features and functions of your website to see what your users like. Then you can use that feedback to help your users get the most out of their experience and engagement.

Chapter **19**

Scaling Up: Funding Strategies for Growth

When you're trying to scale a peak, no matter if it's a hill with a steep slope as in Eric's neighborhood in the Sierra Nevada foothills, or a mountain like Mount Davis in Pennsylvania where Marc lives, you need to be physically able to climb and have the tools needed to get to the top.

Scaling hills and mountains are also harder because humans don't judge distances well and underestimate the time and effort it takes to get the job done. The same is true in your own business, because even though you're excited about scaling your business and you may have heard about doing so from different sources, excitement isn't the right mindset you need to have to, you know, actually grow your business.

If you're going to attract investors, you'll need to show them that you not only have the mindset to scale but you've also actually put that mindset into action. So, if you've come to this chapter champing at the bit to learn how to get bigger *now*, you'll be disappointed. But if you want to get your gear checklist together to make the climb, then grab your hiking stick because you've come to the right place.

Scaling the Mountain

Scaling a successful startup goes beyond securing funding. Although capital fuels growth, it's just one piece of the puzzle. To truly thrive in the scaling phase, entrepreneurs need to focus on several key areas. These are just examples, and the specific details will vary depending on your industry, target audience, and business model.

So, feel free to adapt and expand on these points to create a comprehensive and tailored guide for your business. We've categorized them into three areas: team building, operations, and marketing. And as always, we give you permission (not like you ever needed it) to write notes in the margins next to each bullet point so everyone knows what they need to do to grow.

Team members assemble

You not only need to recruit your team, you also need to keep them engaged and motivated so they stick around because, as you may have heard before, employees don't leave companies — they leave managers.

Recruit A-player talent

It's a long road to reach your ultimate destination, and the only way you'll do that is to bring on the best people who do things better than you. But how do you find those A-listers? Focus on these five areas:

>> **Define your ideal candidate profile:** Identify the skills, experience, and cultural fit needed for each role.

>> **Use diverse recruitment channels:** Go beyond traditional job boards and tap into your network, industry events, and targeted online platforms.

>> **Offer competitive compensation and benefits:** Attract top talent with competitive salaries, equity options, and attractive benefits packages.

>> **Focus on company culture and values:** Clearly communicate your company culture and values to attract candidates who align with your vision.

>> **Implement a rigorous hiring process:** Hold thorough interviews, review skill assessments, and check references to ensure you've found the best fit.

WARNING

You may have heard of the concept "hire slowly and fire quickly," and though it's hard because your ego is tied up in a hire, you need to adopt this practice to keep everyone focused on growing the business. Define what hiring slowly and firing quickly means before you hire someone, and with every hire check your definition to find out whether that hire has met the criteria to be fired. That definition may need to change over time as your business grows.

Empower and motivate your team

Your company culture takes care of your people. Culture is the spoke in all the wheels of your business vehicle, because without it, your business can't continue down the road. So, focus on these four areas:

>> **Foster a culture of ownership and accountability:** Delegate tasks effectively and empower your team to make decisions within their scope.

>> **Provide regular feedback and recognition:** Offer constructive feedback, celebrate achievements, and acknowledge individual contributions. Make sure these are important events in all the calendars you use.

>> **Invest in employee development:** Offer training programs, mentorship opportunities, and conferences to help your team grow and learn. Factor employee development into your cash flow statements.

>> **Promote a healthy work-life balance:** Encourage flexible work arrangements, generous leave policies, and initiatives for employee well-being.

WARNING

Flexible work is harder to manage, so you'll need to clearly define what flexible work is and have discussions about what needs to be done, regardless of how cool and flexible you are.

Optimizing your operations

Just like a car, you need to know that everything is set up and working properly in your business so you can hit the road and reach your milestones.

If you've read the preceding chapters in this book, some of these requirements will help remind you and your team to do these things — or you can bookmark this page so you can get up to speed.

Streamlining processes and workflows

If you don't keep your processes and workflows running smoothly, it won't be long before you have employees and customers complaining about things not getting done and things not working. Nobody likes that. So, focus on these four areas:

>> **Identify and analyze existing workflows:** Map out current processes and identify areas for improvement.

>> **Implement automation and technology:** Use software and tools to automate repetitive tasks and improve efficiency.

>> **Standardize procedures and documentation:** Establish clear, written guidelines, step-by-step instructions, and best practices for consistent execution.

Developing and updating your policies, procedures, and documentation should be part of every team member's job.

REMEMBER

>> **Track and measure performance:** Monitor key metrics to identify areas for further optimization.

Implementing robust data analytics

You won't be able to make good decisions unless you constantly see how your business is performing. So, you need to focus on four areas:

>> **Collect and analyze relevant data:** Track key performance indicators (KPIs) across different departments and functions.

>> **Use data visualization tools:** Transform data into actionable insights through dashboards and reports.

>> **Leverage data for decision-making:** Use data to inform marketing campaigns, resource allocation, product development, and other strategic decisions.

>> **Build a data-informed culture:** Encourage data-informed decision-making and foster a culture of continuous learning and improvement.

Scale your infrastructure and technology

You won't realize your business (and life) dreams unless you plan how you'll use technology and implement it properly and safely. So, here are the four areas that you need to button up:

>> **Choose scalable solutions:** Invest in technology and infrastructure that can accommodate your growth without significant bottlenecks.

>> **Implement cloud-based solutions:** Use cloud platforms for flexibility, scalability, and cost-efficiency.

>> **Develop a robust disaster recovery plan:** Ensure business continuity with backup systems and data recovery protocols.

>> **Invest in cybersecurity:** Protect your data and systems from cyberattacks and vulnerabilities.

Refining your marketing and sales strategies

If your marketing has worked for you so far, it may work as you grow — but it's more likely that it won't. You'll need to up your game, and here are the areas you should review to see if any of them need tweaking or an entirely new structure.

Reaching your target audience at scale

We're betting you dollars to donuts that you want to reach as many potential customers as possible, so here are the four areas you need to focus on to do just that:

>> **Identify and segment your target audience:** Define your ideal customer profiles and personalize your messaging accordingly.

>> **Use targeted marketing channels:** Implement effective multi-channel marketing campaigns across social media, search engine marketing (SEM), content marketing, and other relevant channels.

>> **Leverage data and analytics:** Use data to identify and target high-value segments, optimize campaign performance, and personalize customer experiences.

>> **Partner with influencers and strategic partners:** Collaborate with relevant influencers and businesses to expand your reach and credibility.

Refining your sales funnel and go-to-market strategy

With sales and marketing, you can't set it and forget it. So, here are the basic things you and your team need to focus on every day:

>> **Optimize your website and landing pages:** Ensure a seamless user experience and clear conversion paths for leads.

>> **Implement a strong lead nurturing strategy:** Convert leads into paying customers through personalized communication and follow-up processes.

>> **Develop a data-driven sales process:** Track key metrics throughout the sales funnel and identify how your sales team can improve.

>> **Offer excellent customer service:** Build customer loyalty and positive word-of-mouth through exceptional customer service experiences. Without them, your business won't last for much longer.

Building a strong brand identity and customer experience

People are bombarded with messages every day, and to stand out, you need to build not only a strong brand identity but also attract people with your customer experience by focusing on these four areas:

>> **Develop a clear and consistent brand voice and messaging:** Define your brand values and communicate them effectively across all touchpoints.

>> **Create a memorable brand identity:** Invest in professional branding, including logo design, website design, and marketing materials.

REMEMBER

Your brand is more than a logo — it's a part of your culture that's experienced by customers, strategic partners, investors, your team, and you, too. When you create your brand, ask yourself, your team, and your partners what it means to live that logo, those colors, and that feeling of working with your business.

>> **Focus on customer experience at every stage:** Ensure a positive and seamless customer journey, from initial awareness to post-purchase support.

>> **Gather and analyze customer feedback:** Use customer feedback to improve your products, services, and overall customer experience.

Creating a Strategic Growth Plan

Strategic planning is an area where many startup business owners struggle, and though it's natural, you bought this book because you're smart enough to not be like your competitors.

So, we have a general strategic plan outline just for you that includes a presentation that Marc developed and uses in his own business. After each explanation of each point in the outline, we have an example slide with ideas that you can use to produce your own plan.

What's more, you can use these slides in your presentation to your team, your employees, and your potential investors to prove to them that your business is worth investing in.

TIP

We have the full presentation template available for you to download and adapt in your own business on the book's website at Dummies.com.

Vision and mission statement

This statement defines the long-term vision and immediate mission of the organization, emphasizing core values like integrity, client focus, leadership, and teamwork (see Figure 19-1).

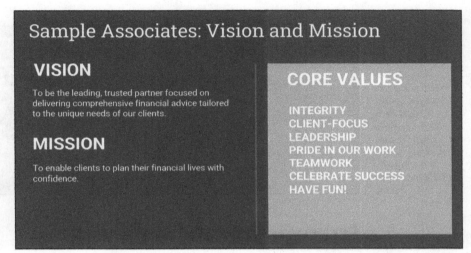

FIGURE 19-1:
A vision and mission statement for a financial company.

Client value proposition (CVP)

As shown in Figure 19-2, the CVP outlines the unique value offered to clients, focusing on specific areas that the company serves and how each area meets client needs and beliefs.

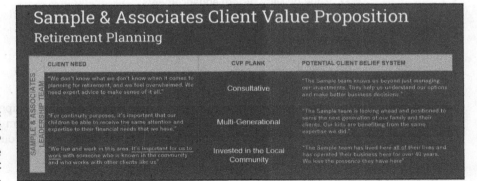

FIGURE 19-2:
A CVP with client needs, the CVP category, and the potential client belief system.

Employee value proposition (EVP)

The EVP shows the value proposition for employees to work at the company for the long term, focusing on aspects like recognition, career path, and work-life balance (see Figure 19-3). Like the CVP, the EVP shows how the company understands employee needs and meets their expectations from their belief systems.

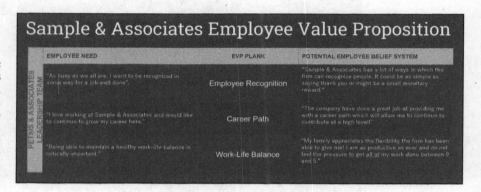

Sample & Associates Employee Value Proposition

EMPLOYEE NEED	EVP PLANK	POTENTIAL EMPLOYEE BELIEF SYSTEM
"As busy as we all are, I want to be recognized in some way for a job well done".	Employee Recognition	"Sample & Associates has a lot of ways in which the firm can recognize people. It could be as simple as saying thank you or might be a small monetary reward."
"I love working at Sample & Associates and would like to continue to grow my career here."	Career Path	"The company have done a great job at providing me with a career path which will allow me to continue to contribute at a high level."
"Being able to maintain a healthy work-life balance is critically important."	Work-Life Balance	"My family appreciates the flexibility the firm has been able to give me! I am as productive as ever and do not feel the pressure to get all of my work done between 9 and 5."

(PETSIS & ASSOCIATES LEADERSHIP TEAM)

Strategic growth framework

The framework shown in Figure 19-4 includes seven strategies that you can get started with:

>> Maximizing existing clients

>> Attracting new clients

>> Innovation in services

>> Value-delivery system enhancements

>> Mergers and acquisitions

>> Geographical expansion

>> Exploring new business arenas

REMEMBER

You may think of other growth strategies based on your competition and your industry that you can add to the framework, and ask your team and prospective investors if they have some strategies that you need to add. (Your investors may come to you with some straightaway.)

Sample & Associates Strategic Growth Framework

1. **Maximizing Existing Clients** - Penetrate existing Sample & Associates clients to increase their share of wallet leveraging digital marketing programs and focusing on meeting their unmet needs with solutions we currently have.

2. **Attracting New Clients** - A second way for us to grow is by attracting new clients that meet our ideal client profile, thereby expanding the size of its client franchise.

3. **Innovation of New Services** - Among the most common ways we can grow is the introduction of new services that extend our ability to service new and existing clients. Examples of this are expanding into providing education services, elder care planning, etc.

4. **Innovation of the Value-Delivery System** - Redesigning the business system by which our client service is delivered. A good example of this would be to redesign the process by which onboard new clients.

5. **Mergers and Acquisitions** - At its simplest, this can mean buying books businesses to capture market share, expand into new verticals, and some types of greenfield capacity expansion. Multiple acquisitions would enable us to create economies of scale, obtain hard-to-find talent, and help us expand into new geographies.

6. **Geographical Expansion** - Move into new regions where the barriers are low, and the market conditions align with our ability to deliver. A good example of this would be to expand beyond this area into other local markets.

7. **New Business Arenas** - Grow by competing in new arenas by seeking opportunities vertically along the industry chain or finding new areas in which to specialize. An example of this would be to provide tax preparation for clients.

FIGURE 19-4: Descriptions of all seven growth strategies in the framework.

When you create a slide describing the framework, have your descriptions be as brief as possible so your audience doesn't get dreaded PowerPoint poisoning. What's shown in Figure 19-4 is to help get you thinking about how to describe your framework.

Growth initiatives

You need to detail specific initiatives planned over a 3-year period, such as from 2024 through 2026, based on the objectives contained in the strategic growth framework. Figure 19-5 below provides an example of a table that's easier to fill out in Year 1 than it is in Year 3.

2024 – 2026 Growth Initiatives

Growth Initiative	2024 (10+% Organic Growth)	2025 (X% Growth)	2026 (X% Growth)
Maximize Existing Clients	1. Create written LTC Plan for every client meeting	1. Leverage HolistiPlan for A clients	
Attract New Clients	1. Launch special needs practice 2. Systemically leverage existing clients and COIs for new client referrals		
Innovation of Products and Services	1. Create and implement Family Meeting to establish relationships with children of clients	1. Implement Family Meeting Phase 2 to establish relationships with the children of clients	
Value Delivery System Innovation	1. Create Value Record for clients 2. Use digital marketing to drive client engagement		
Mergers & Acquisitions	1. Acquire new practice	1. Acquire additional practice	1. Acquire additional practice
Geographic Expansion	1. New York and California		
New Business Arenas	1. Launch special needs planning practice 2. Launch education planning service	1. Launch 401k/403b/Executive Compensation planning service	

FIGURE 19-5: Sample initiatives based on the seven areas in the strategic growth framework.

Key performance indicators (KPIs)

You learned about KPIs in Chapter 18, and now you can list them as measurable goals you will track monthly as shown in Figure 19-6. Your goals can include revenue targets, client acquisition targets, and satisfaction benchmarks.

2024 Sample & Associates KPIs

ON TRACK GREEN	BELOW TARGET AMBER	AT RISK RED	⭐ KPI ACHIEVED	2023 Results	2024 Target
Achieve organic revenue growth of 10%+				~10%	10%+
Create written LTC Plan for every client meeting				N/A	100%
Conduct 25 Family Meeting discussions				N/A	25
Obtain 20 client referrals for existing clients and COIs				N/A	20
Conduct 2 referral events				N/A	2
Onboard 10 new special needs household relationships				N/A	10
Implement client satisfaction survey and create benchmarks				N/A	100%
Create personal development plans for every employee				N/A	100%

FIGURE 19-6:
A sample KPI table that's color-coded for different results.

Marketing strategy

Provide a broad strategy outline for attracting new clients, engaging existing ones, and establishing a centralized system to manage sales and marketing data. Neuroscientific studies have shown that Following the rule of three helps people remember better, as you can see in Figure 19-7.

2024 Marketing Goals

1. **Attract new clients** through a comprehensive and data-driven marketing strategy

2. Penetrate deeper with **existing clients** through coordinated activities across the firm

3. Create a **centralized source of truth** for Sales & Marketing through use of the CRM and marketing automation solutions

FIGURE 19-7:
Three points about your marketing strategies is a good way to help people remember them.

6

The Part of Tens

Chapter **20**

Ten Tips for Successful Startup Funding

B
uilding a business is like driving across the country on a road trip. Not only do you have to be reasonably confident that your car is in good enough shape to make the trip, you also have to plan to determine where you're going to stop at the end of each day, how much money you need to keep you and others fed, and where you're going to get more fuel to keep you going.

You need help getting the monetary fuel to get your startup on the road and going all the way to your final destination. So, here are ten complete tips for getting startup funding to see if you need to check and see that you haven't forgotten anything before you start the engine and move out.

Design a Clear Value Proposition for Potential Investors

Potential investors aren't interested in just throwing money around like the irresponsible ones did during the initial days of the Internet revolution. They want to avoid the dot-com bomb or any other correction that leads them to losing money somewhere along the way. So, by following these steps and tailoring them to your specific business, you can craft a value proposition that grabs investors' attention and paves the way for successful funding conversations.

Uncover the compelling narrative

When you're talking with potential investors, you're not just giving them a bunch of numbers; you're sharing your story and inviting them to write your business (and life) story with you. Start by talking about the following five topics:

>> **Identify your target market:** Pinpoint the specific segment of people who face the problem your solution addresses. Understand their demographics, pain points, and unmet needs.

>> **Articulate your customers' problem:** Dive into your target market's core pain points. Use vivid language and relatable anecdotes to paint a picture of the frustration, inconvenience, or financial burden they experience.

>> **Craft your unique solution:** Explain how your product or service addresses the identified problem directly. Highlight its innovative features, technical advantages, and user-friendly design.

>> **Quantify the impact:** Don't just say it's better — prove it! Use data, customer testimonials, and market research to showcase your solution's tangible benefits. Show how it increases efficiency, reduces costs, improves customer satisfaction, or solves a specific problem.

>> **Embrace emotional connection:** Go beyond technical details and connect with investors on an emotional level. Share stories of how your solution has positively impacted real people, highlighting the human element behind your business.

Differentiate yourself from the competition

Potential investors want to put their money into a business that has a good chance of beating its competition and increasing their chances of profit. So, they're going to want to see that you've done the following four things, and if you haven't done one or more of them, start now:

>> **Conduct competitor analysis:** Research existing solutions in your market and identify their strengths and weaknesses. Understand their market positioning and how you differentiate yourself.

>> **Highlight your unique selling proposition (USP):** What makes you stand out? Is it your proprietary technology, superior customer service, or a disruptive business model? Clearly articulate your USP and demonstrate how it gives you a competitive edge.

- » **Showcase your team's expertise:** Investors back people, not just ideas. Emphasize the experience, skills, and track record of your founding team. Share their past successes and demonstrate their ability to execute on your vision.
- » **Create a memorable brand identity:** Develop a consistent brand voice, messaging, and visual identity that resonates with your target market and investors. This helps establish trust and recognition.

Craft your value proposition statement

You need to have a value proposition statement that rings in the heads of potential investors when they hear it. Here's how to do that:

- » **Condense your narrative into a powerful, concise statement:** Aim for a clear, impactful sentence that summarizes your problem-solution fit and unique value proposition.
- » **Make it investor-centric:** Focus on how your solution creates value for investors, not just your target market. Explain how your success translates into their financial returns and strategic benefits.
- » **Test and refine:** Get feedback on your value proposition from potential investors, industry experts, and even customers. Iterate and refine it based on their input to ensure it resonates and effectively communicates your core message.

Define Clear Funding Objectives

By demonstrating a clear road map to success, supported by robust financial models and responsible financial practices, you can convince investors that your funding request is well defined, achievable, and ultimately beneficial to their portfolio.

Before they sign a check, they'll want to be confident that the funding dovetails with what you want to do and that you know how to spend your money responsibly as we cover in this section.

Align funding with your growth strategy

You wouldn't put fuel in your car or truck if you didn't know where you were going with it, and you need to have a clear idea of how investors' money will fuel your startup to infinity and beyond. Here are the three things you need to work on so potential investors know how you'll put their money to work:

>> **Define your vision and mission:** What do you want to achieve in the long run? Your answer to this question will guide your overall growth strategy and determine the amount of capital you need to secure.

>> **Identify key milestones:** Outline the specific steps you need to take to achieve your vision. These could include product launches, market expansion, or reaching specific revenue targets.

>> **Map funding to milestones:** Break down your total funding needs into smaller allocations that directly support each milestone. This demonstrates how investors' capital fuels your growth journey.

Develop comprehensive financial models

Building on your work to tie funding to milestones, you need to build comprehensive financial models to prove to potential investors that you can reach your milestones with their money, like so:

>> **Create detailed financial projections:** Forecast your revenue, expenses, and cash flow over the next few years. Use realistic assumptions and industry benchmarks to build credible models.

>> **Conduct sensitivity analysis:** Test your models under different scenarios to understand the impact of potential market fluctuations or unforeseen challenges. This shows investors your preparedness and risk mitigation strategies.

>> **Develop funding scenarios:** Explore different funding options and their impact on your financial projections. This helps you make informed decisions about the amount, type, and terms of the funding you seek.

Prioritize financial discipline and transparency

Investors are human, and they hate wasting money just as you do. But they're not going to just take your word for it that you'll spend their money wisely. The rule is deeds, not words, and here are the deeds you need to deliver on:

>> **Demonstrate responsible spending:** Show investors how you plan to use their funds efficiently and effectively. Highlight cost-saving measures and resource allocation strategies.

>> **Communicate openly and regularly:** Keep investors updated on your progress and financial performance. Share key metrics, milestones achieved, and any challenges you're addressing.

>> **Establish strong governance practices:** Implement internal controls and financial reporting systems to ensure transparency and accountability. This builds trust and fosters a positive relationship with investors.

Review Different Funding Options That Suit Your Startup's Stage and Needs

Before you can fund your business, you need to know what types of funding are available and then match them to your needs. You also need to realize what level of risk you're willing to tolerate with each funding type, because each type comes with risk. Here's a rundown of the funding types and how to get sound advice about which one is best for your business right now.

Understanding the funding landscape

The realm of investor funding has a wide landscape with many different options for you to choose from, but you must know the type of funding you need not only for the opening round but for subsequent rounds:

>> **Seed funding:** Ideal for early-stage startups with high potential but limited traction. Angel investors and venture capitalists often focus on innovative ideas and disruptive technologies.

>> **Series A funding:** Typically for startups with a proven product-market fit and demonstrated customer traction. Investors seek strong growth potential and clear paths to profitability.

>> **Series B and C funding:** Focused on scaling established businesses with rapid growth and expanding market reach. These rounds typically involve larger investments from venture capital firms and private equity groups.

Beyond traditional funding

If none of the traditional funding methods we listed in the previous section work for you, familiarize yourself with other forms of funding:

>> **Debt financing:** This can be attractive for startups with strong cash flow and predictable revenue streams. Loans offer fixed repayment schedules but can burden cash flow and increase risk of default and your ability to get future funding.

>> **Government grants and programs:** Available for specific industries, research and development projects, or social impact initiatives. Requires rigorous eligibility criteria and adherence to specific deliverables.

>> **Crowdfunding platforms:** Can validate product ideas, build community engagement, and raise smaller amounts of capital from a large pool of individual investors.

Matching funding options to your needs

Now that you know the available funding options, here are the guidelines you need to follow to decide which one is best for your needs and how much you're willing to stomach:

>> **Stage of development:** Early-stage startups require smaller amounts for proof-of-concept or initial market validation. Later-stage companies seek larger investments for scaling operations and rapid growth.

>> **Funding needs:** Analyze your specific needs for product development, marketing campaigns, team expansion, or infrastructure upgrades. Match your needs to the typical funding sizes and objectives of different options.

>> **Risk tolerance:** Consider your comfort level with debt, equity dilution, and potential for investor control. Certain funding options offer more flexibility but may come with higher risk or longer repayment periods.

Seek expert guidance

If you think you have the expertise to get funding from outside investors single-handedly, we'd be happy to take bets (for charity) to find out how long you'll last before you run into trouble. Life's too short to have unnecessary stress, so here's our advice for finding the help you need:

- **Consult with financial advisors or experienced entrepreneurs:** Gain insights into the current funding landscape, industry trends, and negotiation strategies for different funding options.

- **Use online resources and funding databases:** Research specific investors, venture capital firms, and government grants that align with your sector and stage of development.

- **Network with other startup founders and investors:** Learn from their experiences, gain valuable advice, and build connections that may lead to future funding opportunities.

Build Relationships with Potential Investors Before You Need Funding

Cultivating genuine connections with potential investors before the need for funding arises is a strategic move that can significantly enhance your startup's success. It's not about empty promises or forced networking; it's about building trust, demonstrating value, and establishing yourself as a reliable and promising startup entrepreneur. Here's how you can build solid relationships with potential investors well before you need their capital.

Engage in meaningful networking

If we say it once, we'll say it ten times over: You're building a funding team and you need to find team members. Here's what you need to do:

- **Go beyond attending industry events:** Participate in online forums, relevant LinkedIn groups, or industry-specific conferences to actively engage with potential investors.

- **Provide value, not just pitches:** Share your expertise by writing articles, offering webinars, or contributing to industry discussions. This showcases your knowledge and builds credibility.

- **Seek genuine connections:** Focus on building long-term relationships, not just securing quick deals. Listen actively, offer help, and build trust over time.

Offer strategic insights and expertise

Finding funding isn't just an opportunity to find people who will ride the highway to glory with you. It's also a way for you to share you, your business, and your expertise with others. Here are three ways to do that:

>> **Become a thought leader:** Publish articles, speak at conferences, and share your insights on relevant topics. This positions you as an authority in your field and attracts interest from potential investors.

>> **Connect investors with valuable resources:** Introduce them to other experts, potential partners, or relevant information that benefits their interests.

>> **Offer pro bono consulting or advisory services:** Help other startups in your network, demonstrating your skills and building goodwill within the investment community.

Cultivate relationships beyond the pitch

At the core of investor funding is building relationships with people who will be with you for years to come (we hope). You're also going to build connections with other companies you could partner and grow with. So, here are three ways to start connecting:

>> **Don't disappear after the initial connection:** Stay in touch with potential investors through regular updates, invitations to events, or even casual coffee chats.

>> **Celebrate your successes and share your journey:** Keep them informed about your progress, even if it's not directly related to funding. This shows your commitment to building a successful venture.

>> **Offer support and resources to other startups:** Be an active member of the startup community, willing to help and share your knowledge with others. This builds goodwill and strengthens your network.

Connect with Centers of Influence and Strategic Partnerships

In the dynamic world of startups, leveraging the expertise and influence of others can be a game-changer. Two key allies in your quest for success are centers of influence (COIs) and strategic partners.

Identifying your ideal COIs

So, where can you find your centers of influence and build around them? Here are three areas to explore:

>> **Industry experts and thought leaders:** Look for respected individuals with deep expertise and strong connections in your target market. Their endorsements can lend credibility and attract investor attention.

>> **Successful entrepreneurs and business leaders:** Consider partnering with individuals who have built and scaled ventures in your space. Their experience and guidance can be invaluable.

>> **Media personalities and public figures:** If your startup aligns with a specific niche or cause, partnering with relevant influencers can widen your reach and generate positive buzz.

Building relationships with COIs

Okay, now you've found your COIs, but how do you make your connections valuable? Start with these three guidelines:

>> **Give, don't just take:** Offer your expertise, share valuable resources, or collaborate on projects that benefit both parties. This builds trust and demonstrates your willingness to contribute.

Don't offer to buy someone coffee and "pick their brain," because busy professionals often don't have time for that. Instead, offer something of value first and explain why they would want to spend their time with you.

>> **Seek genuine connections:** Attend industry events, participate in online communities, and actively engage with potential COIs. Focus on building long-term relationships, not just one-time transactions.

>> **Offer testimonials and recommendations:** If you've worked with other COIs, leverage their positive feedback to build trust and credibility with new ones.

Exploring strategic partnerships

In your quest to find centers of interest, you may consider strategic partnerships that can benefit you and the other business. Here are strategies to find businesses to partner with:

>> **Identify complementary businesses:** Look for companies that offer non-competing products or services but share your target audience or market

reach. Partnerships can expand your offerings, cross-promote each other, and access new resources.

>> **Joint ventures and co-marketing initiatives:** Collaborate on developing new products, services, or marketing campaigns. This can leverage each other's strengths and increase brand awareness.

>> **Synergistic alliances:** Seek partnerships that combine your expertise with another company's resources, technology, or distribution channels. This can accelerate growth and reach new heights together.

Maximizing the benefits of COIs and partnerships

Any partnership without rules means that one or more of the partners suffers damage and ill feelings. So, get the most out of your relationship by following these three principles:

>> **Clearly define roles and responsibilities:** Ensure a mutually beneficial agreement that outlines each party's expectations, contributions, and communication channels.

>> **Leverage each other's networks:** Introduce your COIs and partners to your network and vice versa. This expands your reach and opens doors to new opportunities.

>> **Measure and track results:** Regularly assess the impact of your COI and partnership collaborations. Analyze metrics like brand awareness, customer acquisition, and revenue generation to ensure they're driving value.

Construct and Negotiate Investment Agreements

As they said in *Schoolhouse Rock*, knowledge is power. (If you don't know what *Schoolhouse Rock* is, look it up on YouTube.) By equipping yourself with the language of finance and understanding the intricacies of investment agreements, you can negotiate investment terms with your investors confidently.

Essential financial terms

Funding has its own lexicon, and here are the basics to make you familiar:

>> **Equity:** Ownership stake in a company, represented by shares. Investors receive equity in exchange for their investment, giving them voting rights and potential future profits.

>> **Convertible note:** A debt instrument that converts into equity at a predetermined valuation or event, like a future funding round. Often used for early-stage startups.

>> **Pre-money and post-money valuation:** Pre-money valuation is the company's worth before the investment. Post-money valuation is the company's worth after the investment, including the new capital. Understanding both is crucial for determining equity dilution.

>> **Term sheet:** A non-binding document outlining key terms of the investment, including amount, valuation, liquidation preference, and investor rights. Negotiate carefully before signing.

>> **Exit strategy:** A plan for investors to realize their investment returns, such as through an acquisition, IPO, or stock buyback.

Know your agreement provisions

When you draft your investor financing agreement, here are the five main provisions you need to know and include in the agreement:

>> **Liquidation preference:** Specifies the order and priority in which investors receive their investment back in case of a company sale or liquidation.

>> **Anti-dilution provisions:** Protect investors' ownership percentage from being diluted by future funding rounds with lower valuations.

>> **Drag-along and tag-along rights:** Allow investors to sell their shares alongside the founders or other investors in certain situations, ensuring liquidity and alignment of interests.

>> **Board representation:** Investors may receive board seats to influence strategic decisions and protect their investments.

>> **Covenants:** Restrictions placed on the company's operations, such as limitations on debt or dividend distributions, to mitigate investor risk.

Mastering the negotiation game

Investor funding is a negotiation, and in this game you need to come to the table prepared. Here's how to do that and to get the most for you and your business as you deal with your investors:

>> **Seek professional guidance:** Consult with a lawyer or financial advisor to understand the legal and financial implications of each term.

>> **Understand your value proposition:** Articulate your company's potential and growth trajectory to secure favorable terms.

>> **Negotiate key terms:** Don't be afraid to negotiate terms like valuation, liquidation preference, and board representation.

>> **Focus on win-win scenarios:** Aim for mutually beneficial agreements that align your goals with those of investors.

Prepare Your Documentation for Due Diligence

Due diligence is an opportunity to showcase your business's strengths and build investor confidence. By preparing comprehensive documentation, anticipating inquiries, and presenting information effectively, you can turn this scrutiny into a springboard for securing the resources you need to fuel your startup's success.

But what documentation, you ask? Here's everything you need to produce at the minimum; your investors may ask for specific information as well. Then we tell you how to arrange and present your documents.

The essentials

There are six things you need to bring to discussions with your potential investors to get the conversation started:

>> **Financial statements:** Audited financial statements for the past 3 years (if available), along with projected financials for the next few years. Provide detailed breakdowns of revenue, expenses, cash flow, and key financial metrics.

>> **Business plan:** A well-crafted document outlining your business model, market analysis, competitive landscape, growth strategy, and funding needs. Ensure it's clear, concise, and data-informed.

>> **Marketing materials:** Brochures, website content, customer testimonials, and other materials showcasing your brand, marketing strategy, and target audience.

>> **Legal documents:** Incorporation documents, intellectual property filings, contracts with key partners or suppliers, and any relevant legal agreements.

>> **Organizational chart:** A clear diagram illustrating your team structure, key personnel, and their responsibilities. Highlight relevant skills and experience.

>> **Product or service documentation:** Technical specifications, user manuals, design blueprints, or any materials that showcase your product or service's functionality and value proposition.

Anticipating investor inquiries

Investors are going to look at your business under a microscope, with a fine-tooth comb, or whatever trite idiom you prefer. So, do your homework in five subjects so you can pick up gold stars:

>> **Market opportunity:** Be prepared to demonstrate the size and potential of the market you address. Back up your claims with market research data and industry trends.

>> **Competitive landscape:** Analyze your competitors' strengths and weaknesses, and clearly articulate your unique selling proposition and competitive advantage.

>> **Team expertise:** Highlight the skills and experience of your team members, and showcase their track record of success in similar ventures.

>> **Financial projections:** Present realistic and well-supported financial forecasts for revenue, expenses, and profitability. Be prepared to explain assumptions and potential risks.

>> **Growth strategy:** Clearly outline your plan for achieving your goals, including milestones, key initiatives, and resource allocation. Demonstrate a clear path to sustainable growth.

Organizing and presenting documentation

If you don't have organized documentation and make it easily available to your investors, you're going to get a failing grade and you'll have to repeat the process. To avoid that, follow these four guidelines:

>> **Create a due diligence data room:** Use a secure online platform to organize and share all relevant documents efficiently. Allow investors to access and review materials at their convenience.

>> **Maintain consistent document formats:** Ensure all documents are professionally formatted, dated, and easily navigable. This demonstrates attention to detail and professionalism.

>> **Prepare executive summaries:** Provide concise summaries of key documents, highlighting key points and financials. This saves investors time and facilitates efficient review.

>> **Be proactive and responsive:** Anticipate potential questions and prepare answers in advance.

Demonstrate the Ability to Execute

Building investor confidence is an ongoing process. By consistently demonstrating your ability to execute plans, learn from setbacks, and adapt to challenges, you can cultivate a strong track record that attracts and retains valuable partners on your journey to success.

Your track record of success

Showcase any previous ventures or projects where you successfully implemented plans and achieved desired outcomes. Quantify your results with metrics and data to demonstrate your effectiveness.

Seek endorsements from past clients, partners, or collaborators who can vouch for your ability to deliver on promises and execute your vision.

Strong planning and execution framework

Outline your key goals and milestones, illustrating how you plan to achieve them. Break down complex projects into actionable steps with clear timelines and responsibilities.

This is your opportunity to show potential investors your skills with project management tools and methods, or promote the skills of the person you've tasked with that job. That leads directly to happier investors who are more comfortable knowing that their money is going to a company that knows how it will get from Point A to Point B and beyond.

Data-driven decisions and adaptability

Use data and market research to inform your strategies and change your course if you have to. Show investors you're not afraid to adapt to changing circumstances and pivot when necessary.

Demonstrate a commitment to learning from past experiences and incorporating feedback to refine your approach and optimize execution.

Build a capable and committed team

Surround yourself with talented individuals who possess the skills and experience needed to execute your plans. Highlight their achievements and track record of success.

If you want to succeed, empower your team to take ownership of their tasks and hold them accountable for achieving their goals. This builds trust and investor confidence in your team's capabilities, and lets team members know you're all on the road to prosperity together.

Maintain Open and Transparent Communication with Potential Investors

Transparency is not about revealing everything — it's about building trust and fostering a collaborative environment. By actively communicating, being open to feedback, and demonstrating a genuine commitment to shared success, you can cultivate strong relationships with potential investors that will secure your funding and create a culture of support as you grow your business.

Communicate proactively

Investors don't follow the adage, "no news is good news." Instead, they think, "no news means there's something wrong, and I wonder if I should bail." Never let this thought cross their minds by doing these three things:

>> **Don't wait for them to reach out:** Schedule regular updates, even if there's no major news. Transparency breeds trust and shows you're engaged.

>> **Share both good news and bad news:** Sugarcoating challenges will only erode trust and make it more likely investors will shy away from you. Be honest about setbacks and proactive about solutions.

>> **Go beyond just financial updates:** Share company culture, employee wins, and market insights. Investors want to see the human story behind the numbers.

Embrace multiple communication channels

You may be tempted to use one communication channel as your official voice, but it's important to remember that investors have different ways of communicating. Here's how to broadcast as widely as possible:

>> **Don't rely solely on email:** Use phone calls, video conferences, and even casual coffee chats to foster personal connections with your investors.

>> **Leverage online platforms:** Create a dedicated investor portal to share documents, updates, and progress reports.

>> **Be accessible and responsive:** Address investor inquiries promptly and be available for unscheduled conversations when needed.

Be clear, concise, and honest

Your potential investors are busy people, and they need information that's direct, useful, and, most importantly, truthful. Here's how to deliver that information in your investor communication:

>> **Avoid jargon and technical speak:** Use simple, understandable language that resonates with investors from diverse backgrounds.

>> **Present data-driven insights:** Don't overwhelm your team and prospective investors with numbers. Focus on key metrics and trends that tell a compelling story.

>> **Be up front about uncertainties and risks:** Don't shy away from potential challenges, but demonstrate your preparedness and mitigation strategies.

Actively listen and welcome feedback

The ancient Greek philosopher Epictetus said, "We have two ears and one mouth so that we can listen twice as much as we speak." Use your ears more often and encourage connection by following these steps:

- >> **Don't just talk:** Engage in a dialogue. Encourage questions, address concerns, and show genuine interest in their perspectives.

- >> **Use feedback to improve your communication:** Be receptive to suggestions and adapt your message based on investor needs.

- >> **Align your visions:** Show investors you're not just pitching for funding but building a partnership with mutual benefit.

Build long-term relationships

We've mentioned this at least a dozen times in this book: Investor funding is about building relationships with your investors at its core. Take care of your investors as you would with any of your other team members by following these guidelines:

- >> **Don't disappear:** After the initial funding round, maintain communication, share your progress, and keep them involved in your journey — because they are.

- >> **Connect investors with other relevant players in your network:** This demonstrates your commitment to building a strong ecosystem and fostering trust.

- >> **Seek their guidance and support beyond funding:** Treat them as valuable partners who can contribute to your long-term success.

Be Ready to Pivot

Although securing funding is the ultimate goal, rejection is an inevitable reality when you're a new business. By preparing for rejection and embracing the power of the pivot, you can turn setbacks into springboards for even greater success. Here's how you can navigate the bumps and emerge stronger.

Anticipate rejection and reframe your mindset

If you aren't ready to accept failure, then you are much more likely to fail. Here's how to build the right mindset:

- >> **Adapt to grow:** Reframing your perspective on rejection and embracing the power of the pivot can transform it from a roadblock into a catalyst for growth. By learning from your mistakes, adapting your strategy, and maintaining a positive attitude, you can turn every "no" into fuel to get farther down the road.

>> **Focus on the positives:** Celebrate the progress you've made and the valuable insights gained. Every interaction, even a "no," provides valuable data to reach the next milestone.

>> **Develop mental resilience:** Embrace a "fail forward" mentality. Learn from your mistakes, adapt your strategy, and keep moving.

Analyze and learn from the feedback

If you have only one-way communication from your place on the mountaintop down below to potential investors, you'll quickly find yourself talking to no one. So, here's how to get and use feedback from your investors:

>> **Seek detailed feedback:** Ask investors for specific reasons behind their decision. This will help you identify areas for improvement and tailor your pitch to resonate with future investors.

>> **Don't take it personally:** Separate constructive criticism from personal attacks. Focus on the actionable insights and use them to refine your value proposition and business model.

>> **Share learnings with your team:** Debrief your team and discuss the feedback received. This fosters a culture of learning and prepares everyone for future challenges.

Refine your approach

The road to glory is filled with twists, turns, and hazards that you can't anticipate when you embark on your journey, so build up your mindset to be flexible by following these three guidelines:

>> **Don't be afraid to adjust your strategy:** Be flexible and willing to adapt your plans based on market feedback and investor insights. Pivoting is not a sign of weakness, but a mark of agility and resilience.

>> **Explore new funding avenues:** Research alternative funding sources like angel investors, crowdfunding platforms, or government grants. Don't be afraid to think outside the box.

>> **Strengthen your value proposition:** Refine your pitch based on the feedback received. Highlight your unique selling proposition and demonstrate the potential for growth and profitability.

Rejection is part of the process

Life is a lot about finding the right match, and inevitably your business won't be a match with some investors. It's not a repudiation of your business or you personally. Go with the flow by keeping the following in mind:

>> **Every "no" brings you closer to a "yes":** View each rejection as a stepping stone toward finding the right partner or investor who truly believes in your vision.

>> **Focus on the long game:** Don't get discouraged by short-term setbacks. Keep your eyes on the ultimate goal and remain committed to building a successful venture.

>> **Embrace the growth mindset:** See every challenge as an opportunity to learn, grow, and become better for your business, your team, your investors, and yourself.

Chapter **21**

Ten Common Mistakes to Avoid in Startup Funding

Y ou may be the type of person who needs negative visualization to convince you about what could happen if you don't do something, which is what the Romans called *premeditation malorum* or *premeditation of evils*.

No doubt that if you do any of the bad things in this chapter, you're going to be doing a postmortem of your business much sooner than you realize. Instead, let's do a premortem to prevent the postmortem from ever happening.

Rushing the Funding Process

Here are five ways you could go down the wrong rabbit hole by not doing your homework:

>> **Chasing the wrong funding:** Without a defined strategy, you might chase funding sources that don't align with your stage, industry, or values. This can lead to unfavorable terms, diluted ownership, and a disconnect between your vision and the expectations of your investors.

- » **Attracting the wrong investors:** Investors are drawn to businesses with a clear vision, a solid plan, and a dedicated team. Rushing the process can project a lack of seriousness and preparedness, deterring valuable partners and attracting those more interested in short-term profits than your long-term success.

- » **Undervaluing your startup:** Failing to properly research your market and negotiate favorable terms can lead to accepting funding that significantly undervalues your company's potential. This can leave you with less capital than you need and set you back when you go back bowl in hand for more money.

- » **Wasting precious resources:** Rushing the process often leads to haphazard spending and inefficient resource allocation. Without a plan, you might burn through funds on unnecessary expenses or activities that don't contribute to your core goals.

- » **Erosion of control:** Accepting funding without a well-defined execution plan can lead to investors dictating your direction and making you an employee in all but name.

Failing to Create a Detailed Financial Plan

Without creating a financial plan for your business in favor of winging it and just "enjoying the ride," here's how you'll crash and burn more quickly than you expect:

- » **Inefficient resource allocation:** Without a clear understanding of your income, expenses, and cash flow, you're likely to waste resources on non-essential activities or overspend in areas that don't contribute to your core goals. This can leave you scrambling for funds later on and impede your operations.

- » **Your investors make faces:** Investors are wary of ventures with vague financial projections and unproven financial viability.

- » **Unrealistic projections and expectations:** Flying blind often leads to overestimating revenue and underestimating expenses, setting unrealistic expectations for yourself, your team, and your investors. This can lead to disappointment, demotivation, and ultimately, a loss of confidence in your ability to execute your plan.

>> **Your decisions suck more often:** Every decision you make, from hiring new employees to launching a marketing campaign, has financial implications. Without a comprehensive financial plan, you're essentially making these decisions in the dark, increasing the risk of costly mistakes and missed opportunities.

>> **Loss of investor trust and confidence:** Investors rely on your financial plan to assess your potential and make informed decisions. A poorly conceived or non-existent plan can erode their trust, damage your credibility, and hinder your ability to secure future funding.

Underestimating or Overestimating the Valuation of Your Startup

The story of Goldilocks told us about the value of getting things right, and there are two ways you can screw up the valuation of your business: You value your business too low or too high.

The pitfalls of undervaluation

If you think too little about your own business when you approach investors for funding, stress is going to set up shop in your brain in four different ways:

>> **Leaving money on the table:** By undervaluing your startup, you miss out on securing the capital needed to fuel your growth plans and potentially cede future control to investors who acquire a larger stake at a lower price.

>> **Damaging your credibility:** A low valuation can send the wrong message to investors, suggesting a lack of confidence in your potential or a shaky business model. This can deter valuable partners and make it harder to secure future funding.

>> **Hindering future fundraising rounds:** A low initial valuation can set a precedent for future fundraising rounds, making it more challenging to raise the capital you need to scale your business.

>> **Demotivating your team:** A low valuation can demoralize your team, who may feel undervalued or question the company's future survival.

The risks of overestimation

Why not be optimistic with your valuation? After all, you have big dreams and you're confident that you can meet them, right? You'll soon find that you're in that scene from *The Simpsons* where you're at the top of the escalator to nowhere:

>> **Scaring away investors:** An inflated valuation can deter potential investors, who may find it unrealistic or perceive your team as lacking financial discipline. This can lead to missed opportunities and a prolonged funding process. And if the funding process takes too long, you could find your business out of fuel in the middle of the desert.

>> **Setting yourself up for failure:** Overestimating your worth can lead to unrealistic expectations and pressure to deliver results that may not be achievable in the short term. This can damage your credibility and lead to disappointment for both investors and your team.

>> **You're the owner, but you're not:** To secure funding at a high valuation, you may be forced to surrender a larger portion of your company's ownership to investors. This can dilute your control and decision-making power in the future.

>> **Behind the eight ball:** Investors are unlikely to offer favorable terms if they believe your valuation is inflated. This can lead to a disadvantageous deal with potential long-term consequences.

You Don't Understand Dilution

Share dilution, which is also called *equity dilution* or *stock dilution*, is the decrease in ownership percentage for existing shareholders when a company issues or reserves new shares of its stock.

It's a necessary part of startup life, and you can employ different anti-dilution provisions such as full ratchet and weighted average to help protect ownership percentages.

If you're curious, *full ratchet* works by applying the lowest sale price for any ordinary share after the issue of an option or convertible share. *Weighted average* uses a weighted formula to reduce the price at which preferred stock can be converted into common stock. (The "More You Know" music you're hearing in your head is free of charge.)

If you don't use those provisions, it could lead to investors with large percentages taking advantage of shareholders who own a smaller percentage. And that could leave you on the outside looking in at your own company.

Choosing the Wrong Investors

If you choose the wrong investors, let's count all the ways things will go south:

>> **Constant friction and clashing visions:** When your investor's goals and priorities diverge from yours, it creates constant friction and hampers your ability to execute your vision effectively. This can lead to micromanagement, pressure to deviate from your plan, and ultimately, a sense of discord within your team.

>> **Loss of control and autonomy:** Investors who prioritize short-term gains or have significantly different risk tolerances may pressure you to make decisions that compromise your long-term vision. This can lead to a loss of control and autonomy, leaving you feeling like your own venture is slipping away.

>> **Difficulty attracting and retaining talent:** Top talent is drawn to companies with clear values and a defined mission. When your investors clash with your values, it can deter talented individuals from joining your team, hindering your ability to attract and retain the best people.

>> **Reputation damage:** A discordant relationship with investors can damage your reputation and make it difficult to secure future funding. Investors are wary of supporting ventures with internal conflict and unclear direction, making it harder to attract the capital you need to grow.

Setting Unrealistic Expectations

If you think it's no big deal to set expectations for your investors that are optimistic because you think that way, your strategy will come back to bite you several times:

>> **Eroding investor trust:** Making exaggerated claims about your growth potential or setting unrealistic timelines can shatter investor confidence. When you fail to meet these expectations, it can damage your reputation and make future fundraising rounds significantly harder.

>> **Burning all the candles:** Unrealistic expectations trickle down, pressuring your team to achieve the impossible. This can lead to burnout, decreased morale, and ultimately, a decline in performance.

>> **You can't pivot:** Committing to overly specific goals can limit your ability to adapt to market changes or unforeseen challenges. This inflexibility can hinder your ability to pivot and seize new opportunities.

>> **Setting yourself up for a crash:** Striving for unrealistic milestones can lead to cutting corners, compromising quality, and ultimately, failing to deliver on your promises. This can have severe consequences for your company's reputation and future prospects.

REMEMBER

Always err on the side of caution in your projections, because if you want to have surprises, you want to have *good* surprises.

Not Nurturing Long-Term Investor Relationships

Your investors are along for the ride with you, and you're going to have a lot of time to get to know them. If you think that investors are just there to give you money, then here's everything that you'll have to deal with:

>> **Erosion of trust and confidence:** Inconsistent communication and a lack of engagement can erode investor trust, leading to doubts about your commitment and ability to execute your plan. This can make it harder to secure future funding or negotiate favorable terms.

>> **You can't build a strong network:** Investors are often connected to other key players in your industry. By failing to cultivate these relationships, you limit your network and miss out on potential opportunities for collaboration and growth.

>> **Loss of credibility and reputation:** A negative perception of your relationship with investors can damage your reputation and make it harder to attract talent, partners, and future investors.

Being Unprepared for Due Diligence

If you don't prepare for your investors' due diligence examination, boy howdy, are you going to go back to the days when you know you failed a test in school and had to answer for it. Let's show you how you'll hurt your business by being lax:

>> **Leaving question marks:** Unpolished answers and incomplete information can fuel investor doubts and leave them questioning your preparedness and execution capabilities. This can lead to missed opportunities to showcase your strengths and secure favorable terms.

>> **Loss of control over the narrative:** Lack of preparation allows investors to fill in the blanks, potentially painting a skewed picture of your venture. This can damage your credibility and make it harder to steer the conversation towards your strengths.

>> **Eroding trust and confidence:** Inconsistent or inaccurate information raises concerns about your transparency and commitment to ethical business practices. This can erode trust and make investors wary of partnerships.

>> **Late funding or nothing at all:** Incomplete documentation, missing answers, or a lack of clear vision can stall the due diligence process, hindering your progress and potentially jeopardizing your funding timeline.

No Flex

If you think that your funding strategy is made of cut marble and changing that strategy is as anathema as a politician changing their stance on an issue, then here's how you'll soon find your marble is actually brittle ceramic:

>> **Blown chances:** Rigidly focusing on a single funding source can blind you to emerging opportunities like strategic partnerships, alternative financing models, or even unexpected revenue streams. This can limit your access to crucial resources and hinder your growth.

>> **Inability to adapt to market changes:** A static funding strategy can make it difficult to respond to evolving market conditions, new competitors, or disruptive technologies. This can leave you lagging and struggling to maintain your competitive edge.

>> **Stunted growth:** Failing to secure the right funding at the right time can impede your ability to scale and capitalize on opportunities. This can stifle your growth and threaten your company's survival.

Repeating the Same Mistakes

We're human, and so failure is a part of life. But if you're more interested in your ego and how you appear to others, you may want to look like the unassailable leader who knows everything and is incapable of failure. Here are the ways that will get you to becoming the king of nothing:

» **A vicious circle:** Each failure holds within it a wealth of valuable lessons. Failing to analyze the causes, identify weaknesses, and implement corrective actions traps you in a doom loop.

» **You dishearten your team and investors:** Repeated missteps can erode confidence and enthusiasm within your team, leading to decreased morale and potentially hindering your ability to attract and retain talent. Investors, too, may lose faith in your ability to learn and adapt, making future funding rounds more challenging.

» **Damage to your reputation and credibility:** Perpetually repeating the same mistakes can damage your reputation among peers, investors, and potential partners. This can make it harder to attract resources, build trust, and secure the collaborations needed for success.

» **Left behind:** Clinging to outdated strategies and failing to learn from failure can stifle your ability to innovate and adapt to changing market dynamics. This can leave you lagging behind competitors and struggling to find your footing in an ever-evolving landscape — if you ever find your feet at all.

Index

A

A/B testing, 273
Accelerate Long Island, 118
accelerators
  about, 18, 117–118, 169
  defined, 8
  features of, 171–172
  finding, 174–182
  mechanics of, 173
  professional expertise
    and, 256
accepting realism, 44
accounting procedures,
    inadequate, 208
accounting software, 56
accuracy, of financial models, 44
achievements, displaying, 133
active users/sessions, 270, 272
adaptability
  bootstrapping and, 51
  in planning, 251
advertising, evaluating capital
    requirements for, 29
agreement structure, in
    investment agreements,
    190, 191
agricultural development,
    subsidies for, 115
agricultural support, grants
    for, 120
aligning financial needs with
    business objectives, 25–28
alliances, angel investors
    and, 128
alternative lending options, as a
    type of debt funding, 80–81
American Bar Association
    (ABA), 256

American Institute of CPAs
    (AICPA), 256
amortization of debt, plan for,
    84–85
amount, of repayment terms, 84
analytics, evaluating capital
    requirements for, 32
analyzing
  capital investments, 254
  capital needed by business
    function, 28–32
  customers, 13
  finances, 13–14
  industry trends, 13
Angel Capital Association, 131
angel investors
  about, 18, 123–125
  benefits of, 125–129
  during concept stage, 22
  defined, 8
  during initial stage, 23
  making your pitch, 129–134
  professional expertise
    and, 257
  as sources of equity funding,
    95–98
angel seed investors, business
    goals and, 27
AngelList, 97, 130
AngelPad, 177
annual percentage rate (APR), 83
anti-dilution provisions
  about, 194
  defined, 297
  in investment agreements,
    190, 191
  on term sheets, 187, 188
Antler, 178

app performance KPIs, 271–272
Apple, 124
Aribnb, 18
articles of incorporation, for due
    diligence, 205
the ask, 133
aspirations, 223–224
assignment provisions, 196
associations, professional
    expertise and, 257
attorney sites, professional
    expertise and, 257
audience
  as a guide to success, 41
  knowing your, 197
audit trails, 242
audits, of debt portfolio, 86–87
authorization controls, 242
automation, 55
average revenue per user
    (ARPU), 270

B

bad habits, avoiding, 218–219
balance sheet, 232–234, 260
balance-required funding, nice-
    to-have funding compared
    with, 32–34
bar associations, professional
    expertise and, 258
Basecamp, 57
Beyond Meat, 19
board composition, 187, 193
board governance, 216
board of directors
  minutes for due diligence, 206
  reports, 267

common clauses, 192–196
communication
  absence of, 211
  clarity of, 223
  for finalizing funding, 216, 218
  honesty of, 223
  maintaining with potential investors, 301–303
  venture capitalists and, 143
community realization grants, 119
company model, during growth stage, 24
compensation, 203
competition
  as a disadvantage of crowdfunding, 154
  problems with, 209–210
  researching, 13
competitive advantage, angel investors and, 129
competitive intelligence reports, 266–267
competitive landscape, for due diligence, 299
competitive positioning, 203
competitive posture, weakness of, 209
competitor analysis, 263–264
compliance
  professional expertise and, 255
  regulatory, 221
  updates on, 222
concept stage, funding requirements for, 22
conditions prior to funding, in investment agreements, 190, 191
conferences, professional expertise and, 256
confidentiality agreements, in investment agreements, 190, 192

confidentiality provisions, 195
conflict resolution, 225–226
consulting, with experts, 71
content creation, evaluating capital requirements for, 29
contingency planning, 26, 28, 239
contractual obligations, 202
conversion rate, 270
conversion rights
  about, 194
  in investment agreements, 190, 191
  on term sheets, 187, 188
convertible note, 9, 297
corporate culture, 211
corporate governance, in investment agreements, 190, 191
corporate structure, 202
co-sale agreements, 190, 191, 195
cost of goods sold (COGS), 42, 254
costs
  allocating, 238
  controlling, 238, 265
  as a disadvantage of crowdfunding, 154
  managing, 254
covenants
  about, 195
  defined, 297
  in investment agreements, 190, 191
cover slide, in pitch deck, 39
coworking spaces, 54
CPA societies, professional expertise and, 258
creating
  budgets for startups, 64
  business case, 36–38
  business strategy, 87

crowdfunding campaigns, 165–168
detailed P&L scenarios, 41–45
financial models, 290
growth strategies, 280–284
investment agreements, 296–298
investor relations team, 223
payment strategies, 86
pitch deck, 38–40
pitch for venture capitalists, 143–146
relationships, 293–294
strategies for minimizing expenses, 53–57
value proposition statement, 287–289
creative activity, as a reason for needing startup funding, 15
credibility, reputation of, 16
credit lines, as a form of debt funding, 75
credit reports, monitoring, 70
credit(s)
  for film and entertainment industry, 116
  maintaining, 69–71
  for research and development, 116
  safety of, 65
  using your own, 62
creditworthiness, 74
Crowdcube, 162–163
crowdfunding
  about, 17, 149
  advantages of, 152–153, 155–161
  business goals and, 27
  creating a campaign, 165–168
  debt, 151, 157–158, 166
  debt-based, 163
  disadvantages of, 154–161

investment thesis validation, 200

investments
decreasing debt with, 86
prioritizing, 249
terms of, 193
in your business as a top priority, 56

investor confidence, financial models and, 44

investor relations team, 223

investor reporting, 195

investor self-assurance, professional expertise and, 255

investors
maintaining communication with potential, 301–303
relationships with, 312
selecting, 311

invoices, managing, 253

IP management, 133

issue, in business case, 36

J

JOBS Act, 221
JustGiving, 165

K

Keep It Simple Security (KISS) equity crowdfunding
about, 152
creating campaigns, 167
platforms for, 164
pros and cons of, 160–161

key performance indicators (KPIs)
about, 224, 251, 267–269
app performance, 271–272
customer acquisition and engagement, 269–270
financial performance, 269

growth strategies and, 284
operational efficiency, 271
product and service performance, 270
technology-related, 271–273
website performance, 271–272

Kickstarter, 101, 102, 162, 165, 168

Kim, Ernest (Basecamp founder), 57

knowledge, from angel investors, 96

L

labor and employment laws, 222

lack of control, as a disadvantage of crowdfunding, 154

law schools, professional expertise and, 257

laws and regulations
prioritizing, 225
warning signs for, 209

lawyers
consulting to finalize funding, 214
selecting, 220

leadership, venture capitalists and, 142

leadership inspection, 203

lean strategy, 53–54

legal advice, 218, 222

legal clauses, 194–195

legal compliance
addressing concerns with, 220–222
evaluating capital requirements for, 31
for finalizing funding, 215
in process of due diligence, 202–203

legal documents, for due diligence, 205–206, 299

legal knowledge, professional expertise and, 255

legal risks, 203

LegalMatch, 257

lender, 75

LendingClub, 163

licenses, for due diligence, 206

liquidation preference
about, 194
defined, 297
on term sheets, 187, 188

liquidity buffer, establishing, 85

liquidity ratios, 237

litigation, 203

loan agreements, 88

loans, grants and, 115

local government subsidies, 114

loyalty, discounts for, 56

M

machines, financing for, 81–82

maintaining
credit, 69–71
financial condition, 85
personal finances, 69–71

management warning signs, 211

managing
cash flow, 56–57, 249–250
debt, 64, 85–89
expenses, 238
inventory, 253
invoices, 253
payroll, 253
receivables, 253

mandatory conversion, 194

manufacturing standards, inadequate, 210

market analysis
in business plans, 14
in process of due diligence, 203

open source software, 55

openness, venture capitalists and, 143

operating expenses, on P&L, 42

operating income, on P&L, 42

operational costs
  about, 15
  in financial needs analysis, 26

operational efficiency
  as a financial control, 240
  KPIs for, 269–270

operational expenses, 15

operational infrastructure, inadequate, 210

operational plan, in business plans, 14

operational warning signs, 210–211

operations, optimizing, 277–278

opportunities, planning for, 133

opportunity zones, 114

optimizing operations, 277–278

option pool expansion, 193

org (organizational) chart, for due diligence, 206

organizational chart, for due diligence, 299

overinflation, 218

overvaluation, 310

ownership share, equity funding and, 92

P

page load speed, 271

partnerships, angel investors and, 128

patience, for finalizing funding, 217

Patreon, 162

payment strategies, creating, 86

payment terms, 56, 253

payroll, managing, 253

peace of mind, professional expertise and, 256

peer learning, 170

peer-to-peer lending, as a form of debt funding, 77

pending litigation, 209

perks, evaluating capital requirements for, 30

permits, for due diligence, 206

persistence, for finalizing funding, 217

personal assets, sales of, 63

personal credit, as a type of debt funding, 82

personal finances, maintaining, 69–71

personal funding options
  about, 61–62
  considerations for, 63–66
  maintaining personal finances and credit, 69–71
  risks and benefits of using personal finances, 67–69
  using credit, 62
  using reserves and savings, 62
  using retirement accounts, 63
  using sale of personal assets, 63

personal guarantees, 85

personal resources, bootstrapping and, 50

personality, angel investors and, 96

physical space, 119

pitch
  creating for venture capitalists, 143–146
  defined, 10
  for venture capital, 137

Pitch Book, 99

pitch deck, creating, 38–40

pitch presentation, during initial stage, 23

pivot, being ready to, 303–305

platform stages, for venture capitalists, 138–140

platforms
  for angel investors, 130
  for crowdfunding, 162–165

Plug and Play, 179, 180

post-money valuation, 192, 297

practical estimates, 249

practice, 40, 134

preamble, in investment agreements, 190

pre-money valuation, 192, 297

pre-seed stage, for venture capitalists, 138

preservation, historic, 117

price per share, 193

pricing strategy, 264–265

prime rate, 84

principal, 75

priorities, setting, 33

prioritizing
  financial discipline and transparency, 290–291
  investing, 249

private equity, 10

private investors, 136

private sector, grants and subsidies from, 118–119

problem proposition, in pitch deck, 39

processes, streamlining, 277–278

product and service performance KPIs, 269–270

product development, evaluating capital requirements for, 28–29

product features usage, 270

product or service documentation, for due diligence, 299

Tip icon, 2

total addressable market (TAM), 127

traction, venture capitalists and, 141

trade shows/exhibits, grants for, 120

traditional bank loans
  as a form of debt funding, 75
  as a type of debt funding, 79–80

training and development
  about, 119
  evaluating capital requirements for, 30
  grants for, 120

transparency
  absence of, 211
  as a disadvantage of crowdfunding, 155
  prioritizing, 290–291

U

undervaluation, 309

unique value proposition, in pitch deck, 40

unit economics, 266

universities, professional expertise and, 257

UpCounsel, 257

updates, frequency of, 225

uptime and availability, 272

Upwork, 257

U.S. Commercial Service, 115

US Department of Agriculture, 115, 116

US Department of Housing and Urban Development, 114

U.S. Small Business Administration loans, as a type of debt funding, 80

user acquisition, 11

user experience (UX) metrics, 272

user interface (UI) metrics, 272

V

Valentine, Don (marketer), 124

validation
  angel investors and, 127–128
  crowdfunding and, 101
  venture capitalists and, 141

valuation
  under, 309
  clauses on, 192–193
  defined, 11
  equity funding and, 93
  market, 105
  over, 310
  on term sheets, 186, 187

value proposition statement, creating, 287–289

values
  offering to the client, 37
  weak, 211

variable interest rates, 83

venture capital(ists)
  about, 17, 135–136
  basics of, 137–138
  business goals and, 27
  considerations for, 141–147
  defined, 11
  platform stages, 138–140
  professional expertise and, 257
  role of, 138
  as source of equity funding, 98–100

virtual data room (VDR), 207

vision statement, 281

visual appeal, as a guide to success, 40

voting rights/thresholds, 193

W

Warning icon, 2

website performance KPIs, 271–272

websites
  Accelerate Long Island, 118
  Angel Capital Association, 131
  AngelList, 130
  AngelPad, 177
  Antler, 178
  Budgyt, 243
  Cheat Sheet, 2
  Crowdcube, 162
  The Definitive Startup Glossary: 210 Words Every Founder Should Know, 11
  Expensify, 244
  500 Global, 176
  Founders Factory, 178
  Freelancer, 257
  FreshBooks, 244
  Fundrise, 163
  GoFundMe, 103, 165
  Grantify, 111, 112
  Grants.gov, 111
  Gust, 257
  Gusto, 244
  HAX, 178
  Head Boss in Charge Headquarters (HBICHQ), 117
  Indiegogo, 102, 162
  JOBS Act, 221
  JustGiving, 165
  Kickstarter, 101, 162, 165
  LegalMatch, 257
  LendingClub, 163
  Meetup, 130
  Microsoft Excel, 244
  MicroVentures, 164
  Patreon, 162

About the Authors

Marc Butler is the founder and managing partner of Marc Butler Consulting, which focuses on helping startup and mature fintech companies as well as wealth management firms. He is also the founder and CEO of Wealth Management GPT, an artificial intelligence solution built for the wealth management industry. Marc has extensive experience in fintech and wealth management as a leader, operator, innovator, and board member. He previously held leadership roles with firms including Albridge, BNY Mellon|Pershing, and Skience. He currently serves on the board of directors of Future Capital and SIGNiX, and on the advisory board of FiSpoke.

Marc is passionate about leading people, driving strategy + execution, working with awesome teams, building + delivering solutions that solve unmet user needs, delivering awesome client experiences, and making wealth management easier. When he is not working, Marc can be found with his wife, two sons, and two dogs at home in Bucks County, Pennsylvania, or on Martha's Vineyard, Massachusetts. He enjoys participating in any number of athletic pursuits and loves antique cars. Marc is originally from Syracuse, NY, and is a proud alum of Syracuse University.

Eric Butow is the owner of Butow Communications Group (BCG) in Jackson, California. BCG offers web development, online marketing, and technical writing services for businesses of all sizes. He has written 45 computing and user experience books. His most recent books include *MCA Microsoft Office Specialist (Office 365 and Office 2019) Complete Study Guide* (Sybex), *Digital Etiquette for Dummies* (Wiley), *Instagram for Dummies*, Second Edition (Wiley), *Grow Your Business* (Entrepreneur Press) and *Write Your Business Plan*, Second Edition (Entrepreneur Press). Eric also holds bachelor's and master's degrees in communication from California State University, Fresno, where his master's thesis focused on computer-mediated communication. When he's not working or writing books, you can find Eric enjoying time with his friends, walking around the historic Gold Rush town of Jackson, and helping his mother manage her infant and toddler daycare business.

Dedication

To my wife, our two sons, our two dogs, my mother and father, and the many mentors I've had in life. You couldn't ask for a better fan club!

— Marc Butler

To all my daycare kids, who always ground and inspire me.

— Eric Butow

Authors' Acknowledgments

First, thank you to Maureen Farmer for introducing me to Eric Butow. It was a life-changing introduction. Second, as a first-time book writer, I am very thankful to Eric for his leadership and guidance throughout the book-writing process. He's a pro and a high-integrity person. Also, thank you to Matt Wagner, Steve Hayes, Chris Morris, and our tech editor, Julia Chung. I appreciate the opportunity to learn from each of you and get a glimpse into how a book comes together from start to finish. Lastly, thank you to the readers of this book. Wishing you all the best on your entrepreneurial journey — you got this!

— Marc Butler

I'd like to thank my co-author Marc Butler for being a great co-author and a great person to work with. My thanks as always to Matt Wagner, who served as the agent on this book. I also want to thank all the pros at Wiley who made this book possible, especially Steve Hayes, Chris Morris, and our tech editor, Julia Chung. And I also thank you for buying this book and working to help make others' lives better through your business.

— Eric Butow

Publisher's Acknowledgments

Executive Editor: Steve Hayes
Project Editor: Christopher Morris
Copy Editor: Christopher Morris
Technical Editor: Julia Chung
Production Editor: Saikarthick Kumarasamy

Cover Image: © Rawpixel.com/Shutterstock